Greylord
Justice, Chicago Style

GREYLORD

Justice, Chicago Style

James Tuohy
and
Rob Warden

G. P. PUTNAM'S SONS   NEW YORK

G. P. Putnam's Sons
Publishers Since 1838
200 Madison Avenue
New York, NY 10016

Library of Congress Cataloging-in-Publication Data

Tuohy, James.
    Greylord : justice, Chicago style / James Tuohy and Rob Warden.
        p. cm.
    1. Criminal justice, Administration of—Illinois—Chicago.
2. Judges—Illinois—Chicago.   I. Warden, Rob.   II. Title.
KFX1233.5.T86   1988   88-23493 CIP
345.773'1105—dc19
[347.7311055]
ISBN 0-399-13385-2

Text design by Silvia Glickman/Levavi & Levavi

Printed in the United States of America
1 2 3 4 5 6 7 8 9 10

In memory of
Judge John Marshall Tuohy
and Harry Rollins

CONTENTS

☆

This book is written in narrative form, but it is not a novel. Every scene is real— taken from testimony, court documents, interviews, and our personal observations.

Acknowledgments

We are indebted to many friends for counsel and encouragement, first to those who made it possible for us to pursue controversial journalism—the early financial and moral supporters of our publication, *Chicago Lawyer*: John R. Schmidt, Lois and Bernard Weisberg, J. Roderick MacArthur, Martin C. Hausman, Anthony Haswell, Robert T. Drake, Ronald E. Kennedy, Calvin P. Sawyier, Jetta Jones, Judson H. Miner, and Keith Davis.

Jennifer Alter Warden and Susan Nelson provided invaluable help at every stage of our research and writing. Other knowledgeable persons read all or parts of the manuscript and made suggestions that improved it immeasurably—David W. Andich, Jack C. Doppelt, Mary Mikva, Steven H. Cohen, Jonathan Alter, Joanne and James Alter, Brian Barnett Duff, Edward M. Genson, Daniel G. Donovan, Frederick J. Sperling, Robert A. Korenkiewicz, JoAnne F. Wolfson, Molly Friedrich, and the aforementioned John Schmidt.

We have drawn in some instances on the work and knowledge of other journalists, including Civia Tamarkin, Art Petacque, Peter Karl, Flora Johnson Skelly, Adrienne Drell, Larry Weintraub, Tom Fitzpatrick, and James D. Wascher. Three members of the *Chicago Lawyer* staff—Patricia Haller, Oliver Smith, and Susan Sekuler—contributed research, typing, editing, and proofreading skills.

Finally, we are indebted to our editor at Putnam, Neil S. Nyren, for advice, patience, and judicious editing.

1

The Boys
in the Bag

☆

Ray Sodini awoke late.

His head hurt. His eyes ached. His tongue was dry as a blotter, and it stung from cigarettes.

Ray Sodini had a hangover.

He reached for the telephone. He dialed the number, his fingers twitching. It was answered at the other end.

"I was out late last night," said Sodini. "Tell Cy to put on the robes and do the bum call."

Then Raymond C. Sodini, one of about 350 judges of the Circuit Court of Cook County, hung up the phone, pushed his head into his pillow, and closed his eyes. He had borrowed another hour or so of sleep before he would have to get up and go to his courtroom in the Police Headquarters Building at Eleventh and State streets in Chicago.

As Sodini slumbered in his Near North Side apartment, a police sergeant, Cy Martin, was putting on Sodini's black robes. Martin would handle the 8 A.M. call of vagrants and drunks who had been picked up the night before, mostly for safekeeping, in the downtown area.

It was a good thing Cy was so dependable at the bum call, Sodini must have thought on mornings when he was not feeling so good. It saved a lot of aggravation. Sodini simply called his chambers and talked to the bailiff, Deputy Sheriff Pat Ryan, who would relay the message to Martin. Sodini could then delay his arrival until 10 A.M. for the gambling call.

Sodini and Martin had grown up together during the 1940s on the West Side. Martin made a fine judge, square-jawed and handsome. In fact, if anyone had dared to comment, Martin probably made a better looking judge than Sodini, who, with slicked-back hair and protruding, bag-underlined eyeballs, looked more like a defendant than a judge.

"Let's go see the bozos," said Martin as, fully robed, he strode toward the door of the courtroom, where about a hundred derelicts now waited in smelly torpor for their cases to be heard. They had been charged with disorderly conduct, a technicality to allow the police to get them off the streets. Most were more disheveled and disgusting than disorderly, and their cases would be quickly dismissed.

The courtroom—Branch 26 of the nation's largest court system—was reminiscent of a big, gloomy public toilet, like the ones at baseball stadiums or in the recesses of military bases. Filled as it was this morning in 1979 with those members of society Sergeant-cum-Judge Martin called bozos, the courtroom seemed more like a latrine than ever. It had many more benches than were ever needed, giving it a hollow and lonesome look. It was poorly lit and unadorned. The plaster on the ceiling above the bench was falling out. There were no ornaments on the walls except a sign that said "No Smoking" and another that said

14

"Branch . . ." with the number obscured by a tattered flag on a staff. Sodini did not even have one of those metal plates on which other judges displayed their names and titles. It was just as well, for on a day like this it was not always Judge Sodini who sat there; it was not, for that matter, always a judge.

Deputy Sheriff Ryan, the bailiff, swore all of the defendants in at once. They passed by the bench in a steady line, with Martin banging the gavel and dismissing each defendant as quickly as his name was called, justice on the fly. "My object was to get them out . . . so when other people came in, there would be a little dignity in the courtroom," Martin said some years later. "I didn't want Sodini to be embarrassed by a courtroom full of bums and bozos and no judge to take care of them."

There was an occasional diversion. One day in the lockup behind the courtroom a drunk created a ruckus and had to be restrained, all the time expressing vociferously and profanely his low opinion of the American justice system in general and the present authorities in particular. They saved his case until last. After the courtroom had been cleared, he was presented to Martin, who consulted with the lockup officer and determined the appropriate punishment.

The troublemaker was sentenced to death.

After a few minutes back in the lockup, he was released, but it had no doubt been a rather unsettling way for him to start his day.

By 10 A.M. most days, Sodini, hung over or not, arrived for the gambling call. The activity around the bench took on the atmosphere of a private club. It was not an elegant or graceful club, not one to which most people would want to belong, but, on its own social level, in its own neighborhood, it was a club that was powerful and exclusive— and where there was money.

The members of the club—the clerks, the bailiffs, the prosecutors, the public defenders, and a select group of private lawyers—hovered near the bench, walking freely through the gate in a railing that, like a communion rail in a Catholic church, separated the celebrants from the worshipers.

During the 1970s and into the 1980s, Sodini franchised gambling court to the highest bidders. In exchange for kickbacks, he permitted a time-honored practice known as hustling; time was about the only thing that was honored in his courtroom. The lawyers to whom Sodini granted the hustling franchise openly solicited—or in the vernacular, hustled—business from defendants who were out on bond and who appeared in court without a lawyer.

Illinois law encourages or at least accommodates hustlers by making it possible for defendants to sign over their bond directly to lawyers. And, in a sort of Catch-22, defendants who have posted bond—even if they had to borrow the money—are not eligible to be represented by a public defender. When such defendants showed up without a lawyer, Sodini and his court personnel steered them to hustlers.

The gambling cases that arrived in Sodini's Branch 26 were mostly misdemeanors. Convictions would be punished by a modest fine and probation. In many cases the evidence had been seized without a warrant or there had been a procedural mistake, and the state was prepared to drop the charges. The defendants, however, usually did not know what to expect. The law provided up to a year in jail for gambling, which was about all the encouragement most of them needed to accept the services of a hustler. In return, they signed over their bond refunds.

In 1979, the premier hustlers in Sodini's courtroom were known as the Three Bees—Neal Birnbaum, Lee Barnett, and Howard Brandstein. "Birnbaum and Barnett and

Brandstein have the run of Sodini's courtroom," said a prosecutor assigned there. "They cater to Sodini's every whim. They carry his coat. They take him to lunch. They take him to play golf." Said another prosecutor: "You can't win a case against Neal Birnbaum in Branch Twenty-six. He's too tight with Sodini."

The reason for all the fawning over Sodini, of course, was money. Each of the Three Bees grossed six figures a year in bond refunds. And the reason that Sodini was so helpful to them and to other smaller-scale hustlers also was money—up to a third of the fees in kickbacks.

In the early days of hustling in Sodini's courtroom, it was done subtly. A clerk would place the files of unrepresented defendants on the railing and a hustler, say Lee Barnett, would look through the files, note the name of a defendant in a case likely to be dismissed, and walk down the center aisle calling out the name. The defendant would respond, perhaps thinking Barnett was an official of the court. After a few brief words, they would walk to the rear of the room, to the last window ledge overlooking State Street, and within minutes the defendant was signing a bond-refund authorization form.

The clerks received a portion of each fee, while the deputies assigned to the courtroom received general gratuities, as a mailman does at Christmas. But eventually, as the greed grew, the deputies became more aggressive. They had mobility, while the clerks were confined to their desks. The deputies could intercept defendants before they got to a clerk. After a time, the deputies did not even wait for a defendant to come into the courtroom. They would stop anyone with a bond slip at the elevators in the hallway. Bond slips were to the deputies what blood is to sharks.

One day a loud squabble broke out in the courtroom between Ryan and one of the clerks, Jack Petromella. They were arguing over which of them was referring the most

17

cases to the hustlers. Sodini, the sage of State Street, restored dignity to the court. He ordered Ryan, Petromella, and two other clerks into his chambers.

"You guys will have to work this out among yourselves," he said. "There's enough for everybody." Indeed, there was. There was plenty for all. The clerks and the deputies were making hundreds a week, the lawyers thousands, and Sodini received at least a couple of thousand a month in addition to his salary.

Following Sodini's suggestion, the clerks and deputies agreed on a profit-sharing plan. Generally, it worked to everyone's satisfaction, although occasionally there were minor problems. One day from the bench, Sodini saw Ryan, Petromella, and one of the hustlers passing something among themselves in the rear of the courtroom. He interrupted his call and leaned over to Henry LeClaire, a deputy standing near the bench.

"If they're exchanging money, tell them to go into the back room, away from the window," said Sodini.

A lot went on in Sodini's back rooms. Attorneys regularly came into his chambers with envelopes full of money. They would not give the envelopes directly to Sodini. If he was sitting at his desk, they would simply say something such as, "Hi ya, Ray," and put the envelope into a pocket of his suit coat hanging in an open closet. Sometimes they would open a desk drawer and place an envelope there.

Not all cases in Sodini's courtroom were misdemeanors. Like other branch courtrooms scattered around Chicago and its suburbs, preliminary hearings in felony cases were sometimes heard there. The purpose of such hearings is to determine whether there is probable cause to believe the defendant committed a felony. If the judge at the preliminary hearing determines that there is probable cause, the case is sent to a judge at the Criminal Courts Building for trial.

Preliminary hearings were a lucrative source of income for Sodini. In September 1980, for instance, he received $2,500 for results favorable to defendants who were kingpins of a policy wheel.

Sodini and the boys in the bag often went drinking together, usually leaving the courtroom in the early afternoon and starting at a greasy spoon and saloon known as Mr. Pat's across the street from Police Headquarters. Outside the men's room at Mr. Pat's one afternoon, Neal Birnbaum split a $6,000 payoff from a bookie with Ryan and Sodini.

The carrying-on often occurred at other locations, including the Busy Bee Restaurant on the Northwest Side of Chicago and the Holiday Inn in the blue-collar suburb of Hillside. After a drinking bout, Ryan could sleep off his hangover on a cot in Sodini's chambers. Ryan kept toilet accessories and a change of clothes there, where he sometimes spent the night to be sure he would not be late.

Except for the occasional disputes over distribution of bribe money, the functionaries in Sodini's courtroom got along fine. They even formed a fraternal order of sorts, known as the Cavaliers Club. The members drank, and ate pizza together and collected dues to take Sodini to fashionable restaurants, including Le Francais, a five-star restaurant in north suburban Wheeling, a long way from the Busy Bee.

One summer Sodini hosted a party for the Cavaliers at his summer home in Wisconsin. As luck would have it, a Chicago tavern owner happened to have a case pending before Sodini. Ryan arranged for the tavern to provide a free barrel of beer, and he dispatched a Chicago policeman to pick it up.

A lawyer did not have to be a Cavalier to have a mutually beneficial relationship with Sodini. For instance, one of the legendary fixers of the Circuit Court system, an attorney named Dean Wolfson, known in some circles as Dean the Dream, occasionally got around to Sodini's courtroom, and when he did he was always accompanied by money.

Sodini was on the bench one day when Wolfson showed up. Ryan stepped into the hall with Wolfson, who slipped him $50 for himself and $300 for Sodini. Ryan immediately went up to the bench.

"You've got a phone call, judge," Ryan whispered.

Sodini knew the signal and called a brief recess.

"Deano's got a case," said Ryan, handing Sodini the $300.

Sodini put the money in his pocket. He lit a cigarette and chatted with Ryan, as drinkers do, about their time together the night before at Mr. Pat's and the Busy Bee. Sodini lit another cigarette, and the conversation turned to a case in which other lawyers were expected to pass Sodini money. Then Sodini returned to the bench.

Justice must proceed.

Terrence Hake arrived early at Courtroom Nine in the Chicago Traffic Court Building. He hoped to influence Judge John G. Laurie to rule in favor of a client charged with drunken driving, but Laurie was not there. Hake wandered next door, into Courtroom Eight, where Judge John J. Devine presided.

Devine, who was known as "Dollars" among the hustlers because of his voracious pursuit of money, was on the bench hearing a speeding case. Hake, a former assistant state's attorney who had once been assigned to Devine's courtroom, went up to Harold Conn, a clerk, and explained his problem. Conn said he would try to arrange something. Hake returned to Courtroom Nine and took a seat in the front row. Conn whispered in Devine's ear, and Devine called a recess and left his courtroom.

Standing by the door that offered a view of Laurie's courtroom, now temporarily bereft of a judge, Conn said to Devine, "Judge, why don't you go on this case? You know him."

Devine peered into the courtroom and spotted Hake. "Go ahead and call it right now," he said.

Conn walked into Laurie's courtroom and called the name of Hake's client as Devine sat down in Laurie's chair. After what is known as a pretrial conference, Devine said he would find the defendant guilty, fine him $100, and place him on supervision—a disposition that appeared lenient. The sentence was entered, and Devine returned to his own courtroom.

Moments later, Hake huddled with Conn in a small room behind the empty courtroom.

"Well, it's worth a deuce, you know," said Conn.

"Deuce, sure, sure," said Hake, as money rustled in his hands. "Let's see now, I got a deuce here."

Hake handed over two $100 bills to Conn, who looked at them and then at Hake.

"Here's two for Devine, all right," said Conn with a what's-in-it-for-me expression in his voice.

"That was beautiful," said Hake. "Here's sixty for you."

Two hundred was Devine's going rate in the summer of 1981, although that July he showed special consideration to Hake by charging only $150 in one drunken-driving case.

"He's just starting out, Harold," Devine explained to Conn. "I've got to help him out. He was my state's attorney. I got to look out for him. When he gets on his feet and can afford it, then I'll put the price on him."

The price. From the beginning of his judicial career in 1977, Devine had set the price.

A pinched-face, grumpy man with a tight little mustache, thick aviator glasses, and thinning hair, Devine spent ten years as an assistant state's attorney and six more as an attorney for the Chicago Transit Authority before his Democratic political connections got him named an associate judge of the Circuit Court in 1977. Associate judges are chosen by the court's full judges, who are elected by the voters.

Devine's first judicial assignment was Branch 64, known as auto-theft court, down one floor from Sodini's gambling court at Police Headquarters. Most of the hustlers who operated out of Sodini's courtroom were also welcome in Devine's. But, while Sodini was an amiable crook, Devine was abrasive and short-tempered, even rude. Unlike Sodini, he did not fraternize with the boys in the bag. He raced through his caseload each day and left the building alone.

Well, usually alone. At one auto-theft hearing, the defendant was an attractive woman. Prosecutors were trying to throw the book at her, but Devine persuaded them to reduce the charge to a misdemeanor. He then invited the woman's attorney into his chambers and arranged for an introduction. The judge left court that afternoon in the company of the defendant.

One of the top hustlers in the courtrooms at Police Headquarters was Martin Schachter, who operated primarily out of Branch 40, which handled prostitution cases and was known as women's court, but who also found his way into Sodini's gambling court and eventually into Devine's auto-theft court. On his first day before Devine, Schachter received several referrals. He thanked the judge for his consideration.

"Thanks are nice," said Devine. "But they don't go very far. For those who help you, you should show your appreciation."

Schachter held out for a while, but after he found himself with no cases in auto-theft court, he began to show his appreciation.

Once Schachter objected to paying kickbacks on cases before Devine that were not steered to him by Devine.

"Whatever cases you have in this courtroom," replied Devine, "one-third goes to me. Those are the rules."

Schachter accepted the rules and eventually became the champion bond-receipt attorney for the whole county.

Devine's relentless insistence on kickbacks eventually caught the eye of the Chicago Bar Association, which recommended that he not be retained as an associate judge in 1983. The CBA's action was unprecedented. In response, the full judges decided not to give Devine another term. The word was out.

After he left the bench, Devine tried to establish a private law practice, but his reputation was as sour as his disposition. He was drinking heavily, and he was unable to attract enough clients to make the sort of living he had become accustomed to during his judicial career.

By 1985, he was managing the bar at Little John's Restaurant and Tap, located on a side street just across a parking lot from traffic court.

"I never sold my robe," he said one night at the bar.

The next day he went to prison, having been convicted of selling almost everything else connected with his office.

Judge Frank V. Salerno sat in a downtown restaurant one evening with his girlfriend and Vic Albanese, his close associate and sometime bagman. There was a pile of $100 bills on the white-linen-clothed table, tucked away in an alcove out of sight of the other customers.

Albanese, an investigator for the Chicago City Council Finance Committee, counted the money, putting it in stacks.

"How about some for me?" asked Judge Salerno's girlfriend, Wilma Peto. Albanese tossed her a C-note.

It was 1983 and a lucrative time for Salerno. He was assigned to license court, where he not only could take payoffs to fix court cases but also, through arrangements with Albanese and another Finance Committee investigator, Vito Stella, to fix city license violations and arrange zoning changes. They all worked in cooperation with Edward Margoscin, the head of the city Department of Consumer Services, which oversaw license violations.

Salerno had other contacts, too. He had once been a heavy bribe taker in traffic court, so he knew the ropes there. He could get tickets fixed, for a price, and Albanese was often the carrier of the money. Sometimes Wilma was the carrier of money from someone who wanted something done. Salerno, Albanese, Stella, or Margoscin got it done. Payoffs were pouring in from several directions.

It was ironic how Salerno had managed to get into such a lucrative position. In 1980 he had been assigned to Branch 29 at Belmont and Western avenues on the Northwest Side. Hustling was rampant in Branch 29 when Salerno was there, but one day he became a little too bold. There had been a case before him in which the defendant had a little black book with the names of many prominent Mafia figures in it. The state had had the book entered into evidence, but then, on a motion by the defense, Salerno had given it back to the defendant.

Salerno's action, questionable law, had the potential for a lot of bad publicity. Charles P. Horan, the judge who presided over all of the branch courts in Chicago, heard what Salerno had done and had him transferred immediately to traffic court, which is not considered a prestigious assignment. It is a dumping ground for errant or incompetent judges and a training ground for neophytes. After a tour in traffic court, Salerno was shuffled over to license court, where business blossomed.

Salerno had met Wilma Peto in 1982, when he was fifty.

24

She was sixteen. Although that was quite an age difference, Salerno could see right away that Wilma was mature for her age. He met her in a west suburban striptease club, where she worked. Apparently feeling a joint like that was no place for a swell kid like Wilma, Salerno soon got her a job as a cocktail waitress at a restaurant conveniently located near Salerno's courtroom in the Richard J. Daley Center in the Loop.

Wilma was too young to serve drinks legally, so Salerno arranged for her to get a driver's license saying she was twenty-one. After Wilma got the job in the Marina City office and apartment complex, Salerno and Albanese would lunch there almost every day. Wilma often visited the judge in his chambers. He would simply recess court when he saw her arrive. Albanese was usually there too, lining up deals for the judge and himself.

Through Albanese, Wilma would have overdue parking tickets fixed for her friends. She would collect half of the face amount of the tickets and offer that to Albanese. "But usually Vic told me to keep the money and took care of it for nothing," said Wilma. Salerno, Wilma estimated, gave her about $10,000 during their two-year relationship, carried on, of course, without the knowledge of Salerno's wife and family in suburban Oak Park.

The judge sent her roses by the dozens and showered her with gifts. One Christmas he gave her a mink coat. When she wanted to exchange the coat, Salerno told her she couldn't.

It was hot, he explained.

In June 1980, when Judge Salerno was suddenly transferred out of Branch 29, he was replaced by Associate Judge Thaddeus L. Kowalski, a former supervising public defender with a well-deserved reputation for honesty. Kowalski quickly got rid of the hustlers. His method was

25

simple: He refused to authorize the bond payments to crooked lawyers. They soon left for courtrooms where more cooperative judges presided, mostly at Eleventh and State.

Then, in December 1980, Judge Horan retired as head of the Chicago branch courts and was replaced by Judge Richard F. LeFevour, elevated from chief of traffic court. Traffic court under LeFevour had been a wild place, where a group of lawyers known as "miracle workers" had a steady arrangement with LeFevour to fix drunken-driving cases for $100 apiece. The lawyers would send the money to Judge LeFevour through his first cousin, James Le Fevour, a Chicago policeman who later admitted fixing at least one drunken-driving case a day through his cousin for seven years. There was a pool of judges who would accommodate any request for a fix by Judge LeFevour in exchange for being assigned to courtrooms where there was an opportunity to make money for themselves.

The traffic court is divided into two divisions, minor courtrooms and major courtrooms. Judges in the minor courtrooms hear charges on lesser offenses, such as speeding and wrong turns. The major courtrooms handle more serious charges, such as drunken driving and leaving the scene of an accident. Cases were assigned to courtrooms, not to individual judges. Judge LeFevour assigned judges to courtrooms on a daily basis.

After Jimmy LeFevour turned government witness against his former cohorts, including his cousin, he explained that the miracle workers would leave a list of the cases they wanted fixed and in what courtrooms. Judge LeFevour would then assign bribe-taking judges to those courtrooms. Later the attorneys would drop off their payments in Jimmy LeFevour's office, which was just outside Judge LeFevour's chambers.

Judges who did not fix cases seldom lasted more than

a week in major courtrooms. All new judges assigned to major courtrooms were tested immediately by Judge LeFevour, and those who did not accept bribes were not reassigned there.

"A judge didn't sit in a major courtroom very long unless I could see him," Jimmy LeFevour revealed; "see" was his euphemism for "fix." "I usually saw a judge every day," said Jimmy. "Sometimes more than one judge."

One judge in traffic court Jimmy could always see was John M. Murphy, a short, portly, gray-haired man in his midsixties who had been assigned to traffic court since he became a judge in 1972. Murphy was so dependable that, according to a former prosecutor who was there at the time, he once acquitted a miracle worker's client despite her testimony that she was drunk while driving. When the prosecutor, during cross-examination, elicited the admission, Judge Murphy threw up his hands and called a recess.

"This state's attorney got the defendant to admit she was drunk," said Murphy to the miracle worker. "Counselor, I suggest you talk to your client."

The trial resumed and Murphy found the woman not guilty.

"I still have a reasonable doubt," he said.

When Judge LeFevour became the presiding judge over all the city branch courts, he quickly looked to expand his economic horizons. Shortly after his appointment, he visited the courtrooms at Belmont and Western, where Judge Kowalski, who allowed no hustling, presided in Branch 29. Kowalski told LeFevour how he had eliminated the hustlers.

"Good," said LeFevour. "We shouldn't tolerate hustlers."

Within three weeks, Kowalski was transferred to a little courtroom in the Cabrini-Green housing project on the

27

Near North Side. Kowalski was replaced in Branch 29 by Judge Murphy, and the hustlers were soon back in the hallways.

Judge LeFevour had broadened his traffic court concept of organized corruption and formed a "Hustlers Club" in the branch courts. In the spring of 1981, Jimmy LeFevour began collecting $500 a month from five lawyers for allowing them to hustle clients in the courtrooms at Eleventh and State and at Belmont and Western. Later the club expanded to allow in two more hustlers, including James Oakey, a former associate judge who in 1975 had been removed from the bench for running his family's private business from the telephones in his chambers. Oakey was a large man with corresponding Falstaffian appetites—in food, in drink, in women. As a judge, attorneys say, he had been known to spot an attractive woman in his courtroom and have his clerk summon her to his chambers, where he would make whatever sexual moves the situation allowed.

Another member of the Hustlers Club was Bob Daniels, an attorney with no known office address; his office seemed to be whichever hallway he was working. Daniels was the archetypal hustler. He looked exactly like what he was. He was a slight man with a crooked nose and long, oiled hair combed back at the sides to meet in a shiny tangle at the rear of the head. He wore lightweight three-piece suits, always with a boutonniere in the lapel. His wide-collared shirts had long French cuffs, and his large gold cuff links were visible below his jacket sleeves. Daniels frequently appeared in Branch 29 at Belmont and Western.

There was a second courtroom at Belmont and Western, across the hall from Branch 29. This was Branch 42, a felony preliminary hearing court. Branch 42 was presided over by Judge John F. Reynolds, a hearty veteran of the fix wherever he went, just the kind of man Judge LeFevour felt comfortable with. Sometimes called Black Jack, Reynolds had spent time in traffic court, where he was always open to negotiations. One of the star negotiators was Edward (Fast Eddie) Kaplan, who had a code Reynolds understood.

"Judge, I'll be at Fritzel's tonight," Kaplan would say, referring to a State Street restaurant that, before it went out of business in 1972, was frequented by politicians and show-business types. The reference to Fritzel's meant Fast Eddie would have money available for Reynolds in return for a favorable ruling in a drunken-driving case.

One evening, after Reynolds had found Kaplan's client innocent of drunken driving, Kaplan walked into Fritzel's and up to a table where Reynolds sat with some friends. Kaplan greeted everyone and then asked Reynolds if he could speak with him for a minute. The two walked out of the dining room, down a flight of stairs, and into the men's room. Kaplan took out $100 and gave it to the judge.

"Thank you for your courtesy," said Kaplan.

"Anytime," said Reynolds.

Judge Reynolds ran an orderly, efficient Branch 42. Clerks, who previously received a one-third kickback from lawyers for steering clients to them, no longer received anything. Reynolds himself steered the clients—exclusively to Thomas M. Del Becarro and Arthur Cirignani. This eliminated the scrambling present in courtrooms like Sodini's.

Reynolds first met Del Becarro, a handsome young man who wore expensive, not-quite-flashy suits and had carefully styled dark hair, when he was just out of law school and a member of the public defender's staff. Reynolds encouraged Del Bacarro to go into private practice, and by 1979 he was appearing before Reynolds in Branch 42. At first, Del Bacarro did not pay Reynolds any kickbacks. One day Reynolds called the young lawyer into his chambers.

"You were on a scholarship and the scholarship is over,"

said Reynolds, who told Del Becarro he was to pay one-third of the bond receipts he received from cases Reynolds referred to him.

"You're a lawyer, I'm a lawyer, and lawyers pay referral fees," said Reynolds, who added that Del Becarro was naive if he thought it was any other way.

"You didn't just get off the Belmont Avenue bus, did you?" asked Reynolds.

From that day on Del Becarro paid off. He made payoffs by dropping magazines stuffed with cash into a drawer in the judge's desk. He left cash in the judge's suit coat pocket and on the console between the bucket seats of Reynolds's BMW. He slipped it to the judge under the table in restaurants. Sometimes he visited the judge at his Astor Street condominium and gave it to him there.

Business was brisk. In the month leading up to Christmas in 1980, Del Becarro received $8,550 in cash bond refunds from Reynolds's courtroom.

Jimmy LeFevour oversaw the payoffs from the Hustlers Club to his cousin. Jimmy was an aggressive bagman. Members of the club came to call him "Jingles" because he had a habit of rattling loose coins in his suit jacket and demanding, "Fill me up."

"I'm here. Fill me up," Jingles would say with his face pressed nose-to-nose with lawyers in the branch courts. "If you don't fill me up, I'm going to make life rough for you."

For a time in 1982 Judge LeFevour assigned an old crony of his from traffic court, Judge John H. McCollom, to Branch 29. McCollom was such an active bribe taker in traffic court that once, in spite of receiving "a ton of money" for a favorable ruling in a drunken-driving case, he forgot the case was fixed. He gave the defendant the maximum sentence, 364 days in jail. After the sentencing, McCollom was

30

reminded that he had taken money to fix the case. He began to laugh.

"Aw, Christ, I don't know what in the hell we are going to do," McCollom said to Ira Blackwood, a police officer who was his bagman.

"Undo it," said Blackwood.

Within a week McCollom had reduced the sentence to weekends in jail.

The sentence reduction was a relief to the lawyer who paid the bribe, John J. Ward, who did not want a blot on his distinguished record. Ward was then executive director of the Cook County Judicial Advisory Council, a group empowered by the executive branch of the Cook County government to make recommendations on ways to clean up the court system.

Since becoming a judge in 1962, Wayne W. Olson was not one who avoided the appearance of impropriety, either on or off the bench. Olson, in fact, seemed to embrace impropriety eagerly, as if it were a stack of crisp $100 bills.

"I love people that take dough because you know exactly where you stand," Olson told attorney Bruce Roth one day in December 1980. They were discussing whether a certain attorney would take money from a client to fix a case— money, of course, that might be passed on eventually to Olson.

Olson, a fat, hard-drinking man with white hair and a white mustache, presided over Branch 57, narcotics court, in the early 1980s. He made it a haven for hustling. Branch 57 is one of two narcotics courts in the criminal courts building at Twenty-sixth and California on the Southwest Side, adjoining the Cook County Jail. Branch 57 is the busier of the two courts. It has, as one attorney put it, "the nickel-bag stuff," while the other court, Branch 25, has the tougher cases, including so-called Class X felonies, punishable by a minimum of ten years in prison. There was no hustling in Branch 25 because big-time dope dealers arrived there with lawyers on handsome retainers and because the judge in Branch 25, Arthur V. Zelezinski, did not allow hustling.

Outside Olson's Branch 57, however, the hustlers arrived early, rounding up their first customers at 8:30 in the morning at the stand-up coffee shop located around the corner from the courtroom. James J. Costello, Olson's main kickback partner, was almost always there.

"We can make a thousand a week," Olson told Costello in August 1980, when the judge said he would refer cases to Costello in return for half of his legal fees.

The records showed that Olson and Costello were able to make their thousand a week, although not without an occasional misunderstanding. Once, when both were drunk in a restaurant, they began arguing over the cut. Olson threw Costello's eyeglasses across the room, smashing them. He then poured a glass of red wine over Costello's shirt and shouted, "You're thrown out of Twenty-sixth and California!" Costello responded with a torrent of profanity and threw a bottle of wine across the room.

There was no lasting breach in the business relationship, however. Costello gave Olson $1,000 the very next day.

Public brawling was not new to Olson. At four o'clock on the morning of September 22, 1965, outside a bar called the Alibi Inn in the western suburb of North Riverside, Olson got into an argument with a man named Frank Benner. Next thing anybody knew, Benner went down, hit his head on the sidewalk, and died of a skull fracture. A witness charged that Olson had pushed Benner, but the judge denied it. He did admit he had been drinking since five o'clock the previous afternoon.

Olson was absolved of possible involuntary manslaughter charges when a grand jury refused to indict him, which was curious because grand juries almost automatically indict anyone a prosecutor wants indicted. The Illinois Courts Commission, the agency in charge of judicial discipline, also took no action. After a four-month leave of absence at full pay, Olson returned to the bench.

Neither his conduct nor his reputation improved. One night there was a going-away party for a wealthy South Side contractor in a Rush Street nightclub named Adolph's, a playground for connected swingers. The contractor was going away to prison, having been convicted of bid rigging. Judge Olson was at the party, which was held in an upstairs room. When the party broke up, some of the guests, including Olson, went to the restaurant downstairs. As the host left, he slipped two $100 bills to a couple of large, off-duty Chicago cops.

"Your job for the rest of the night is to look after Wayne and make sure he gets home alive," the host said, tossing a look over to Olson, now yodeling at full volume at the bar with his arm around a pretty young woman.

Olson liked to sing. In court one day in the early 1970s, when he had been assigned to Branch 44, Olson had before him a defendant who had plea-bargained on a burglary charge. Before sentencing, Olson asked the man if he had anything to say. The defendant said it was his birthday. "It's your birthday?" Olson said. He stood up, leaned over the front of the bench with his hands clasped behind his back, and sang quickly: *Happy birthday to you/Happy birthday to you/One year in Vandalia/Happy birthday to you!* Olson turned to the bailiff and said, "Get him outta here."

Olson was nicer to another defendant, Nathaniel Spurlark, who was, among many other things, a drug dealer. Spurlark had been sentenced to a long prison term by a judge who had denied him bail pending appeal. The judge had called Spurlark a menace to society. But two weeks later, the judge retired. Olson temporarily took his place. Spurlark's lawyer, Sam Adam, immediately seized the opportunity. He asked Olson to reconsider granting bond. Olson agreed, requiring Spurlark to post only $1,250, and released him.

"He's a solid citizen," said Olson.

The news organizations came down hard on Olson for that one, causing much consternation for the chief judge of the Circuit Court, John S. Boyle. Boyle transferred Olson to small claims court, where Olson's opportunities to supplement his salary were limited. But two years later Boyle was replaced as chief judge by Harry G. Comerford, who, for reasons he has never explained, assigned Olson to Branch 57. Once again, the cash register in Wayne Olson's heart started dinging.

In Branch 57, Olson had a tight deal worked out with Costello, but Costello was by no means the only lawyer kicking back in Branch 57. And Olson was always open to new propositions. After referring several cases to Bruce Roth one day, the two had a little chat in Olson's chambers.

"I'm a coin collector," said Olson.

"Is two enough, judge?" inquired Roth, who had grossed $765 in bond refunds that day.

"Well, I made a deal with somebody," said Olson, "but I'd rather give it to you. You'd do a better job."

"I gave you a deuce," Roth said. "If it's not enough, just tell me."

"I like a guy that gives me half of what he gets," Olson replied.

Olson had never looked upon his career at the bar as a public trust. He often boasted of his corruption when he had been a private attorney, from 1953 until he became a judge less than a decade later.

"I paid off every judge I appeared before."

He told of a judge who once demanded more money

than he was willing to pay. Olson said he had arranged the transfer of the case to another judge, but he never forgot or forgave the judge he considered greedy. Years later, when he was on the bench himself, Olson became that judge's supervisor.

"And I assigned him to nothing," Olson said with a laugh. "The moral of this story is never kick your janitor in the ass. Someday he might be your landlord."

But the lucrative days for Olson were running short. The FBI and IRS were poking around the courts. They were especially interested in Wayne W. Olson.

The landlord was about to be evicted.

2

The Sting

☆

It was November 26, 1980, the day before Thanksgiving, and Judge Wayne Olson was on vacation.

A team of FBI agents, led by Randall Jordan, walked into Olson's empty chambers in narcotics court. They went right to work, looking over Olson's office, checking the walls, the ledges, his desk. They decided on the desk. They hid a microphone in it.

They were making history of a sort. It was the first time a judge in the United States had ever had his chambers bugged. At least it was the first time it had ever been done legally.

The man who had obtained the authorization, at the direction of U.S. Attorney Thomas P. Sullivan, was agent Jordan. A short time before, Jordan had secretly filed an affidavit with Chief Judge James B. Parsons of the U.S. District Court for the Northern District of Illinois. The affidavit said there was reason to believe crimes were being committed in Judge Olson's courtroom.

Olson had become one of the most visible thieves around. His open favoritism toward attorney James J. Costello and other hustlers wandering his courtroom had attracted the attention of anyone who had spent time there. Jordan had first become suspicious while conducting an investigation—originally independent of Olson's activities—of possible police corruption.

Jordan discussed his suspicions with Sullivan. About the same time, in 1979, two young assistant U.S. attorneys, Charles Sklarsky and Daniel Reidy, also conferred with Sullivan, telling him they believed corruption "had become a way of life" among certain lawyers and judges in the Chicago courts. Sklarsky had recently joined the federal prosecutor's office after six years as an assistant Cook County state's attorney. As a county prosecutor, Sklarsky had been assigned to various courtrooms and had developed opinions about which judges were crooked.

Several other assistant county prosecutors followed Sklarsky into the U.S. attorney's office. They contributed horror stories of their own about the court system.

Sullivan talked to Cook County State's Attorney Bernard Carey, who, frustrated with a string of acquittals that he felt were questionable, was ready to cooperate in an investigation.

"The straw that broke the camel's back as far as I was concerned was the Harry Aleman case," said Carey, after he left office and shortly before becoming a judge himself.

Aleman was a nephew of Joseph Ferriola, a rising mafioso who would eventually become the head of the Chicago mob. Aleman was considered one of organized crime's top assassins. He was the suspect in more than a score of killings. He was thought to have dispatched syndicate enemies in Kansas City, Milwaukee, Indianapolis, Atlanta, Las

Vegas, San Diego, and throughout Chicago and its suburbs. Supposed Aleman victims had been found in car trunks, restaurant booths, kitchens, recreation rooms, parking lots, garages, alleys, basements, airports, movie houses, and horse parlors. Authorities believed his list included the husband of singer Barbara NcNair and onetime Chicago mob boss Sam Giancana.

In May 1977, Aleman was brought to trial for the murder of William Logan, a Teamsters union steward who was shotgunned outside his West Side home. The state's attorney's office went into court with what Carey thought was a strong case. For the first time that anyone could remember, a private citizen who had witnessed a crime syndicate murder was going to testify against an accused hit man. The witness was Robert Lowe, twenty-eight, who was Logan's neighbor. Lowe had been walking his dog when Logan was killed. Lowe said he was approaching Logan to ask him a question when a shotgun, appearing from a double-parked car, blasted Logan. A man got out of the car, walked over to Logan, and shot him again with a pistol, a coup de grace. As the killer turned, and Lowe restrained his dog, their eyes locked for a moment.

"I'll never forget that face as long as I live," Lowe said in court as he pointed out Harry Aleman. Lowe's testimony backed up testimony by Louis Almeida, an outfit killer, who said he was the driver of the car. By the time of the trial, Almeida was doing time in a federal prison, so he had a motive for turning government witness, but Lowe had no such motive. He would have to live the rest of his life with fear and a new identity.

The defense demanded a bench trial—which was a defendant's right then in Illinois—and the judge was Frank J. Wilson. Despite the vivid eyewitness testimony of Lowe and Almeida, Wilson acquitted Aleman. A few weeks later, after a sustained outcry from the press and Carey, Wilson retired from the bench.

"That was one of the best-evidenced trials I ever saw," Carey said several years later. "We had two eyeball witnesses—one who was the driver and one who was an independent party. You can convict people with one or the other, but when you have both, and a pattern, I don't know how any judge could decide it the way Wilson did. What is anybody's life worth, if the syndicate can spring a hit man when there are two eyewitnesses?

"Our frustrations were great, and we were hot to do something. Sullivan and I got together. Then we had some meetings and started considering how the investigation could be done. The U.S. attorney's office did hours and hours, weeks, months of research."

Eventually, Sullivan went to Washington, D.C., and discussed the Cook County Circuit Court situation with Justice Department officials.

By that time, the Justice Department had become enamored of sting operations. Abscam, which eventually led to the convictions of Senator Harrison A. Williams, Jr., of New Jersey and six congressmen, was the most highly publicized of the government stings. FBI agents posed as employees of Abdul Enterprises, a fictional multinational corporation whose principal was supposed to be an Arab sheik who needed help on immigration matters. Melvin Weinberg, a career swindler, led the officials to the sheik, played by an FBI man. They met in hotel rooms where cameras were hidden. Perhaps the most lasting single image from Abscam was Representative Richard Kelly of Florida stuffing money into his pockets while the FBI cameras rolled. It made great television and delighted FBI Director William H. Webster and top Justice Department officials.

Until the mid 1970s, the FBI had not engaged in many

39

sting operations. FBI Director J. Edgar Hoover did not like them. He considered them a waste of resources: Sting operations, especially those involving electronic surveillance, are hugely expensive. He was also afraid agents who acted corruptly might become corrupt. Hoover died in 1972, however. Morale in the bureau was low and became lower with the unfolding of Watergate, when Hoover's successor, Acting Director L. Patrick Gray III, was forced to resign because he was part of the cover-up.

In 1975, the FBI began what became known as the D.C. Sting, a joint effort with the Washington Police Department. It was, simply, an undercover fencing operation for stolen goods. The word was passed around the streets of Washington that hot items could be sold at a certain location. Then the cops and feds just waited for the thieves to arrive. Scores were arrested and convicted. FBI morale soared with the ensuing publicity. Undercover sting operations came into vogue. In 1977, the Justice Department was involved in fifty-three undercover operations, including twenty conducted jointly with local investigators. By 1980, the yearly average was three hundred.

The operations raised constitutional questions. Should government be in the business of committing crimes, no matter to what admirable ends? A sting operation such as Abscam is not an investigation in the traditional sense, in that law enforcement officials are not confined to looking for someone responsible for a crime that has already been committed, and surveillance is not confined to people who may have committed crimes.

An Abscam-style sting solves no existing crime; rather, it tests the capacity of citizens to commit hypothetical crimes. The sting is—to quote the government's own language in cases arising out of Abscam—"conceived to create opportunities for illicit conduct" by people who are "predisposed" to crime. It might be argued that dangling $50,000 in front of someone, as the government did in Abscam, might make almost anyone agree to help a project through, especially if the project was supposed to be good for the city. The person would not have to be "predisposed" to commit a crime. Thus, critics argue, sting operations merely prove that if you offer enough people enough money, sooner or later someone will take it. But juries and appeals courts have sided consistently with the government's point of view in the sting cases: The act of accepting the money shows a predisposition to do so. Guilty. Case closed.

As the Justice Department's appetite for stings grew, agents sometimes got a little sloppy. In Cleveland, for instance, the feds launched Operation Corkscrew. They contacted a hustling court bailiff named Marvin Bray, who took money from agents who were offering up to $3,000 to get traffic cases fixed. Bray said, sure, he'd arrange for the money to get to judges. He set up meetings between agents and two judges, Lillian Burke and Clarence L. Gaines; the meetings were videotaped. The judges told the agents to give the money to Bray and everything would be fixed. The agents kept going back, twenty-six times in all, passing out more than $100,000.

After about a year of this, one of the agents saw Judge Burke on television and realized the Judge Burke he was looking at was not the same Judge Burke he had been paying off all those months. It turned out that Bray had friends posing as the judges. He was pocketing all the money himself. Most of the cases that the FBI agents thought they were fixing were being dismissed by the real judges on the merits.

In Chicago, at about the same time, the Justice Department was bringing to trial a series of defendants accused of robbing mail carriers of mailbox keys. A minor crime wave of key thefts was under way. But the perpetrators were getting caught, thanks to the undercover work of

41

Gregory Jones, a small-time thief facing a jail sentence. The postal service was employing Jones as a mole to help catch other thieves. Jones was, in essence, a bounty hunter. He got $1,000 per arrest. For several years, he earned $15,000 to $18,000 annually.

"All of a sudden we were getting mail-key cases from all over the city," said Richard F. Walsh, a former federal public defender who represented several of the defendants. Then Walsh found out why. Jones was going to patients at methadone clinics around the city and telling them he had someone who would pay them $4,000 for stolen mailbox keys.

"Can you imagine offering a junkie four thousand dollars?" asked Walsh. "He'll do anything."

What they were doing was grabbing the keys from mail carriers and then contacting Jones, who would simply have the junkies arrested with keys in their possession. He was enticing them to commit crimes, turning them in, and collecting a bounty. Walsh went to the U.S. attorney's office.

"You're going to get a mailman killed if you let this go on," he said. But the cases did keep going on, and some mail carriers did get injured, although not seriously. One was Maced and one beaten up. Walsh won several of the cases with an entrapment defense.

"We were winning them, but they kept bringing them," said Walsh. Finally, Jones overstepped himself. He was caught plotting to steal a key and plant it on an innocent man. He was indicted and convicted, but federal prosecutors, in consideration of Jones's past work for the government, recommended a light sentence. He got one year, which was suspended after a few months.

"It's a fact of life that your dirtiest people are sometimes your best informants," said an assistant U.S. attorney familiar with the case.

Joseph Meltzer was pretty dirty. During the Abscam

sting, but before it had become public, he was working as an FBI informant out of Florida. He had offered his services to the government after being convicted of possession of stolen securities. When he got wind of the Abscam operation—how something called Abdul Enterprises had been set up by the FBI, and how an agent was posing as a sheik who was willing to pay bribes to guarantee good investments—his swindler's heart was touched. He began contacting small businesses and telling them he could get the sheik to invest in their companies. Abdul Enterprises was a multinational company, he told them, with almost unlimited resources. This might be the break the businesses were waiting for, a chance to get some real money behind their operations. Meltzer would want a fee, of course, $10,000 in processing costs—not much when one considered the type of investment Abdul Enterprises would make.

Meltzer gave his potential clients the name and number of Abdul Enterprises and the name of a Chase Manhattan Bank vice-president who could confirm the sheik's assets. When Meltzer's marks called Abdul Enterprises, FBI agents answered the phone and confirmed that it was a legitimate enterprise. When they called Chase Manhattan, the vice-president, cooperating with the FBI, said Abdul Enterprises had $400 million on deposit.

At least fifteen people paid Meltzer $10,000 each in processing costs.

One couple, whose interior decorating business went broke after they got involved in Meltzer's scam, sued the government for $65,000. In the suit they claimed that the FBI knew for months what Meltzer was doing but allowed him to continue because they did not want to jeopardize the secrecy of the Abscam investigation.

Despite such abuses and complaints from civil libertarians, prosecutors went ahead with more and more undercover operations. They were getting convictions and headlines. In New Orleans, reputed mob boss Carlos Marcello was convicted in a labor union health insurance sting. In Oklahoma, about a hundred county officials were convicted of taking kickbacks after the FBI wired a lumber contractor. In Massachusetts, more than fifty people were convicted after the FBI and state police set up a D.C. Sting–type operation, fencing hijacked goods out of a warehouse while cameras whirred. And in Chicago, Teamsters Union president Roy L. Williams and reputed mob hit man Joseph Lombardo, among others, were convicted of conspiracy to bribe former U.S. Senator Howard W. Cannon of Nevada—in a case that involved the most widespread use of electronic surveillance in the nation's history.

With the tapping of Judge Olson's chambers in the Chicago narcotics court, the government had broken new ground. When it was later revealed that Olson's courtroom had been wired, many judges and lawyers were appalled. "To a degree, the judge's chambers is a sanctuary," said an Illinois Supreme Court justice. "It's kind of like placing a bug in a confessional booth."

The pro-bugging argument ran along the line that eavesdropping was the only way to find out that a crime had been committed when both the briber and the bribee were serenely and silently content in their illegal arrangement. "These crimes are often between two people, both profiting at the public's expense," said the man who initiated the bugging, Tom Sullivan, after he left the U.S. attorney's office. "The victim is society. You have to go undercover."

Once Sullivan had the go-ahead from his superiors in Washington to conduct a sting in the Cook County Circuit Court, the operation needed a name. The FBI had taken to giving names to its investigations—a public relations touch picked up from military assault operations. The names often had a grandiose quality.

After reviewing several suggestions, the special agent in

charge of the Chicago FBI office, James D. Hegarty, decided to call the Chicago sting "Operation Fly Catcher." Unfortunately, that name was already taken. "We learned that, in a Delaware probe in 1973, we had used the same code name, and FBI regulations bar the use of a code name more than once," Hegarty said later.

Chosen as a replacement was "Operation Greylord"—a sarcastic reference to the dignity of the English lord chancellors, who wear wigs, and the lack of dignity in the Chicago courts.

To understand the Chicago courts and the origins of Greylord, it is first necessary to understand how the court system works in the context of Chicago politics.

The Cook County Circuit Court was dominated for many years by Richard J. Daley, the last of the big-city political bosses. Daley derived his power over the courts not from being mayor of Chicago but from being chairman of the Cook County Democratic Central Committee, which was to Cook County what the Politburo is to the Soviet Union.

As chairman of the central committee from 1953 until his death in 1976, Daley controlled tens of thousands of jobs ranging from garbage collector to assistant city attorney. The patronage system provided legions of election workers known collectively, together with the party bosses, as the Democratic Machine.

Daley treated the judiciary as just another part of the county's overall patronage system. He parceled out jobs here and there as rewards for good performance by committeemen, Chicago aldermen, and other politicians. The more votes a politician could deliver, the more jobs Daley gave him. A judgeship was the grand patronage prize.

About half of the county's judges were elected in general elections. To get elected, in most cases, one had to be slated by the central committee. To be slated, one had to be approved personally by the chairman. Thus, although judges were chosen in popular elections, in a very real sense only one vote counted—Daley's.

The elected judges, called full judges, in turn selected the rest of the judges, called associate judges. Daley exercised enormous influence over the full judges in their choice of associate judges. On both levels, selection was by connection.

The full judges also elected a chief judge from their ranks—the ultimate in organizational perversity: a supervisor being chosen in a popularity contest by those he was supposed to supervise.

In addition to Circuit Court judges, the central committee also slated—and therefore assured the election of—eighteen judges of the First District Illinois Appellate Court, which hears appeals of Cook County cases, and three of the seven judges of the Illinois Supreme Court. The Supreme Court was empowered to fill any vacancies on the lower court that occurred between elections, but unofficially delegated the appointment authority in Cook County to its three Cook County members, who in turn unofficially delegated it to Daley.

Republicans hadn't been much of a threat in the city since the Depression. Countywide, the Democrats could dominate because there were more Democrats in the city than there were Republicans in the suburbs. Occasionally, however, Republicans could grab a countywide office. Daley hated that. He particularly hated having Republican state's attorneys—which happened twice during his reign—because they invariably created embarrassing headlines by indicting Democrats. However, by selecting the right candidate—one, say, who was not himself under indictment—the Democrats never stayed out of office long.

The Machine's power was curtailed in 1970 as a result of a federal lawsuit brought by a young lawyer named

Michael Shakman, but, partly through inertia, it kept functioning into the early 1980s. After Daley died, however, the absolute power he enjoyed was never again vested in one person. The mayors who followed him did not chair the Democratic Central Committee.

The Shakman litigation reduced the power of patronage by forbidding firing for political reasons, thus rendering the politicians powerless to compel public employees to perform election work. After Daley's death, further Shakman litigation was settled with a court-approved agreement forbidding hiring for political reasons—the death sentence for the Machine.

During the period pertinent to Greylord, however, the Machine was the mechanism for judicial election. Exceptional legal talents occasionally ascended to the bench under the system—but usually only by accident. In 1975, for instance, Daley had the central committee slate Joseph Gordon for the Circuit Court. Gordon, a bright and highly regarded former law professor, would have been an outstanding member of any judiciary, but that had little to do with why Daley selected him. When Daley's youngest son, William, was having trouble with his grades at John Marshall Law School, Gordon tutored him privately. For this, Daley was grateful. He expressed his gratitude by making Gordon a judge.

Before 1964, judicial terms were four years. To stay in office, judges had to be reslated by the committee every four years, which meant that they had to stay in the committee's favor. This gave politicians tremendous potential to influence cases. Any judge who offended a Democratic politician ran the risk of being dumped at the next slating session.

For many years, pressure had been building to replace the political selection system with a merit selection system. A merit system had been operating effectively since

1940 in the two largest counties of neighboring Missouri. Under the Missouri system, a panel of judges, lawyers, and laymen screens judicial candidates and nominates three for each vacancy. From the three, the governor chooses one.

In 1960, the American Bar Association issued a report praising Missouri's system, saying that a judge there "no longer has to be fearful of any of his judicial pronouncements displeasing the political bosses." The report encouraged merit selection proponents in Illinois. The Chicago Democrats, of course, ardently opposed the idea. However, to head off merit selection, they agreed to a general restructuring of the judiciary.

Under the rubric of "reform," the Illinois General Assembly approved a constitutional amendment, which, after approval by voters, went into effect in 1964. The amendment created a commission of judges with power, in cases brought to its attention by the Illinois attorney general, to remove or suspend judges for misconduct. It also increased the terms of full judges from four to six years and made it possible for judges to stay in office without reslating. To become a full judge, a candidate still had to run in a partisan election, but thereafter only had to stand for retention. The names of judges seeking retention were on a nonpartisan ballot. Retention initially required a majority vote, but that was later changed to 60 percent.

The change made sitting full judges somewhat less susceptible to political pressure, but they still owed the Machine. As Democratic Committeeman Vito Marzullo, one of the crustiest of Daley allies, put it: "Don't think that these people are ingrates. They always cooperate with the party that put them on the bench whenever they can."

In 1980, fourteen years after the so-called reform, forty-five men and women appeared before the committee seeking slating for nine full judgeships. Several spoke of their academic records and the scholarly articles they had written. Committeeman Nicholas B. Blase was unimpressed. "The difference between them is whether they've done their homework for the Democratic Party," Blase said. "We must bring people up from ward organizations and ultimately reward them."

Better to be direct, if you were a candidate. "It is morally proper to reward people for past service to the party," Associate Judge Edward H. Marsalek told the slatemakers.

"I will never do anything as a judge to cast any ill feeling toward this organization," said Associate Judge Arthur A. Ellis.

The reformed system put the major figures of the Greylord scandal on the bench. Ray Sodini, the hung-over gambling court judge who sometimes delegated his responsibility to a police sergeant, was sponsored by Congressman Daniel Rostenkowski, who later became chairman of the House Ways and Means Committee and Democratic committeeman from the Thirty-second Ward. Dollars Devine was sponsored by Neil F. Hartigan, former lieutenant governor and committeeman of the Forty-ninth Ward, who later became Illinois attorney general. Frank Salerno, the judge who gave his girlfriend a hot mink, was sponsored by Edward R. Vrdolyak, alderman and Democratic committeeman of the Tenth Ward, who switched to the Republican Party after Harold Washington, the city's first black mayor, was reelected.

Other legislative "reforms" helped set the stage for the Greylord scandal. In 1963, the General Assembly amended the Illinois Code of Criminal Procedure to eliminate bail bondsmen. Rather than having bondsmen post the full amount of defendants' bonds, levying a 10 percent fee, the new law allowed defendants to be released after posting 10 percent of their bonds with the clerk of the court. After defendants appeared in court, their bonds were refunded by mail. In 1969, the General Assembly amended the Bail Reform Act to allow defendants to sign over bond refunds to attorneys of record.

The hustler was born.

Meanwhile, in 1969, Illinois' first constitutional convention in fifty years was convened. Proponents of merit selection saw this as another opportunity.

Two Illinois Supreme Court justices, Roy J. Solfisburg, Jr., and Ray I. Klingbiel, had just been forced to resign after it became known that they held stock in a bank organized by the state director of revenue, Theodore Isaacs. The court had reaffirmed a lower court decision quashing an indictment against Isaacs.

The scandal suddenly thrust judicial reform into the forefront of the constitutional convention, which proposed establishing, in the body of the new constitution, what was touted as a tough system for policing judicial conduct.

The convention also favored replacing election of judges with a merit system but feared that including the measure in the body of the constitution might prompt the electorate to reject the entire document. Thus, merit selection was submitted to voters in the 1970 general election as a separate proposition. The new constitution was overwhelmingly approved in the 1970 general election, but the merit proposition was defeated.

The constitution, which went into effect in 1971, created a Judicial Inquiry Board and an Illinois Courts Commission. The board, composed of judges, lawyers, and laypersons, investigates complaints of judicial misconduct and, in cases where there is a "reasonable basis" to do so, files complaints with the commission. The Courts Commission, composed of five judges, was empowered to remove, suspend, or censure any judge for "willful misconduct in office, persistent failure to perform his duties, or other conduct that is prejudicial to the administration of justice or that brings the judicial office into disrepute."

For the first six years of its life, the new disciplinary system operated as expected. By late 1977, the Judicial Inquiry Board had brought charges against twenty-two judges, and seventeen of those had been found guilty by the Courts Commission and punished. Then, in 1977, although the constitution provided that "decisions of the commission shall be final," the Illinois Supreme Court took it upon itself to review one of the commission's decisions. The Supreme Court did this despite the fact that, after vigorous debate, the Illinois Constitutional Convention in 1969–70 had deliberately withheld that authority from the court.

The case the Supreme Court decided to review involved a politically connected judge from central Illinois, Samuel G. Harrod III, who had sentenced twenty-six young men to go get haircuts as punishment for what he called their "antisocial attitudes." Since there is no law against such attitudes, the Courts Commission held that the sentences were improper and suspended Harrod from the bench for thirty days without pay.

The Supreme Court reversed Harrod's suspension, declaring that the commission had overstepped its authority. In sweeping language that virtually emasculated the judicial disciplinary system, the court declared that the commission was not empowered to interpret statutes, such as the sentencing statute Harrod was accused of violating. Intimating that the constitutional standards might be vague and overbroad, the court added that only its own rules governing judicial conduct could be the basis for disciplinary action.

The Judicial Inquiry Board issued a press release condemning the Supreme Court for "an extraordinary misreading of constitutional language and intent," but it had no other recourse. The Illinois Supreme Court is the court of last resort in interpreting the state constitution.

Harrod, who had condemned antisocial attitudes from the bench, then began to display some of his own. He was caught forging the names of three members of the Judicial Inquiry Board to orders for magazine subscriptions. Over a period of weeks, the men were flooded with magazines they didn't want. When he was exposed as the forger, Harrod resigned from the bench.

Then, in 1979, the Illinois Supreme Court issued a ruling that almost stopped the Greylord investigation before it began. The court harshly criticized a prosecutor, Morton E. Friedman, for doing precisely what the Greylord prosecutors proposed to do—technically violating the law in an effort to obtain evidence of bribery in criminal cases.

Friedman had been chief of the criminal division of the Cook County state's attorney's office in 1973 when a defense lawyer offered a Chicago policeman a $50 bribe to give false testimony in a drunken-driving case—testimony that would result in an automatic dismissal of the charge. However, the officer happened to be honest and told Friedman of the bribe offer. Friedman instructed him to do what the lawyer requested. The officer did, and the charge was dismissed. A few minutes later, the lawyer paid the officer the $50 and was arrested and charged with bribery.

After Friedman approved a similar sting in a case involving another defense lawyer, Illinois authorities moved not only against the corrupt lawyers—who were disbarred—but also against Friedman. A review panel of the Attorney Registration and Disciplinary Commission, an agency created by the Illinois Supreme Court in 1973 to investigate attorney misconduct, recommended that the Supreme Court formally censure Friedman.

52

Friedman contended that his alleged disciplinary infractions were necessary to bring corrupt lawyers to justice, that no alternative methods to accomplish this were available, that his lofty motive should negate his technical violations of the law, and that censuring him would give more emphasis to the abstract concept of courtroom sanctity than to the more substantive concept of an honest legal system.

Several well-known lawyers filed *amicus curiae* (friend of the court) briefs with the Supreme Court on Friedman's behalf. One of the briefs was from Tom Sullivan. It said, in part:

> From time to time, prosecutors receive what appear to be reliable allegations that defense attorneys in criminal cases are engaged in suborning perjury, or bribing witnesses, bailiffs, clerks, prosecutors or judges, or the like. The prosecutor to whom such allegations are made has a duty to investigate, and to prosecute those found to be corrupting the criminal process. . . .
>
> Usually, to obtain hard evidence of payment, it is necessary to have one or more of the participants in the case pretend to abet the scheme. Payment usually occurs *after* the policeman, witness, prosecutor, clerk, or judge has done whatever he is supposed to do; usually, the payment is made *after* the defendant is acquitted, the evidence is suppressed, the case is dismissed, or the like.
>
> It is respectfully submitted that this court should not hold an Illinois prosecutor guilty of unethical conduct when, in good faith, he carefully seeks evidence to ferret out and prosecute lawyers who are engaged in corrupting the criminal process. Surely Mr. Friedman should

not be censured for doing that which he hon-
estly believed to be a proper and ethical exercise of his sworn duty.

At the time, no one outside the Justice Department knew
that Sullivan had more than an academic interest in the
outcome of the *Friedman* case. But Sullivan knew that
what the Illinois Supreme Court decided here could hinder,
or even wreck, his impending sting in the Chicago courts.

The Supreme Court grappled with the Friedman censure
recommendation and found itself sharply split. Six of the
court's seven judges participated in the case and filed four
separate opinions.

Although speaking with several voices, the court seemed
to say one thing clearly: If prosecutors were going to attempt to deceive the courts for law enforcement reasons,
they should not make the decision unilaterally. They should
consult with some judicial authority first.

The main opinion, written by Chief Justice Joseph H.
Goldenhersh, quoted a famous passage from U.S. Supreme
Court Justice Louis D. Brandeis's dissenting opinion in
1928 in *Olmstead* v. *United States*: "Crime is contagious. If
the government becomes a lawbreaker, it breeds contempt
for law; it invites anarchy."

Goldenhersh wrote that the integrity of the courtroom
"is so vital to the health of our legal system that no violation of that integrity, no matter what its motivation, can
be condoned or ignored." Moreover, said Goldenhersh,
Friedman had an alternative means of uncovering corruption: The corrupt lawyers could have been charged with
solicitation of perjury or attempted bribery, which are
felonies.

However, Goldenhersh went on, Friedman did not de-
serve to be formally censured because he had "served the
public diligently and with integrity," and he had "acted

not out of self-interest, but from a sincere, if misguided, desire to bring corrupt attorneys to justice."

The decision left little doubt that any prosecutor who, from that day forward, phonied a case or suborned perjury without judicial authorization would be disciplined.

It was not a decision Tom Sullivan liked, but it was one he would have to abide by.

In light of the *Friedman* case, Sullivan called several people he trusted and posed a hypothetical question: "If one had to notify someone in the court system of an investigation in order to comply with the *Friedman* opinion, to whom might one go?"

One of those Sullivan called was Dan K. Webb, director of the Illinois Department of Law Enforcement, who would succeed Sullivan as U.S. attorney two years later. Without hesitation, Webb said he would go to Richard J. Fitzgerald, the presiding judge of the Criminal Division of the Circuit Court. Webb said he knew Fitzgerald personally, saw him socially, and was convinced he was honest.

Others contacted by Sullivan shared Webb's view and, in early 1980, Sullivan called Fitzgerald and asked if they could meet. "I'm going to be downtown today," answered Fitzgerald. "I'll drop by your office."

That afternoon Fitzgerald met with Sullivan and two of his assistants, Reidy and Sklarsky. Sullivan told Fitzgerald of the plan to investigate the Circuit Court and his desire to run phony cases through the system. He wanted to know if Fitzgerald would cooperate. "I'll have to think it over for a while," Fitzgerald said, although he felt he had no choice.

Fitzgerald was concerned about corruption. He had heard rumors for years, and this was a chance to do something about it. On the other hand, Fitzgerald, a warm, helpful man whose friends called him "Fitz," hated the thought that men he had known and worked with for years would be under investigation and that he, in effect, would be conspiring against them while continuing to work with them.

"It's that old prison theory that you're ratting on your cellmates," Fitzgerald said in an interview some years later. "So you don't just jump up and say, 'Hey, hey, I'll do it!' "

Fitzgerald met with Sullivan again a week later and agreed to cooperate—to become the point man within the system who brought the investigation into compliance with the *Friedman* decision.

Sullivan was stretching things a bit by selecting Fitzgerald as the judge to whom to entrust knowledge of Greylord. Fitzgerald headed the felony division of the Circuit Court, and none of the cases that the government was concocting were felonies. They were traffic cases and other misdemeanors. The logical supervising authority would be either the Illinois Supreme Court or Fitzgerald's boss, Judge Harry G. Comerford, chief judge of the Cook County Circuit Court.

But it was easy to see why Sullivan wanted Fitzgerald. Some of the judges on the Supreme Court had expressed strong views against introducing phony cases into the legal system. Also, there were seven Supreme Court judges who would have to be informed, greatly increasing the possibility of a leak.

The other possibility—informing Comerford—was even less appealing. Comerford was a former Near North Side precinct captain with so many political connections it would be impossible to trust his discretion. Also, Comerford had been responsible for assigning the notorious Wayne Olson to narcotics court, taking him from exile in a misdemeanor court—where he had gone after beating the manslaughter rap—and placing him in a position where the potential for corruption was immense.

Thus, Fitzgerald became the choice by default. From the far south suburbs, Fitzgerald, sixty-six years old, had a reputation for honesty and had never been an insider in the Democratic Machine. He had become a judge in 1964 and had spent almost his entire career in the criminal courts, becoming chief judge in 1976.

Without Fitzgerald's cooperation, Operation Greylord would have been impossible. "The Justice Department wouldn't have approved the expenditure of manpower and money if you had to go notify the chickens that the fox was on the way," said Dan Webb. "No federal prosecutor would have had the guts to put his law license on the line by not complying with *Friedman*. The investigation could not have gone forward without Fitz."

Fitzgerald said later, "I think I had an obligation to cooperate and uncover whatever corruption there was. It was a reflection upon the entire judicial system, it was a reflection upon me, and if we had any people with their hands in the till, then by God they should be exposed and thrown the hell out."

3

The White Knight and the Hillbilly Judge

☆

Terry Hake wanted to be a G-man.

He had wanted to be one for a long time, since he was a teenager in the northwest suburbs. In high school, he had been a model student and a gymnast. Blond and wiry, he had the face of an altar boy and the demeanor of an Eagle Scout. He went to Loyola University and then to its law school, graduating in 1977.

"He was Mr. Innocent, and Mr. Honesty and Integrity," said one of his fellow students in law school. "He always had a smile on his face, always cheerful, wouldn't ever say anything bad about anybody. So much so that I think he got the reputation of being a lightweight, just because he was so innocent."

While in law school, Hake clerked for the law department of the U.S. General Services Administration in Chicago. Hake's supervisor at the GSA recommended him for a job with the Cook County public defender's office.

"I'm sending you Jack Armstrong, the All-American Boy," the supervisor told Hake's new boss at the public defender's office. Hake looked the part, with a strong jaw, clear complexion, and open, white-toothed smile. In another generation, Norman Rockwell could have used him as a model—the white middle-class American male, innocent but strong, duffel bag in hand, kissing his mother and going off to war. He even lived at home with his mother. He was almost naively enthusiastic and said "Gee" a lot.

Hake's first application to the FBI was rejected in 1978. He applied again in 1979 and was put on the waiting list. In the meantime, he was not without connections. He landed a job in the county prosecutor's office under State's Attorney Bernard Carey, a Republican and former FBI man.

Like most young prosecutors just out of law school, Hake had had a variety of low-level assignments. He started in the felony review unit, rushing to crime scenes in the middle of the night to interview witnesses and oversee police station post-arrest procedures. He handled these sleep-time interruptions with enthusiasm. He missed his official swearing-in ceremony because he was out on Interstate 57 working on a particularly brutal murder case.

He had moved on to trial work in several courtrooms, including narcotics and traffic courts. The general stench of corruption emanating from those venues had disgusted him. He thought about giving up the law. He got himself transferred—actually landing one of the plum assignments for a young assistant, trying felony cases in the criminal courts building, as opposed to the routine pretrial hearings in narcotics court.

It was at this point, when he was twenty-eight years old and two years out of law school, that opportunity came tapping, so to speak, at Terry Hake's door. Tom Sullivan was looking for a volunteer lawyer to go underground with a wire. Sullivan went to Carey, the Republican state's attorney. Carey recommended Hake.

Hake was willing to masquerade as a crooked prosecutor, a kid turned sour on the system and now eager to play ball with the bad boys. He would wear a hidden microphone and see what developed. Carey would cooperate with Sullivan's probe by reassigning Hake to Wayne Olson's narcotics court. Spying on judges and his fellow attorneys might not enhance Hake's future as a lawyer, but it would be a marvelous boost to his ambition to become a G-man. In fact, that was part of the deal.

Hake went back to narcotics court. The transfer, an apparent demotion, was naturally noticed by his fellow prosecutors. "He made that strange move back to narcotics court and started wheeling and dealing," said a former prosecutor after Hake's role in Greylord became known. "The cover story was that he was very unhappy in the trial courts, that he wanted to leave the office, but that they talked him into taking a less pressured job."

He was actually under more pressure, but Terry Hake accepted it eagerly. He was at last working with the FBI. He was not a full-fledged agent, only a "project development specialist." But if he did well at his project—if he got the goods on a few lawyers and judges—the FBI held out the promise of making him an agent in two or three years.

Tom Sullivan would soon have another mole in place in the courts, this one a more flamboyant character than Terry Hake. He was Brocton Lockwood, a thirty-six-year-old associate Circuit Court judge from Marion, Illinois, 350 miles south of Chicago. Lockwood had been assigned several times to traffic court in Chicago as part of an Illinois judicial program that allows judges from one circuit to be transferred to another when there is a shortage. Most of the shortages occur in the huge Cook County system, especially during summer vacations, so visiting judges are common there. Lockwood had reacted angrily to the pervasive corruption he found in traffic court and had gone to the Justice Department in Washington to complain. It was almost natural, given Lockwood's background, that he would do so.

Lockwood was raised on his grandfather's fruit farm outside Carbondale, site of Southern Illinois University, where his mother was a professor of business. Lockwood was exposed to two worlds, the conservative farm community with simple values and loyalties, and the academic environment of the SIU faculty. He was strongly influenced by his grandfather, a lonely liberal Democrat in a conservative Republican area. The grandfather had strong attitudes about everything and read the Bible aloud each morning at breakfast.

Lockwood was short, five feet eight inches, but handsome, a good athlete, a good student, and, prophetically, he acted in the school production of Reginald Rose's *Twelve Angry Men*. Active in the burgeoning civil rights movement of the mid-1960s, he gradually became disillusioned, as his grandfather's politics began to clash with his strong rural patriotism. Lockwood turned against the civil rights activists when they started protesting against the war in Vietnam.

He took a job as a part-time policeman, moving further and further away from the civil rights movement. After graduation from college, he tried to get into the Marines, only to be rejected for bad knees and shoulders left over from his high school athletic career. Instead, he went to Vanderbilt Law School and then took a job with a Carbondale firm that represented the city on many matters. When the SIU students staged protests in the early 1970s, and some escalated into near-riots, Lockwood was out on the streets as city attorney, advising the police and the administration on how best to beat back the students.

In 1978, at the age of thirty-four and after five years in private practice, he was appointed an associate Circuit Court judge in Williamson County. Under the statewide judicial rotation program, he was soon sent to Chicago, first to housing court, and then, in another tour, to traffic court. It was there that the seeds of discontent were sown.

One afternoon while having a few drinks with a court clerk, he was told that a prosecutor had fixed a case that Lockwood had just ruled on. Lockwood felt he had been set up, and he was angry. Up until then, he had thought the Cook County system was lax but not outright crooked. He became determined to find out what was going on.

Lockwood had the Hollywood good looks of a soap opera star—thick, brushed-back wavy hair and a thick mustache—and a resonant voice laced with a southern Illinois twang, making him sound like a judicial Slim Pickens. The whole presentation was a likeable one and, using an innocent hillbilly front, he was quickly able to ingratiate himself with the lowest elements of traffic court.

Lockwood found out who was honest and who wasn't. He learned about Presiding Judge Richard LeFevour's courtroom rental system—where dependable bribe-taking judges would be assigned to the courtrooms where they could make the most money, the ones with drunken-driving and leaving-the-scene cases. These judges would kick back to LeFevour. If they didn't, or, worse, if they were honest, they were soon transferred to courtrooms that heard minor offenses.

Lockwood began to plot ways to strike back for having been used. "I was appointed a judge at a relatively young age," he would recall later. "I was enamored of the position. I thought it was an honor, and I was angry that those jerks in Chicago were robbing me of the job. I thought, well, I'm gonna get even one way or another. I tried to figure out what was gonna hurt them the worst."

Lockwood considered going to the Cook County state's attorney, but he discarded the idea. Although Bernie Carey was a Republican and certainly would not be averse to uncovering corruption in a court system dominated for years by Democratic Machine appointments, Lockwood did not think Carey's office could effectively investigate sitting judges. The assistant state's attorneys, public defenders, and judges were all too intertwined to maintain secrecy, Lockwood thought. For the same reason, he wasn't sure he could trust the local U.S. attorney's office, so he decided to go to the Public Integrity Section of the Justice Department in Washington. By this time, in the fall of 1980, Hake was already taping people in narcotics court, and Operation Greylord was under way.

The feds listened to Lockwood but were afraid he might be a counteragent sent by the Cook County crowd, who might have gotten wind of Sullivan's investigation. Over a period of months, the Washington people tested Lockwood's reliability and finally told him they wanted tapes of traffic court shenanigans.

They wanted a mole. Lockwood, the ex-actor, the ex-cop, the ego-bruised would-be Marine, was ready for the role. By now twice divorced, he would play the part of the womanizing, hard-drinking, free-spending good old boy who needed cash to support his excessive habits, including a couple of lead-footed racehorses back in Marion. He would entertain on Rush Street, Chicago's nightlife strip, preferred by conventioneers and other out-of-towners. He would offer himself for sale.

To get himself into character, Lockwood began reading spy novels. He devoured Robert Ludlum and Ken Follett. He was amazed by their detail. He was wired for sound. The FBI, not up to the technical standards of Follett and

Ludlum operatives, loaded him down with some pretty primitive equipment. They draped a microphone over his shoulder, under his judicial robes, and attached it by wire to a tape recorder that Lockwood hid in his cowboy boots. Normally a back-slapping, bear-hugging extrovert, Lockwood had to curtail his style somewhat. He was fearful that someone would pat him on the back and feel his concealed equipment. But he did fine.

"I can play the role you want me to play," he boasted later. He convinced the LeFevour gang that he was one of them, and they let him in. He arranged to spend more and more time assigned to Chicago. By the summer of 1981, he was in full swing, moving among corrupt judges, lawyers, bailiffs, and clerks with ease.

When Ronald Reagan became president, Democrat Sullivan was out—not reluctantly—and in November 1981, Dan Webb took over as U.S. attorney. Webb, thirty-five years old, was, like Lockwood, a wily downstater who took well to the machinations of Chicago politics. Webb was smart, tough, and an excellent trial lawyer. He had intense ambitions. No one knew exactly for what—but you could sense it, almost see it in his eager, quick eyes.

Webb was born in Macomb, in the west central part of Illinois, and raised in Bushnell, a nearby farming community. His father was a rural mail carrier, driving along gravel roads, leaning over the passenger side of his car, placing mail in tin mailboxes with red metal flags on them. Even at Bushnell Prairie High School, Webb knew he wanted to be a lawyer. He went to Western Illinois University in Macomb, about the only school his parents could afford, and took a special prelaw program that was supposed to get him admitted to the University of Illinois Law School in just three years. But the program was discontinued before Webb made it to the University of Illinois, and he was left hanging with three years of prelaw, no major in any other subject, and no undergraduate degree.

Most law schools would only accept students with degrees, but the dean of the Loyola University School of Law in Chicago took a chance on Webb. After a year, however, Webb ran out of money. He had to take a job as a paralegal at the First National Bank of Chicago, which paid tuition for him to attend Loyola at night. The bank experience taught him that he didn't want to be a corporate lawyer. He wanted to try cases.

After receiving his juris doctor degree in 1971, Webb was hired by U.S. Attorney William J. Bauer. At the time, Richard Nixon was waiting for an opening so he could appoint Bauer to the federal bench. It was common knowledge that the next U.S. attorney would be James R. Thompson, who was then Bauer's first assistant.

A few weeks after Webb joined the office, the expected promotions occurred. Thompson quickly came to like Webb and assigned him to prosecute a group of police officers accused of shaking down tavern owners. There was a series of trials, ending in the convictions of nineteen police officers from the Austin and East Chicago Avenue police districts, including a district commander, Clarence Braasch, the highest ranking Chicago police officer ever convicted of a felony.

After that, Webb won convictions against a Chicago alderman, seven state legislators, and Cook County Clerk Edward J. Barrett, who was accused of taking kickbacks from a voting-machine manufacturer. By the time Webb resigned as an assistant U.S. attorney in 1976 to begin a lucrative private practice, he had prosecuted forty-five jury trials. He had lost only one.

Thompson's tenure as U.S. attorney had been marked by the convictions of a stream of Chicago politicians, most accused of taking bribes. Thompson, who had always had frank political ambitions, used his perch as a crime-busting federal prosecutor to propel himself into the governor's mansion in 1976. That lesson of political success was not lost on Webb, Thompson's most apt protégé, who had tried some of the corruption cases.

After a short stint in private practice, Webb was appointed—by Thompson—as director of the Illinois Department of Law Enforcement, a powerful agency that oversees the state police and has broad powers to investigate vice and official corruption. His tenure was relatively uneventful, and he returned to private practice briefly before he was named U.S. attorney.

"I never have harbored any desire to run for public office," said Webb when he took over as U.S. attorney. "I don't intend to use the office as a political stepping-stone."

Somehow, hardly anyone seemed to believe him.

On Webb's first day on the job, Sullivan went to see him. "There are two sensitive matters I thought I should tell you about personally," said Sullivan. "Cardinal Cody is under grand jury investigation, and we are, with the knowledge of your friend Fitzgerald, conducting an investigation of judicial corruption known as Operation Greylord."

"Jesus," Webb told Sullivan, "my wife is a Catholic, and you're investigating my entire goddamned profession."

The Cody investigation came as a surprise to Webb. It would later be disclosed that John Cardinal Cody, the archbishop of Chicago, had done a number of unusual things with church money, including helping support a longtime woman friend. Cody died before the grand jury's investigation was completed, thus sparing Webb and Sullivan the wrath Catholics might have visited upon them for indicting a cardinal.

Greylord was not a surprise, however. Two years earlier,

Sullivan had consulted Webb—hypothetically—concerning which judicial authority to inform of the investigation so as to comply with the dictates of the *Friedman* case. Thus, Webb knew that some kind of judicial sting had been at least under consideration.

After Sullivan briefed him on Greylord, Webb was delighted. This was just the sort of investigation that would get national headlines when it broke.

Webb flew to Washington for several meetings with Justice Department officials, particularly FBI director William Webster, a former federal judge. The FBI was involved in Greylord in a big way.

An FBI agent named David Grossman was already working as an assistant state's attorney at Belmont and Western. Another agent, David V. Ries, joined Hake as a defense lawyer, in the underbelly of the courts. Using the name D. Victor Ries, he began trolling traffic court with ready cash on behalf of his clients—who were also FBI agents.

One of the first Greylord decisions Sullivan had made was to use cases that were phony from the outset, instead of trying to fix legitimate cases already in the system. Webb thought that decision made sense. "There were discussions about fixing real cases," said Webb after he left office. "But the risks were too great. What could we say to the widow of a man killed by a drunken driver whose case we fixed— 'Look, this is okay because we're going to do good'?"

Under Webb's direction, additional federal agents fanned out across the city. The agents began faking crimes, creating a network of phony cases that they hoped would ensnare crooked lawyers, clerks, bailiffs, or judges. Agents posed as both victims and perpetrators and enacted elaborate scenarios, hoping to get caught. Their efforts resulted in some ludicrous situations.

In March of 1982, a man named Jesse Clugman walked out of Water Tower Place, a posh high-rise shopping complex on North Michigan Avenue. As Clugman started to enter a waiting taxi parked near the Ritz-Carlton Hotel, a man ran by, snatched Clugman's attaché case, and sprinted down Michigan Avenue. Clugman took off after him. The two zigzagged through lunch-hour pedestrians, Clugman yelling all the while. After a block-long chase, Clugman tackled the thief, and the two wrestled on the sidewalk while bystanders summoned a nearby police officer. Clugman subdued the perpetrator, and when detectives arrived, they took the two to the East Chicago Avenue police station.

The man who took the attaché case identified himself as Mark S. McGee. Police searched him and found his identification. It said his name was Mark Bingston and that he was an FBI agent. Clugman was an FBI agent, too. It was an obvious setup, and an inept one at that. The cops came to believe that the cab driver and many of the bystanders were working for the feds, too. "The witnesses were climbing all over themselves to offer statements," said one of the officers. "Things don't normally happen that way."

The police were infuriated. There had never been any bond between them and the FBI. To the police, the incident confirmed what they already thought—that FBI agents basked in an undeserved glory while, for the most part, they were naive and bungling.

The FBI told the police their investigation centered on the courts, not on the police, but the officers from the East Chicago Avenue Police District, among the most suspicious outside the Soviet KGB, did not believe them. They thought the FBI was trying to establish a police corruption sting. In order to keep the lid on Greylord, the FBI and the U.S. attorney's office began to consult with Chicago police superintendent Richard J. Brzeczek, but that didn't stop other goofy incidents from happening.

On the morning of January 19, 1983, for instance, detectives received a tip that a man with an attaché case full of cocaine was in a fast-food restaurant on the North Side. Police arrived and spotted a man in a white shirt, tie, and fedora sitting in a booth. He was holding an attaché case by his side.

"What's in the case?" asked one of the officers.

"Cocaine," replied the man, almost cheerfully.

The cops looked inside and found twenty-three one-gram packets of cocaine. They took the man to the area headquarters. There the man began offering police money or cocaine or both if they would not press charges against him. The cops, of course, suspected all along that he was an FBI plant. They charged him with everything they could. Bond was set at $20,000. The man made a phone call, and someone came and bailed him out.

The afternoon of the same day, police received another tip, this one from the Northwest Side. The caller said there was a drug pusher sitting in a car in a park. Police converged on the scene and found a man neatly dressed in a tie and hat in a rented car with its license plates bent so that the number could not be read. The man had no drugs, but in the car, in full view, were a Browning blue steel nine-millimeter automatic pistol and an ammunition clip.

Police arrested the man. He, too, wanted to know if the cops were willing to make some kind of deal. The cops were having no part of it. The man called the same number that the happy cocaine dealer had called, and someone appeared to post bond. Neither man was ever heard from again, so far as Chicago cops were concerned.

Another time, the FBI poured liquor on an agent's shirt, faked a one-car accident, and awaited the inevitable arrival of the Chicago police. The cops came and found the agent sitting in his car, an open bottle nearby. But the cops were getting ready to change shifts and did not want to get caught up in the paperwork involved in a single-car, no-harm accident. They dropped the agent's keys down a sewer, poured the booze into the gutter, and told the man to go home.

Sometimes the FBI would manage to get a guy charged, but the case would come to trial on a day when the targeted judge was on vacation or off sick. The whole elaborate effort would be wasted. Little by little, though, the feds were getting some phony cases introduced into the system. One agent poured whiskey over himself and drove erratically until he was stopped and arrested for drunken driving. Another agent slipped two sterling silver candlesnuffers under his coat at Marshall Field and Company and was nabbed by store security. Still another was caught breaking into a car by the car's owner, who was an agent, in full view of several witnesses, who were also agents.

All of the fake cases were in the First Municipal District, which includes traffic court and the branch courts. The district became the target of the sting by default, not because it was necessarily more corrupt than other divisions. As difficult as it was to simulate shoplifting and traffic cases, it was beyond the Justice Department's means to simulate a case in, say, the Chancery Division, which handles many big-money civil cases.

Faking a chancery case would have required elaborate phony documents and having agents play various roles over long periods of time. Likewise, to fake a divorce case, agents probably would have had to set up and maintain a household for a couple and then a separate apartment for one spouse. It would have been necessary to create an appearance of substantial assets, and then wait a couple of years for the case to become ready for a ruling. Then it might end up before an honest judge. "It was just too much to contrive," said Webb.

When the fake misdemeanor cases that were put in the system finally came before the suspected crooked judge for trial, it was important for the government to observe the proper bribery etiquette. Number one on the list of scam manners: Never offer too much money for a fix.

It wasn't that the FBI was frugal. It was that overpaying would have aroused suspicion. Besides, it would have been like stuffing bills into the maid's dress at a private dinner party. Some things simply are not done.

Terry Hake had been wearing his microphone around narcotics court since May of 1980.

In November of that year, his boss, Bernie Carey, had been defeated for re-election by Democrat Richard M. Daley, son of the legendary mayor. In February of 1981, Hake was transferred out of narcotics court, in what appeared to outsiders to be a routine reassignment. If he had stayed much longer, someone might have become suspicious. The reassignment served as a cover to give Hake an excuse to quit the prosecutor's office and stay in narcotics court, now posing as a corrupt defense attorney.

The closest association Hake developed in the state's attorney's office was with Arthur R. Cirignani, whom Hake would later describe as his best friend. Cirignani graduated from John Marshall Law School in 1977, the same year Hake graduated from Loyola. Cirignani joined the state's attorney's office immediately after graduation and met Hake the following year, when Hake transferred from the public defender's office.

Like Hake, Cirignani worked several different assignments, including traffic court, where he had a chance to watch some of the most infamous members of the Chicago judiciary in action. Cirignani and Hake shared their experience together in social evenings. When Cirignani decided to propose to his girlfriend, one of the first people he told was Hake. Hake attended Cirignani's bachelor party and was a member of the wedding. He slept overnight on occasion at the Cirignanis' home. When Cathy Cirignani had a baby, Hake was one of the first people Art called.

In May of 1980, the month Hake began his undercover work, Cirignani left the state's attorney's office. From his experience in traffic court and from comparing notes with Hake, Cirignani did not think the system was legitimate. He went into private practice with bribery on his mind.

Cirignani's partner was Thomas M. Del Becarro, who was Judge Black Jack Reynolds's understudy in Branch 42 at Belmont and Western, kicking back on each case. When Reynolds, under heat, was transferred out of Branch 42, Judge John Murphy was transferred in. This was fine for the Cirignani–Del Becarro partnership, since Cirignani and Murphy knew each other from traffic court. Cirignani switched places with Del Becarro in Branch 42, kicking back to Murphy on referred cases.

Almost as soon as Hake went undercover for the FBI, he began surreptitiously taping Cirignani. He asked Cirignani a lot of questions about payoffs. On one occasion Cirignani gave Hake $100 to give to Judge Olson. It was not for Cirignani's case. It was on behalf of another attorney. Cirignani was only the conduit. Cirignani did not know Olson at that time, but, together, Hake and Cirignani arranged for Cirignani to meet Olson. Hake made the introductions. Cirignani was then ready to do business in narcotics court on his own.

When Hake left the state's attorney's office in early 1981, Cirignani offered to take him into his firm, but the government had different plans. The FBI set Hake up in an office in west suburban Villa Park, in DuPage County. Art Cirignani gave Hake some office furniture to help him out. The FBI could have supplied Hake with all the furniture he needed, but Hake accepted his friend's generosity instead, in order to maintain the cover of a struggling young attorney. Each night in his office, Hake would record into a cassette the day's adventures in corruption, including any involving Cirignani.

One day Cirignani told Hake about $200 he had paid a judge.

"Art, wouldn't it be better if you just tried the case straight up and let the evidence speak for itself—whether the evidence is there or whether it's not there, just try the case without paying the judge?" asked Hake.

"Things aren't done that way," answered Cirignani. "In order to be successful in the court system, you have to pay the judges to get what you want. To protect your client's interest, you have to pay the judges."

Hake later testified he went home that night, told his mother about the conversation, and cried.

But he had everything on tape.

Hake met and fell in love with a girl named Kathleen Crowley, a law student and the daughter of a retired Circuit Court judge. She eventually became an assistant state's attorney. They were married in 1982. Both before and after the wedding, Kathy and Terry socialized with Cathy and Art.

Cirignani was a member of Terry and Kathy's wedding party, and Terry's new, seamy friends were invited, in order not to blow his cover. Following FBI instructions, Terry did not tell Kathy he was a mole until they were married. He did not tell his mother, either.

"A mother is always the last to know," she said when the news hit the papers.

Hake had a secret identity for these FBI reports—Leo Murphy.

"This is Project Development Specialist Leo Murphy," he would begin. Sometimes, if something good had developed and he had an opportunity, he would not wait to get back to the office to begin his report.

"This is Project Development Specialist Leo Murphy," he reported one day from traffic court. "The time is now two thirty-eight P.M., approximately eight minutes after I paid Harold Conn in the back of the jury room. Today is July seventh, 1981. Thank you."

Even as a mole he remained polite.

The FBI also had a code name for Hake, alias Murphy— The White Knight.

Hake had only ten legitimate clients. The rest were phony. When the agent who poured whiskey over himself appeared in traffic court, Hake represented him and paid clerk Harold Conn $150 to fix the case before Judge Devine. In the meantime, Ries, the FBI agent who was also posing as a crooked lawyer, was set up in offices across from the Daley Center courtrooms. When the agent who had broken into the other agent's car appeared in court, Ries represented him, thus producing a phony case with a phony plaintiff, defendant, witness, and lawyer. In a similar case, in which Brocton Lockwood was the judge, it was almost a clean sweep—everybody but the prosecutor was wired.

The first rumors about an FBI mole's wearing a wire in the branch courts appeared in the newspapers in August of 1983. Cirignani had an uneasy feeling that the mole might be his old friend, Terry Hake. In November, Cirignani was stopped by two FBI agents, including Ries, and was asked to come in for a chat.

Cirignani showed up a couple of days later with counsel to see what evidence the government had against him. He found out there were many recorded conversations with Hake, both in person and on the telephone, including those about Hake's wedding plans.

Cirignani agreed to cooperate with the government in exchange for immunity from prosecution. He eventually testified against Judge Murphy, as did Hake.

Cirignani was disbarred.

As promised by the FBI, Terry Hake, The White Knight, became a G-man.

4

Hustlers and Miracle Workers

☆

Although the prosecutors and moles were having a lot of fun running their stings, their bag of potential indictments was still pretty light. But in 1981 two journalistic investigations opened new possibilities.

In March of that year, *Chicago Lawyer*, a monthly publication circulated in the legal community, carried a story detailing hustling in the branch courts. The story, which was done in cooperation with the Better Government Association, a watchdog group, explained how the bond refund procedure worked, how judges steered clients with bond refund slips to certain lawyers, and identified the lawyers who had earned the most through bond refunds.

Chicago Lawyer began its investigation at the suggestion of Keith Davis, a defense lawyer who had spent a lot of time in the branch courts and was disgusted with what he had seen.

"There's just a tremendous amount of hustling going on," Davis said one day as he stood in the rear of Branch 40, sometimes called women's court. In the morning, most of the cases in Branch 40 were prostitution misdemeanors. In the afternoon, most of the cases involved retail theft, almost all shoplifting. The afternoons were when the action got heavy, and on this afternoon, in December of 1980, Davis had brought along a reporter from *Chicago Lawyer* to watch.

A couple of lawyers sat on a short bench in the very rear of the court, Room 800 at Eleventh and State. Windows ran along one side of the long, narrow room, and in front, Judge Donald E. Joyce was presiding. Joyce, short and stocky with an extremely short, out-of-fashion crew cut, was an ex–FBI agent, ex–assistant U.S. attorney, and ex–Republican committeeman from suburban River Forest. The lawyers in the back were Vincent F. Davino and Martin Schachter, and for both of them the bench they were sitting on was the closest thing they had to an office. The bench was a convenient spot to make initial contact with clients because it was against a wall on which the call sheets for the day were posted. When someone began studying the sheets one of them would say something like, "You need help?" or, "What are you here for?" and the dialogue would begin. Together they did a lot of business in this courtroom, especially when the shoplifting defendants began to arrive.

"Shoplifting cases are made to order for these hustlers," said Keith Davis. "Many of the cases involve first-time offenders who at the most will be given six months' or a year's court supervision. They are happy that they didn't go to jail, and they don't mind paying their bond money to the lawyer. It's very lucrative."

Lucrative enough so that in the months leading up to

the investigation Davino and Schachter were collecting bond refunds at a clip that would gross each of them more than $100,000 a year.

That afternoon Davino and Schachter had nine cases apiece assigned to them by Judge Joyce.

"Look, there goes the CBA lawyer," said Davis, referring to the Chicago Bar Association attorney who was officially assigned to the court to represent people who didn't have lawyers. Joyce had ignored him, and he left in disgust. A case would be called and an unrepresented defendant would stand before the judge.

"Do you want to go to trial without a lawyer?" Joyce would ask.

"Yes, sir," a defendant might answer.

"You're charged with a Class A misdemeanor punishable by one year in jail. I don't think you want to go to trial without a lawyer. You're going to get one year in the county jail."

A deputy would usually lead the defendant over to the first row of benches, where Davino and Schachter now sat, having moved up from the rear when the cases began to be called. After a short conference, one of the lawyers would plead the defendant guilty. Joyce would sentence him to supervision, and his $100 cash bond would be turned over to Davino or Schachter.

By 3 P.M. the courtroom was nearly empty. Davino, looking for a final score, walked down the center aisle, away from the bench. He stopped where a young woman sat. He placed his hand solicitously on the woman's shoulder.

"What are you here for?" he asked in his most polished manner.

Vinnie Davino, short, chunky, and balding, wore suits that fit too tightly and a tie loose on a shirt collar that was unbuttoned. He looked like he might have been a lineman for a Public League football team. His manner, even at its most polished, was not what one might term courtly. He tended to talk to people the way cops do when they make an arrest.

The woman looked up at Davino.

"Get your fucking hand off me," she said.

Keith Davis let out a loud laugh.

Davis's laugh hid an anger that had been simmering for a long time about the unethical behavior of hustlers and their abuse of defendants' rights. Davis was a practicing Lutheran minister, the only ordained Protestant minister in the Illinois bar. His was an inner-city ministry, his people poor and powerless; one of the reasons he became a lawyer was to offer them some power.

If ever there were people who did *not* share Davis's concerns, they were hallway hustlers—Edward Nydam, for example. In January of 1981, Nydam stood poised outside Black Jack Reynolds's courtroom at Belmont and Western, on the site of what once was Riverview, one of the world's largest amusement parks. Nydam worked the courthouse there with shifty-looking Bob Daniels, who had the quick, furtive moves of a ferret. They were known around the branches as "the bar flies."

A young black woman carrying a baby entered the building, which houses two courtrooms and a police station. She fumbled in her purse and pulled out a bond slip, checking for the courtroom number. Nydam approached.

"May I help you?" he asked. Nydam was tall and slim with dark hair, and when he tried he could look contemplative. He usually carried a scholarly looking reference book and when he said, "May I help you?" one's instincts were to allow him to try. The woman and Nydam began to talk, and she told him her problem. She was facing time because she had been picked up for prostitution while on probation for an earlier felony conviction. Nydam made one trip into the courtroom and then another. The first time he talked to the assistant state's attorney. The second time he did not, but now he lied.

"I just talked to the state's attorney again. She's got everything," said Nydam.

"Everything?" asked the woman. "That alcohol stuff, too?"

"Yeah, she's got that," Nydam said. "She knows everything. She wants to give you six months. They were talking about two years, but I talked and they said they'd be willing to go for six months. Now I've got them down to thirty days. But they want you to start serving time today. If you go for a continuance or a trial, they might go for the two years. It's a pretty good deal."

What Nydam was doing was trying to get the woman to plead guilty. She had come to court prepared to plead not guilty or to get a continuance. In order to get a bond slip turned over to him, a lawyer has to dispose of a case. If a defendant pleads not guilty the case is then assigned for trial to another judge in the criminal courts building. In order to get a fee Nydam would have to follow the case to the South Side. Hustlers never did this. If a defendant refused to plead guilty, and the case was assigned for a later trial, the hustler withdrew as the attorney.

In trying to convince the woman to plead guilty, Nydam was using a technique common among hustlers: making trips back and forth from the courtroom to the hallway, pretending to be conducting difficult negotiations. The lawyer starts by saying the state wants a big sentence, but after a couple of trips he is able to come up with a contrasting light sentence—if the defendant is willing to plead guilty and begin serving time immediately.

The woman facing parole violation was with two companions, possibly relatives. They talked it over among themselves and decided that they could get the baby looked after, if it came to that.

"What I'll do is tell them you are willing to do it at this point, or you might be willing to, and I'll see if I can get you less time, maybe twenty-five days or two weeks or seven days—whatever. You just relax and I'll go talk to her."

Nydam went through a side door to the courtroom.

"Some of those guys come in and ask what we are willing to give on a guilty plea," said an assistant state's attorney who negotiated with hallway hustlers in various branches in those days. "We tell them. Sometimes they don't even pitch for a lower sentence. The back-and-forth stuff is just for show."

Later that afternoon the woman's case was called.

"Cindy Johnson!" the clerk yelled.

"Judge, there's been a pretrial conference," said the state's attorney. "She's agreed to plead guilty to violation of probation for thirty days in the House of Correction."

There was some hugging and kissing between Cindy Johnson and her two companions, and then she was led off to the lockup by a white-shirted sheriff's deputy.

"Thirty days on that particular charge is probably not an injustice," said Keith Davis, who had watched the whole solicitation performance. "Cases like that are hard to win. But the whole operation is so sleazy it disgusts you."

The main thrust of the *Chicago Lawyer* article was that hustling was not only unethical and unseemly but also damaging to the interests of defendants. Some of the hustlers did not do anything but plead defendants guilty so that the bond refund would be forthcoming quickly. When hustlers worked out good deals for their clients, it was just a coincidence. Clients' interests were secondary to the goal of getting cases over immediately.

Chicago Lawyer made no accusations of criminal activity on the part of the hustlers or the judges who allowed them to operate. It simply told what was happening, giving examples, in branches around the city, including the courtrooms of judges Sodini, Devine, Joyce, Reynolds, Salerno, and Olson.

The story caused a mild stir at the time, prompting Harry Comerford, chief judge of the system, to make a few transfers, but nothing major. Joyce and Reynolds were moved away; Salerno, romancer to the teenybopper go-go dancer, had previously been transferred.

Although Comerford made only a desultory follow-up to the *Chicago Lawyer*'s hustling story, federal authorities were interested. They did not move on it at once—they were still enamored of their sting adventures—but eventually they began checking the income tax records of the lawyers mentioned in the story who had earned the most in bond authorizations. Dan Reidy and some other assistant U.S. attorneys reasoned that if the judges were allowing the lawyers to hustle in their courtrooms, perhaps they were not doing it out of friendship, or respect for the status quo. Perhaps they were receiving kickbacks from the lawyers. And if the lawyers were paying part of their bond earnings back to judges, the prosecutors asked, what were they declaring as income? If a lawyer earned $300, for instance, from a case referred to him by a judge, and if he paid the judge $100 of it, say, what did he declare as income? The whole $300, as the law required of him? Or only the $200 he kept after he paid the judge?

Thus began a long and tedious process—classic investigative work, not some *I Led Three Lives* production—of examining records. FBI and IRS agents checked the hustlers' bond-money earnings against their declared incomes. Earnings day by day, month by month, year by year. Since some of the lawyers made little or no money outside of what they hustled, their total income was easy to figure. The investigators discovered that, indeed, some of the hustlers were reporting only what they kept as income, not what they had paid the judges. Faced with income tax charges, some of the lawyers eventually began to cooperate with the government.

None of this was quick. It took years to develop—Sodini and Reynolds were not indicted until four and a half years after the *Chicago Lawyer* story—but in the end this traditional sort of investigation produced more indictments than the sting techniques.

The second journalistic investigation that affected Greylord was conducted by Peter Karl, a reporter from WLS-TV news, the ABC-owned station in Chicago. Karl's investigation, which was broadcast in October 1981, exposed larceny in the Chicago traffic court.

The traffic court building sits, alone and apart, in a converted redbrick warehouse, flush against the Chicago River on La Salle Street, just over the bridge from the north edge of the Loop. Physically isolated, traffic court seemed to function within a kind of judicial ecosystem of its own, separate from more civilized society. The hustlers lurking in the messy, crowded hallways seemed a natural part of an untamed wilderness, like hyenas on the Serengeti Plain or piranhas in the Amazon River.

The press had done periodic stories on traffic court. In the old days, the stories tended to be critical, usually disclosing one ticket-fixing scam or another. In the 1970s, however, most of the stories were complimentary, often concentrating on technical innovations. The reporters liked the supervising judge there, Richard F. LeFevour, and gave him good press. One of the reasons reporters liked LeFevour might have been that he was so cooperative in dismissing their parking tickets—ostensibly obtained while on stories, but really accumulated through standard negligence.

LeFevour was widely touted as an exceptionally good administrator, at least by the standards of the Cook County courts. The defects in the system, such as hustlers, were somehow thought by the press to be congenital, perhaps too ingrained for any one man to correct in the time allotted him. But Karl turned up evidence that LeFevour, contrary to his public image, was an aggressive crook, and at times somewhat careless.

Karl's investigation had begun routinely. More than four million parking tickets are issued each year in Chicago, and the city has a backlog of millions of unpaid tickets. Karl was going to do a series on the backlog, with a side look at the hallway hustlers.

Karl's first installment, describing the jammed-up traffic court collection system, ran on October 28, 1981. Minutes after the story aired, Karl received a telephone call from a viewer named Lauren Sacks, who had an example of how mixed-up the system was.

Sacks said she had paid $220 to have eleven tickets dismissed, and now somehow they were still after her for the money. She said she paid half the money that was owed on the tickets to a police officer by mail.

"What proof do you have that you paid him?" asked Karl.

"I've got the check," said Sacks. "I've got the canceled check at home."

Karl left immediately for Sacks's apartment. She showed him a check made out to cash and endorsed by one Arthur W. McCauslin. The check had been cashed at a restaurant-bar named the Beef 'n Brandy, located in the Loop next to the Palmer House.

McCauslin was a Chicago police officer assigned to the

traffic court's parking ticket scofflaw unit, which was responsible for tracking down motorists with ten or more unpaid parking tickets and collecting the fines they owed.

It turned out that McCauslin and his partner in the scofflaw unit, Lawrence E. McLain, had had an arrangement with Judge LeFevour to fix parking tickets at a cut rate since 1977. As McCauslin and McLain—the Macs—later testified, LeFevour approached them in a busy first-floor corridor of the traffic court building.

"There's a lot of money to be made on these multiple parkers," said LeFevour. "We can all make money if we can settle for half."

LeFevour meant that instead of issuing warrants to citizens, the officers should strike a deal—offer to clear the record for half the money owed. The ticket holders would think the officers had authorization to offer the deal, and in a way, of course, they did.

McCauslin and McLain went to a coffee shop on La Salle Street, within walking distance of traffic court, to discuss LeFevour's offer.

"I'm really shocked at the way the judge approached us like that in the hallway," said McCauslin, but the two agreed to go into business with LeFevour. They would contact the ticket holders, either in person or by phone, offer the cut-rate deal, and tell them to bring the money down to traffic court. When the money arrived, one of the officers would get a computer printout of the unpaid tickets and take it to LeFevour. The judge would either dismiss the tickets or enter an order of supervision, requiring the person to remain ticket-free for a year.

McCauslin began delivering money to LeFevour the week after their hurried conversation in the hallway. "I went to the side of the desk and gave him the money," McCauslin testified later. "He took the money and swiveled a little bit in his chair. He counted the money, put it in his pocket, and swiveled back."

The Macs had assumed that LeFevour would give them a percentage of what they brought in, although no specifics were ever discussed. But after six weeks of repeated deliveries, the officers had still not been paid. The next time he brought money to LeFevour, McCauslin asked for a clarification.

"Don't I get a piece of this pie?" he asked.

LeFevour finished counting the money and looked up.

"Art," he said. "Whatever comes in this office, stays in this office. You make yours out there."

From then on the Macs either added to the price they charged, understated to LeFevour what the people brought in, or made some private arrangement.

One woman who had twenty-five overdue parking tickets was told by McCauslin to be prepared to pay $500—$20 a ticket—but that he would see if he could settle it for half. That was a standard technique. Use a high figure at first, and when a lower one was actually required, the person holding the tickets was grateful to pay it—with no questions asked. The woman waited for a short time in the lobby of LeFevour's office while McCauslin had the judge nonsuit the tickets. He returned and said the fine would be only $250.

"Put the money in that magazine," said McCauslin.

"Why?" asked the woman.

"How would it look handing a police officer money?" asked McCauslin.

The woman agreed it would look a bit odd. She put the money in the magazine, got a computer printout receipt, and left, somewhat perplexed but satisfied that justice had been served.

The ticket-fixing was supposed to be strictly a cash-and-carry business—no checks. But, in a weak moment, to do a favor for Lauren Sacks, McCauslin had made an exception to the rule.

In September of 1981, he contacted her about her outstanding tickets. She said she was willing to pay the full amount of her fines, but that her work schedule—she was a dialysis-machine technician at Evanston Hospital—made it inconvenient for her to come to court. In that case, said McCauslin, she could send in a check—for $220. He told her to make it out to cash and mark the envelope to his attention. She did what he asked.

The check arrived at McCauslin's office on September 22. McCauslin was ready to go on vacation. He took the check with him to the Beef 'n Brandy, one of his regular hangouts. He had a few drinks, cashed the check, and had a few more drinks. Then he went home. He left on vacation the next day, forgetting to take Sacks's tickets to LeFevour to get them dismissed.

A few weeks later, Sacks received a notice that her tickets were still due. She was threatened with the revocation of her driver's license. At that point she saw Karl's report and contacted him.

The next day, Karl went to traffic court and pored over the records. He discovered how frequently tickets were nonsuited by LeFevour.

That night, Karl went on the air with a report about how LeFevour was having all these tickets dismissed, and how McCauslin had taken one check and cashed it in a tavern, and the money had never made it to traffic court. The story made it clear that there appeared to be ticket-fixing going on in traffic court.

Within a few days of Karl's report, all records involving LeFevour and the Macs had been taken out of the files. They were never found. But there still was a paper trail. Every time LeFevour received payment from a defendant

who had multiple tickets, he initialed the computer printout to indicate that the matter had been settled. This ini-
tialing was only for the court's own records. But, unknown
to LeFevour, McCauslin was giving a copy of the printout
with LeFevour's initials to the defendants.

"McCauslin is kind of an idiot," said Karl. "He was
giving people receipts with Judge LeFevour's initials on
them, which was his signature to corruption. It was done
to avoid any problems. This cop in his own way was saying,
'You paid me, and I want to make sure that I take care of
you for corrupting me, and if you ever have a problem
with these tickets, you take this receipt down to traffic
court and show it to the people.' "

Karl's report set the feds on an investigation that led
directly, for the first time, to LeFevour. Terry Hake, who
had initially operated only in narcotics court, where his
cover job as an assistant state's attorney kept him, had by
now been set up in private practice and could roam freely
about the courts. He immediately headed for traffic court.

The FBI discovered that LeFevour fixed tickets not only
for individuals but for businesses as well. One was Hanley
Dawson Cadillac-Datsun, which through its Kirkway Leas-
ing subsidiary was facing seven hundred tickets acquired
by people who had long-term car rentals. The owner of the
company, Hanley Dawson, Jr., met LeFevour at an Irish
Fellowship Club party. Dawson told LeFevour about the
tickets.

"That's no problem," said LeFevour. "Just send me the
tickets. I'll see that the proper party gets billed."

From then on Dawson sent the paperwork to LeFevour,
who made sure the person who leased the car got the violation notice and not the company. Dawson was grateful.
A few months later LeFevour dropped by the Hanley Dawson showroom. He said he wanted to lease a car. Dawson
would not hear of such a thing.

"We told him we would provide free use of the car," said Dawson. It was the beginning of a beautiful relationship. LeFevour kept taking care of Dawson's tickets, and Dawson kept giving LeFevour cars and other things.

Between 1976 and 1982, LeFevour received seven Cadillacs from Dawson—a new one each year. For a couple of years, his wife got one, too. Three of his sons got summer jobs at Hanley Dawson. When one of the boys was married out of state, Dawson provided the LeFevours with a fleet of limousines to drive to the wedding. When they took a vacation in 1976, Dawson gave them a van to use. In 1978, LeFevour borrowed $16,000 from Dawson to pay for one of his sons' college tuition. He never paid it back. By the early 1980s, the relationship between Dawson and LeFevour had become somewhat strained.

However, by that time, LeFevour was also getting cars from Avis. The law firm that represented Avis picked up a $2,500 rent-a-car tab for the judge and his wife when they went to Ireland in 1982 and when they traveled around America the next year. At the time, the City of Chicago was suing Avis for $200,000 for 13,000 unpaid traffic tickets. The judge who was deciding the case was LeFevour, who assigned it to himself and then never did decide it.

LeFevour took care of other tickets for an office machine supplier and got a free photocopier for his wife. In fact, he got two of them; she didn't like the first one, so she sent it back. He took large campaign contributions, even when he wasn't running for anything, from businessmen for whom he dismissed tickets. He accepted $51,800 in loans over a five-year period from lawyers and judges—including the Honorable Frank Salerno, who always seemed to have a pile of ready cash—and Pro Football Hall of Fame quarterback Sid Luckman.

*　*　*

The parking ticket investigation led the FBI into other areas, ultimately unmasking the most crooked court operation in the history of American jurisprudence.

The FBI discovered that LeFevour had organized the traffic courtrooms in such a way that judges who were honest were separated from those who were on the take. The honest judges were assigned to courtrooms that heard minor cases, such as parking and speeding violations, while dishonest judges were assigned to courtrooms where major cases, such as drunken driving, were heard. The potential for making money was much greater, of course, in the major courtrooms, where citizens faced with license revocations or jail terms would willingly pay bribes.

LeFevour's rules were simple. A judge in a major courtroom could steal as much as he wanted, any way he wanted. It was up to him to make his own deals. In exchange, judges in those courtrooms had to favorably dispose of any cases in which LeFevour had a personal interest. As supervising judge, LeFevour did not have a courtroom of his own, but he still took bribes to fix cases. Then he would assign the cases to one of his crooked cronies, and they would take care of it for him.

Almost all new judges on the Circuit Court do a tour of duty at traffic court. LeFevour had an immediate test to find out if they were honest or not. He sent his first cousin and chief bagman, Jimmy LeFevour, to give them money.

On one of his first days as a judge in traffic court, Brian L. Crowe was assigned to a major courtroom. Jimmy told Crowe that Judge LeFevour had "an interest" in a certain case before Crowe that day. Crowe dismissed the case on its merits and thought nothing more of it.

That afternoon, Judge Crowe, holding books in both arms, pushed open the door leading out of his courtroom. Jimmy walked up and slipped something into Crowe's suit coat pocket. Crowe felt the pressure, but had no idea what it was until he got to his chambers. He found a $100 bill.

Crowe raced out of his chambers, found Jimmy, unbuttoned his uniform shirt pocket with one hand, and stuffed the money into it with the other.

"You son of a bitch," said Crowe. "Don't you ever do that again!"

Jimmy looked at Crowe for a moment and, then, without saying anything, turned and walked away. He walked into his cousin's office and said, "He didn't want it."

Judge LeFevour shrugged, "Who has the money now?"

"I do," answered Jimmy. The judge stuck out his hand, and Jimmy gave him the bill.

Brian Crowe was never assigned to a major courtroom again.

Jimmy LeFevour, in a life devoid of grace, was notable in one respect. Of all the liars, cheaters, chiselers, blackmailers, bribers, extortionists, squealers, scoundrels, womanizers, double-crossers, drunks, phonies, and finaglers connected with Greylord, he appeared to be the one with the least redeeming social value. Even the vilest of the lawyers occasionally helped someone with a legal problem. Jimmy LeFevour never helped anyone.

In twenty-eight years as a police officer, he never rose above the rank of patrolman in a career that was distinguished only for his drinking. His binges were legendary, sometimes lasting as long as nine days and ending only with his hospitalization. He would drink a case of beer and more a day. Between the mid-1960s and early 1980s, he turned himself into alcoholic rehabilitation programs almost once a year. He also gambled, spending many long afternoons or nights at the local racetracks. He had the clout he needed for protection when his first cousin became a judge in 1968. Dick LeFevour kept Jimmy nearby.

Jimmy and Dick, three and a half years apart in age, grew up together. Jimmy was born in 1928, Dick in 1931. Their fathers were brothers, both of them Chicago policemen. Dick's father became a captain in the Austin District on the far West Side, which borders the quiet suburb of Oak Park. Jimmy was one of five children. His mother died when he was twelve, and Dick's mother frequently looked after him as he grew into adolescence. The cousins bunked together at summer camp.

Dick went to Campion Academy, a Jesuit boarding school in Prairie du Chien, Wisconsin, where he won the oratorical contest, and then on to Loyola University in Chicago. After receiving a degree in education, he joined the Marine Corps, but received a medical discharge after he severely injured his leg in boot camp. Then, in 1953, he married his childhood sweetheart, Virginia McHugh. Known as Ginger, she was the daughter of a legendary Chicago newspaperman, LeRoy "Buddy" McHugh, who was the model for the character Buddy McCue in Ben Hecht and Charles MacArthur's classic 1928 play about Chicago journalism, *The Front Page*.

Dick taught high school English while going to Loyola School of Law at night. Then, in 1958, he started a private law practice in Oak Park.

Jimmy, somewhat shiftless, had trouble in school, didn't go to college, and joined the Army. Three years later, the family name carried enough weight to get him hired by the Chicago Police Department. He was married, but his wife divorced him because of his alcoholism. A few years later, when Jimmy's older brother, Robert, was dying—as a result of alcoholism—he asked Richard to look after Jimmy, the inept black sheep. In 1968, at age thirty-six, Dick was appointed a magistrate. In 1969, he was assigned to traffic court. Almost immediately he arranged for Jimmy to get a cushy job in the building.

"We can make some money, Jimmy," said Dick.

They did. In 1971, Richard LeFevour became supervising judge of traffic court, with a big office on the first floor. Jimmy's office was next door. Together they formed one complex personality: Richard, tall, distinguished-looking, with graying hair and an engaging, witty manner—the elegant Dr. Jekyll, accepting awards from civic and legal groups for his innovative administrative techniques in the courts; and James, heavy-set, flaccid-faced, and crude, wandering the corridors of traffic court as Mr. Hyde did the alleys of London, menacing and loathsome, accepting money.

From 1971 until 1981, while Dick ran traffic court, Jimmy never had it so good. He made more than $100,000 a year, tax free. When Dick was elevated to presiding judge of the entire First Municipal District, which included all the courts inside the city, Jimmy had it even better. Dick moved to a spacious office on the twelfth floor of the Daley Civic Center, and Jimmy went with him. They then organized the branch courts the way they had traffic court—replacing honest judges with crooks from the traffic courtrooms. Even more money rolled in.

Then one day the FBI wanted to talk to Jimmy. Hake had some interesting tape of him. Jimmy did not hesitate. He immediately flipped. He told the FBI he could give them Judge LeFevour if they would go easy on him. Not easy on the judge. Easy on Jimmy.

Prosecutors liked the idea. They let Jimmy plead guilty to three misdemeanors, which allowed him to keep his police pension. Then he started squealing. He told a federal grand jury about, among other things, a group of attorneys known as "miracle workers" who practiced nowhere but traffic court and never lost a case—at least not a case they paid for, which seemed to be every serious one.

Then, in exchange for leniency for themselves, some of

the miracle workers started talking. One of them, Bruce Campbell, said he paid at least $70,000 in bribes during Richard LeFevour's reign in traffic court. He spread the money among, probably, thirteen different judges—he wasn't quite sure. "I didn't count them, I just bribed them," said Campbell. "I did it every morning. It was kind of like brushing your teeth."

The miracle workers, with a revolving nucleus of eight to twelve lawyers through the years, systematized their bribery. Attorney Melvin Kanter later explained how it worked. Every morning he would give Jimmy LeFevour a list of cases that were to be dismissed or, at worst, given a sentence of court supervision. Jimmy would then go to Dick, who would assign cooperative judges to the courtrooms where the cases were to be heard.

Jimmy and Kanter would meet again around noon and Kanter would hand over envelopes—one for each case— containing money for both the LeFevours. Jimmy roamed the hallways doing this over the noon hour, going from one lawyer to the next, collecting envelopes.

Kanter was a longtime miracle worker. His miracles predated Judge LeFevour's tour as head of traffic court. He admitted that, in 1968, when he was a new lawyer around the building, LeFevour's predecessor, Raymond K. Berg, told him, "If you want to win your cases, it's going to cost you a hundred dollars a case." LeFevour's methods were steeped in tradition.

The dean of the miracle workers was Joseph E. McDermott, who admitted that, over more than two decades, he had bribed twenty-three judges. Each Christmas, in the later years, he had collected $200 from each miracle worker as a present to Judge LeFevour. Most years, the total was more than $2,000.

In 1986, shortly before McDermott's admissions became public, he was slated by the Cook County Democratic Central Committee for a judgeship in city-only voting. Addressing the committee, Edward R. Vrdolyak, the chairman, gave McDermott a rousing endorsement dripping with irony. "He knows how to assist his fellow man," said Vrdolyak. "He'll make an excellent judge."

McDermott, sixty-eight years old, easily won the Democratic primary over four independent challengers and was elected without opposition in the general election eight months later. Before he could take office, however, McDermott was jailed for refusing to testify before the federal grand jury handling the ongoing Greylord investigation. McDermott had been granted immunity from prosecution, which stripped him of his Fifth Amendment right to remain silent. When he still refused to talk, he was held in contempt of court by Chief Judge John F. Grady of the U.S. District Court and packed off to the Metropolitan Correctional Center, a medium-security federal penitentiary in downtown Chicago.

McDermott defiantly announced that, if necessary, he would take his oath of office in his federal jail cell—an unseemly prospect even for Chicago. After only one week behind bars, however, McDermott emerged a new man and agreed to cooperate with the government. He signed an affidavit agreeing to "decline and resign" his Circuit Court seat. He also voluntarily relinquished his law license.

McDermott's reluctance to cooperate blew the potential benefits of his immunity. The kind of immunity that the government had given him—called "use immunity"—only meant that he was immune from prosecution for his testimony. In other words, anything he said could not be used against him, but the government could still prosecute him, using evidence developed independently of his testimony against others. In practice, this sometimes means that government witnesses can escape prosecution entirely by being expansive when they testify. Other times, it means that a witness will be allowed to plead guilty to a misdemeanor instead of facing a felony prosecution.

The government was no longer willing to let McDermott off easy. He was prosecuted for racketeering and tax evasion. He pleaded guilty and was sentenced to a year and a day in prison and fined $30,000. He would have gotten a harsher sentence, except that he agreed to testify in whatever investigations the government wanted him to.

Some of McDermott's unreported income was cash he received from defendants ostensibly to bribe judges, although the bribes were never paid. It was a common practice among some lawyers to tell their clients that a bribe was needed when it wasn't. The lawyer would just keep the money, leaving the client thinking that the case had been fixed. This practice was known as "rainmaking."

Sometimes bagmen also participated in rainmaking. Jimmy was his cousin's chief bagman, but there were others—including Ira Blackwood and Harold J. Conn. While the miracle workers had direct deals with judges, inexperienced lawyers had to deal entirely through a bagman. This way, neither the lawyers nor their clients would have direct knowledge—knowledge they could testify to—that a judge took a payoff.

Conn, Blackwood, and a couple of policemen brothers, Joseph and James Trunzo, would take money from the new lawyers and pass it on to the appropriate judges.

Blackwood was a dependable bagman, but Conn and the Trunzos, who were identical twins, developed reputations as rainmakers. They often told lawyers they would fix cases, but didn't. If the lawyer won the case on its own merits, the rainmakers would take the credit. If he lost, the rainmaker would give the money back with some excuse. Suspicious lawyers started to catch on to the rainmakers, however, and after they won a case they would sometimes ask the judge if he had "seen" the bagman. The rainmaker could then be in trouble. Judges hated to find out they had been fixed and didn't know it.

Terry Hake had given Joseph Trunzo $200 to give to Judge John Murphy in January of 1982. Not long before, Murphy had been transferred from traffic court to Branch 29 at Belmont and Western, but he continued to use some of his old traffic court bagmen.

Hake had a client he wanted acquitted of a theft charge in Branch 29. Hake paid the $200, and the client got off. Later Hake spoke to Murphy, trying to get an admission on tape that Murphy had gotten the money. It was the first Murphy had heard about it. The conversation alerted Murphy that Trunzo had pocketed the payoff.

Murphy went down to traffic court looking for Trunzo. He found him in a hallway. Trunzo, knowing what was up, reached into his pocket.

"I got some money for you from Terry Hake," Trunzo said sheepishly.

"Don't worry about it. It's all right," said Murphy, speaking the obtuse language of fixers; he did not mean it was all right, and Trunzo knew it.

"I got some money in my hand," said Trunzo, as the two strolled toward the La Salle Street lobby. They shook hands at the entrance. Trunzo went up the escalator, his hands now empty. Murphy went out the revolving door clutching two $100 bills.

Peter Karl's 1981 report did not worry LeFevour much, but McLain was worried. He called LeFevour.

"Maybe it's time to shut down the operation," said McLain.

"Continue as you're doing. It's just a ripple on a pond and will blow over," said LeFevour.

McLain asked what if things did not blow over; could he rely on LeFevour for support?

"Did you ever accept any checks?" asked LeFevour.

"I don't think so," said McLain.

"Don't worry about it," said LeFevour. "They can't trace cash."

For another year, through all of 1982, LeFevour continued to run the First Municipal District as a gigantic judicial tollbooth, collecting from scores of insiders using the courts to their advantage.

It apparently did not enter Dick LeFevour's mind that he and his subordinates were under official scrutiny until the Greylord story broke in 1983, and he was identified by Karl—who by then was working for WMAQ-TV, the NBC-owned Chicago station—as a target of the investigation.

LeFevour became enraged at Richard M. Daley, the state's attorney. LeFevour and Daley were close. When Daley became state's attorney in 1980, LeFevour swore him in. Ginger LeFevour had worked as chairman of Women for Daley in the campaign. When Daley ran for mayor in April of 1983—he was defeated in a three-way primary race won by Harold Washington—Ginger LeFevour worked full time for him.

It is true that Daley knew about the investigation. But Daley trusted LeFevour and thought him honest. When Karl reported on the air that LeFevour was a Greylord target, Daley reiterated his trust in LeFevour to friends.

"So far as I know, there isn't anything against LeFevour other than allegations and innuendo," Daley said.

Years later, a Daley associate reflected on Daley's relationship with LeFevour. The associate said that Daley did not believe LeFevour was a crook. Perhaps psychologically Daley had to believe that.

"It's interesting from a human standpoint," the associate said. "If Daley had started from the premise that LeFevour was a crook, then he'd have had to deal with the fact that he had betrayed a friend by not telling him he was under investigation. Not that Daley would have told him, anyway. I don't think he would have. But it was easier for him to believe in LeFevour's honesty."

LeFevour, a man not troubled by moral shadings, had no sympathy for Daley's dilemma. "That little bastard!" shouted LeFevour. "He knew about it and he never told me."

He tore Daley's picture off his wall and never spoke to him again.

He never spoke to his cousin Jimmy again, either.

5

The Drug Misconnection

☆

While the investigations of traffic court and the First Municipal District branch courts were going on, Assistant U.S. Attorney James Schweitzer was trying another approach to broadening Greylord.

Schweitzer was a tough prosecutor. There were stories about his dedication, his absorption in his work, his tenacious pursuit of indictments and convictions. He had stayed at the office all night working on cases, napping on couches, brushing his teeth and washing in little basins in the men's room, and wandering the corridors in the empty hours in his underwear.

Schweitzer was a man of little warmth and less humor. Taller than six feet, he was unusually lean, and his skinny neck protruded from shirt collars that always seemed to fit too loosely, as if he had just lost weight. He had the posture of a vulture, and when he sat in a courtroom he hunched over his legal pad and shook his right leg nervously. From this slumped position, he periodically peered around the courtroom, swiveling his head like a periscope, sneering at the testimony of witnesses. A person would not want to be in a position where James Schweitzer could cause him trouble.

In 1980, the two leaders of a West Side drug organization, Green Smith and Milton Kelly, whom Schweitzer had prosecuted, were sentenced to twenty and fifteen years respectively, both without parole.

During the Smith-Kelly trial, one of the government's witnesses, a former street seller named Kalvin Shannon, said he had paid bribes to Marquette District patrolmen Joe Pena and Dennis Smentek and two officers known to Shannon as "the Billys."

Joseph Pena and Dennis Smentek were Marquette District Tactical Unit officers. So were "the Billys"—William Haas and William Guide. The Marquette District covers a large part of the tough, poor, black West Side. During the 1970s the Marquette tac unit included four sets of partners who were regarded as among the best the Chicago Police Department had to offer: Pena and Smentek, Haas and Guide, Curtis Lowery and James Ballauer, and Thomas Ambrose and Frank DeRango.

Ballauer was named policeman of the year in 1974 by the Junior Chamber of Commerce. Altogether they had more than 1,700 commendations for their police work. Haas, Smentek, and Lowery were Vietnam veterans. Lowery had been wounded twice.

Every police district in Chicago has a tactical unit. Tac officers are patrolmen without a beat. They roam their districts freely, and they are some of the most streetwise cops around. Their assignment is "aggressive patrol." They do a lot of rousting, popping in on places where they think something illegal is going on, confiscating weapons or dope.

"They were head-bangers, there's no question about it," said Jo-Anne Wolfson, a lawyer who eventually represented Billy Guide. "They shook up a lot of people, including the dope dealers."

The Smith-Kelly ring and another drug operation headed by C.W. Wilson were in the Marquette District. Through the years, the tac officers were responsible for hundreds of arrests of members of the rings, including the leaders. Most of the cases were thrown out of court because the arrests were executed illegally. The officers said they didn't care. They had grabbed dope or guns during the bust. The dope sellers would go back on the streets, but the guns and drugs would not. That was their assignment—get those things off the street.

But Schweitzer had developed a theory: If indeed the Marquette tac officers were taking bribes to protect the drug dealers, perhaps they were involved in something more serious. Maybe, Schweitzer's theory ran, the cops were passing money to judges to protect the dealers in court. If that was true, the cops, if they could be made to talk, could give the government the judges. And that would bolster Operation Greylord, the biggest thing the U.S. attorney's office had going.

On Schweitzer's recommendation, a task force of Chicago Police Internal Affairs Division detectives and FBI agents was formed to snoop around the Marquette District. Schweitzer began talking to the convicted drug dealers. He was prepared to make a deal.

West Side drug dealers knew how to deal.

Smith and Kelly operated at Twenty-second and Avers, Wilson near the corner of Sixteenth and Christiana, five blocks east of Avers and six blocks north.

C.W. Wilson, who started large-scale dealings in 1976, began working out of an alley that ran between Christiana and Homan and opened onto Sixteenth Street. Soon, though, he moved his base of operations around the corner to a building he bought at 1618 South Christiana. He also bought a hot dog stand at the corner of Sixteenth and Christiana. He named it the Jones City Sandwich Shop. A "Jones" in drug parlance is a habit.

The Wilson and Smith-Kelly drug distribution centers, although unconnected, were set up similarly and displayed a certain sophistication. Heroin was purchased and cut—diluted with quinine—in a location away from the street where it was sold. Wilson, for instance, would buy heroin in half-kilo amounts once or twice a week. Each "half key" would cost $21,000, which he would hand over in cash. The diluted heroin would be divided and placed in aluminum foil packages. Each package sold for $10. The packaged heroin would be delivered—not by Wilson—to sellers on the street. The number of sellers varied according to the time of day and the amount of business.

Buyers would drive, or walk, down Christiana and stop at one of the sellers standing at the curb and order what they wanted. The sellers were strung out from Sixteenth Street past the Howland Elementary School a block away. The seller would run to his stash, grab the order, run back to the buyer, and collect the money. Knowledgeable in the rudiments of search-and-seizure law, Wilson, Smith, and Kelly had set up their systems to minimize the time the seller actually possessed the heroin. This made it extremely hard for police to make possession arrests.

In addition, the ringleaders employed lookouts throughout the neighborhood, from kids riding bikes to elderly men standing on street corners. In the Avers Street operation, Smith and Kelly supplied the kids with bicycles, and the kids developed an early warning system, using whistles. On Christiana, Wilson's chief lookouts were Blue Barnett and John Mosby, known as The Butler. They would yell "Heads up!" if police were in the general area, and

"Roll it" if they were actually coming down Sixteenth or Christiana.

Frog Williams and Lump Winfield were Wilson's middlemen, who distributed the heroin to the street sellers and picked up the cash. Or, as Wilson put it: "Frog and Lump was the guys that collect my money and pass out the bags."

The sellers worked on a sixty-forty split; they kept $4 every time they sold a $10 bag. If, for instance, they were given fifty bags at the start of the day and had none left at the end, they were expected to turn over $300 to Wilson, keeping $200 for themselves. Wilson (or Smith or Kelly) paid everyone else a wage. There were no other commissions, and it was unwise to take an unauthorized one.

In 1975, a neighborhood hanger-on and junkie who went by the name of Charlie D. was suspected by the sellers of dipping into their stashes. The sellers told Rock Calhoun about these suspicions. Calhoun was Wilson's prefect in charge of discipline, according to the government, which in 1981 offered him a deal and put him in the federal witness protection program. Calhoun said he told Wilson about Charlie D. and Wilson said to kill him. According to Calhoun, the method Wilson selected was to arrange for Charlie D. to receive a packet of white powder that contained, among other things, battery acid and rat poison.

A few days later, on May 23, 1975, a man who lived on the first floor of an apartment on Homan near Sixteenth noticed a foul odor coming from the basement. He checked and found the decomposing remains of Charlie D. He was sitting on the basement floor, his back propped up against the concrete wall, a heavy string tied around his left arm, and a hypodermic needle protruding from his forearm. Nearby was a bottle cap, a small piece of cotton, some burnt matches, and a small piece of paper.

The police assumed Charlie D., whose real name was

Charles Whittaker, had died of a drug overdose. They took the body to the morgue. The examining pathologist did not think of testing for rat poison or battery acid in Charlie D.'s system and listed the cause of death as acute cardiac dilation of unknown causes.

Keeping the neighbors in line, Wilson was king of the 'hood. By 1977, he was buying at least two kilos a week from his man, Skadoolie Napue. Sometimes Wilson would buy from his half-brother, Rabbit Parker, who had introduced Wilson to Skadoolie while they were serving time together at the federal prison in Terre Haute, Indiana. Business was so good that Skadoolie wore a beeper and C.W. would give him a beep whenever he needed a fast shipment of heroin.

To get money for drugs, many of the indigenous West Side junkies went on criminal forays into the rich suburbs along the North Shore. But some of the wealthy white kids up north did not wait for their money to be stolen from them. They brought it to the West Side. Easily a third of the heroin customers of the two rings were white.

With business so brisk it was natural that a few ambitious entrepreneurs would crop up to challenge Wilson's kingpin crown. It was a dangerous undertaking. One day in May 1977 an ex-con named Pepilo Perry showed up at a neighborhood tavern with a sawed-off shotgun. Perry looked around and left. A little later he saw Rock Calhoun, C.W.'s enforcer, walking near Fifteenth and Kedzie. He jumped out of his car—a 1973 Pontiac Firebird with black vinyl top and silver-gray bottom—whipped out the shotgun, and announced that he was going to start selling drugs on the corner of Sixteenth and Trumbull, which is two corners west of Sixteenth and Christiana. He said he would kill Calhoun if he tried to stop him. Perry, thirty-two, had just finished a long stretch away from the neighborhood and perhaps was a little out of touch with the prevailing sentiments there.

Rock Calhoun held a hurried conference with Wilson, Arkansas Baker, and a few other boys. It was decided that they would kill Pepilo Perry and any associates he might have as soon as possible. Later that day Calhoun spotted Perry riding in his Firebird with his buddies, Henry Hughes and Little Chief Hennigan, and a couple of women.

A little before 10 P.M. Perry, still with the same passengers, was driving down Millard Avenue, where Henry Hughes lived. A black 1973 Fleetwood was parked on the right side of the street and a burgundy 1976 New Yorker was parked on the left. As Perry's Firebird approached, the New Yorker suddenly pulled in front of it and stopped. The Fleetwood pulled out from the curb and blocked Perry from behind.

From gangways between buildings on both sides of the street, men with automatic weapons opened fire on the Firebird. Spent cartridges pinged off the concrete, glass shattered, and bullets ricocheted off metal. The driver of the New Yorker, Arkansas Baker, was out of the car and pumping bullets into Perry's side of the Firebird. A bullet grazed Perry's skull. He looked out of the rearview mirror and saw a slight opening between the Fleetwood and the cars parked to his right. He slammed into reverse and sped backwards through that opening, past the Fleetwood and down the street. Arkansas Baker jumped back into the New Yorker and peeled away in the other direction. The Fleetwood, with Rock Calhoun in the front passenger's seat, followed.

In the meantime, Perry was still speeding backward, blasting through two busy intersections, finally whipping the silver-and-black Firebird around from Millard onto Twenty-third Street and racing east. The window on the right side had been shot out, and in the right backseat Henry Hughes lay sprawled, blood running out of his head. Perry squealed to a brief stop near Farragut High School, and the women and Little Chief Hennigan scrambled out of the car. Then Perry dashed to St. Anthony's Hospital, where Henry Hughes was pronounced dead. Perry was treated for a crease on the left side of his head and released. He was never seen in the neighborhood again.

The police questioned Arkansas Baker. He said he had, indeed, been the driver of the New Yorker, but he had merely dropped off his girlfriend and had accidentally pulled in front of the Firebird when all the commotion started. One cold night in December 1980 he was murdered.

Three months after the Millard Street shooting, during the muggy days of August, another drug dealer surfaced with more ambition than sense. He told people he was going into business for himself. Rock Calhoun warned the new dealer, twenty-eight-year-old David Willis, that, in essence, if he wanted to see his twenty-ninth birthday he should stay off Sixteenth Street. Willis refused.

Calhoun relayed this information to Wilson, who told Calhoun to make whatever arrangements were necessary to have Willis killed. Calhoun went to Herbert Carlton, who said that he was not interested in committing the murder himself, but that he knew a couple of members of a South Side street gang, the Disciples, who might get the job done. He introduced Calhoun to Steven Steward, a twenty-one-year-old gang member with a game leg to show for past actions, and Little Charles Glover, a nineteen-year-old warrior with a lumpy, scarred face.

The next day Carlton drove Glover and Steward to the West Side, where they picked up Calhoun in the early afternoon. They cruised the area until they spotted David Willis and his brother, Harold. They returned to Calhoun's house, where they got weapons, a chrome-plated sawed-off shotgun for Steward and a nine-millimeter automatic pistol for Glover. At about 6:30 on the evening of August 23, Carlton dropped Steward and Glover off a block away from Sixteenth and Christiana.

As usual on a hot summer night, the corner was jumping. David and Harold stood outside the Jones City Sandwich Shop talking to a friend. Outside Wilson's headquarters at 1618 South Christiana—or "1618" as it came to be called— were Harry "Dog" Cannon, Wilson's right-hand man in the heroin organization, and four other ring members.

As the Willis brothers talked on the corner and Glover and Steward approached from Christiana, a boy who lived next door to Wilson rode his bike up to the Jones City Sandwich Shop. Harold Willis took the bike for a ride as the boy went inside to get a hot dog. The ride saved Harold's life. At that moment, Steven Steward and Little Charles Glover were about to cross Sixteenth Street, Steward to shoot David Willis and Glover to shoot Harold. When Harold rode away, Glover stopped.

Steward continued across the street, not hurrying, limping at a measured pace, the shotgun in a case. Just before he reached David Willis, he took the gun out of the case and, with the chrome-plated barrel glistening in the setting sun, shot a single blast through Willis's throat. Steward had trouble with the trigger device, pinching his right hand between the thumb and forefinger. He dropped the weapon and the case on the sidewalk and hurried back south across Sixteenth Street, following the already fleeing Glover. A block away they jumped into Carlton's car and drove back to the South Side.

Willis was pronounced dead on arrival at Mount Sinai Hospital at 7 P.M.

Calhoun showed up on the South Side an hour later and gave Steven Steward and Little Charles Glover $200 to split.

It did not take the police long to make a connection between the Wilson gang and David Willis. They questioned Dog Cannon and others, who said they had wandered down to the corner out of curiosity after the shooting but really didn't know anything.

Wilson was not around after the shooting, but the cops found him the next day and took him to the station for questioning. He said he was at 1618 playing cards with Lump and Blue when they heard the shot. They ran outside, Wilson said, and determined what had happened. Wilson, displaying admirable public-spiritedness, said he went to get his car so he could drive Willis to the hospital. But, alas, when Wilson arrived on the scene in his Eldorado, the police were already taking care of the transportation, so he had driven off to see if he could find Willis's mother and gently tell her of the tragedy.

It was a touching story. The interviewing officers didn't believe him, but they could not hold him on their suspicions. He was released. It was not until March 1981, when Rock Calhoun told his story under the protection of the federal government, that the police arrested Carlton, Glover, and Steward, all of whom confessed. The authorities still did not feel they had enough evidence to charge Wilson, though, since his part in the affair was so indirect.

Wilson was living high in the late 1970s, especially for a fifth-grade dropout. Born in Greenville, Mississippi, Wilson had come to Chicago to live with an aunt in 1967, when he was seventeen. His first job in the city was washing cars at a Pontiac dealership, but apparently he was doing more than just running a sponge over them. He was sentenced to two years at Terre Haute for crossing state lines in stolen autos. After that he turned to dope, first as a small-time dealer and then, in 1975, as chief of the ring that thrived on Christiana Street.

By 1977, Wilson owned the 1618 building and one in the

suburb of Oak Park and, finally, a house in Broadview, a suburb west of Oak Park. He paid cash for these properties, as he did for everything else. He paid cash for so many cars at Marolf Cadillac that they began letting him charge them. He lived with a woman, Pee Wee Rhone, who did not cramp his style. He headed luxury-car caravans to Chicago area racetracks.

Often the crowd would get together at a Holiday Inn just west of the Loop for crap games that lasted as long as two weeks. Utilizing three or four rooms in the motel, they flipped mattresses off the beds and onto the floor, threw down their money, and rolled the dice on the mattresses. The participants in the games represented the elite of West Side dope society—C.W., Dog Cannon, Long Money Adams, Hundred Street Sam, Rabbit Parker, Skadoolie, Reno the Lady (who wasn't a lady, or even a female), Menky and Jimmy Wilson (C.W.'s brothers), and West Side Dog, not to be confused with just plain Dog. Wilson explained the difference when he testified at Skadoolie's trial: "Dog is the Dog that I just identified in the picture—West Side Dog is another Dog that live further west."

In the crap games Wilson often bet $1,000 a pass and, in a side game called "bigger pay the littler," as much as $10,000. One night during a nine-day game at 1618, Skadoolie ran out of money. He got $2,000 from another crap shooter by giving him a ring to hold. Skadoolie was quite fussy about his jewelry, and he noticed the man slipping the ring on and off his little finger.

"Look man, don't be playing around with my ring," said Skadoolie. "I want my ring back in a few minutes."

"Give me my money and you can get it," replied the other shooter.

Skadoolie, angry, picked up the phone, and a few minutes later a teenager drove up, came into the house, and gave Skadoolie a roll of bills. Skadoolie peeled off $2,000, barely reducing the wad, and gave it to the man, who turned over the ring.

Sometimes C.W. liked to go with the boys to Las Vegas for extended weekends of cabarets and casinos. Occasionally they would go to Los Angeles, meeting with dope-dealing buddies there in fancy hotels for craps and cards and womanizing. Of course, they needed transportation during these excursions, so C.W. rented cargo airplanes at Midway Airport. C.W. and one or two of the others would drive their Cadillacs aboard and take off.

By 1979 Wilson was ready to branch out. He turned the day-to-day operation of his "stroll"—his drug beat—over to Dog Cannon. Wilson went into a side business buying and selling cars. Cannon then purchased the heroin and oversaw the books. Records were kept on how many bags each street seller was responsible for and how much money was owed Wilson. The Wilson organization, as well as Smith-Kelly's, kept meticulous records. It is interesting to note, in light of what eventually transpired, that there were never any records of payments to policemen.

The Wilson and Smith-Kelly operations were thriving. Cars from the city and suburbs lined up to buy heroin at both locations on the West Side. To accommodate them during the winter months, Wilson had the streets and sidewalks on Christiana cleared of snow. Green Smith and Milton Kelly, to mollify the residents of the 2200 block of Avers, held block parties, distributed presents, including bikes to kids who could then be used as lookouts, and had the tromped-down grass resodded.

As good as business was, however, both organizations were heading for a bust—literally. A special task force of federal Drug Enforcement Agency agents and Chicago narcotics detectives was formed. After a five-month effort that included camera surveillance and undercover heroin buys,

Green Smith and Milton Kelly were indicted in 1979, along with fifteen members of their ring. In October 1980, C.W. Wilson was indicted.

The convictions of Wilson and Smith-Kelly could have been of major significance if the government had been interested in squeezing dope pushers to get to the sources of their drugs. Prosecutors typically use the retailer to get the wholesaler and follow the trail up the ladder, getting convictions against sellers on each ascending rung until they reach a top dealer—a "French Connection" type.

But in the case of the West Side dealers, the government did not apply pressure for the names of higher-ups. Schweitzer wanted cops. It was cops who could deliver judges for the greater glory of Greylord, according to Schweitzer's theory that the cops were working with judges to protect drug rings.

In April 1981, he had brought Wilson before a grand jury. Wilson was given immunity from prosecution so that he could not invoke his Fifth Amendment privilege against self-incrimination. Nonetheless, Wilson still refused to talk, and he was thrown in jail for contempt.

Schweitzer kept trying. On May 22, U.S. District Court Judge Charles P. Kocoras sentenced C.W. Wilson to thirty-three years without parole. Smith and Kelly, previously sentenced, had already begun talking to the grand jury. Now Wilson, brooding over his long stretch plus additional time for contempt, decided to sing a tune of his own.

Wilson knew what Schweitzer wanted. When Wilson had been granted immunity in April, he thought Schweitzer was going to ask him about his drug sources. He had decided going in that he would take the Fifth, even though he would be held in contempt. But he quickly found out what Schweitzer was really after.

111

"He was concerned about the Marquette Ten more than he was anything," Wilson said later, when he testified against his old pal, Skadoolie Napue.

Smith and Kelly knew, too.

"When the deal was proposed, Schweitzer made it clear it was cops, not sources, that they wanted," said defense attorney Robert Bailey, who was involved in both the Smith-Kelly and Marquette Ten defenses. "I think it was unconscionable. They told Smith and Kelly right off that they just wanted cops; they were not interested in drug dealers. Smith and Kelly would not be telling on their friends. Once they got in the fold they could get forty or fifty other people in the organization as witnesses. Kelly or Smith or Wilson could say, 'They ain't after us. All they want are cops. Let's give them cops. All it can do is help us. You won't be hurting anyone but the cops.' It was an open invitation to commit perjury. These are greedy people without moral compunctions, and you are telling them in advance they don't need to worry about lying."

The main problem facing the government in building a case against the Marquette Ten was to find a federal crime they had committed.

If the tac officers had merely been busting dealers and stealing their money and drugs, their crimes would not be federal. They would be state crimes, such as armed robbery. But by getting kingpins Wilson, Smith, and Kelly to testify that they had paid the officers a continuing surcharge—more than $600 a week in the case of the two Billys, the dealers said—Schweitzer and his boss, Dan Webb, contrived to charge the policemen with aiding a continuing criminal enterprise and, since they were all in it together, with conspiracy.

At Schweitzer's urging, the investigators were relentless in their efforts to accumulate physical evidence against the officers. The government wanted something other than the word of men like C.W. Wilson, not exactly known as a sentinel of veracity. Wilson, after all, had once testified on behalf of Dog Cannon.

"You lied the whole time you were on the stand, correct?" he was later asked about that testimony.

"Well, I told them what my name was. I didn't lie about that."

The government tailed the officers, tapped them, bugged them, audited them, and, it was strongly suspected, broke into their cars and homes. The FBI and IRS examined every financial record the officers had. Agents traced spending patterns. They felt sure they would find someone living beyond his declared income. They didn't. No hidden bank accounts. No fancy cars. No boats on lakes at summer homes. No summer homes. No lakes.

The officers lived like what they were—middle-class working men. No fine clothes for the wives. No fancy schools for the kids. The wives worked. So did the kids. Even the only bachelor in the group, Billy Haas (who the government said was getting hundreds a week in payoffs), gave inexpensive gifts to girlfriends and, when the occasion arose, took them to characterless motels on Cicero Avenue. Decent places, certainly, but not the swinging opulence the feds had hoped to find. Most of the cops worked second jobs, some as security guards at Comiskey Park for White Sox home games. Not hard work, but not much pay, either.

"From the beginning—during the investigation, before the indictments—Webb let it be known that his door was open if anyone wanted to talk about lawyers and judges," said Paul Bradley, who represented Billy Haas.

Webb hoped the impending indictments would frighten some officers into flipping and testifying for the government, since the mandatory minimum for aiding kingpins in narcotics conspiracies was ten years without parole. But the policemen unswervingly maintained their innocence of the threatened charges and denied any knowledge of lawyer or judge wrongdoing.

In November of 1981, ten officers were indicted—nine tactical unit patrolmen and one other. Still, the Greylord-style surveillance of them continued, much of it typically amateurish. Dope dealers the government had flipped would walk up to officers and engage them in conversation, trying to get them to make incriminating statements. Armed with transmitters, the informants would ask questions like, "Do you remember the time you let me keep the dope?" These do-you-remember-style questions were invariably met with street-cop-style answers like, "Get fucked, asshole."

One of the Marquette defendants, Frank DeRango, a tough cop who had received dozens of police commendations, held a part-time job as a bouncer at the Home Run Inn, a pizza parlor near Comiskey Park. A little after 10:30 one night in March of 1982, a few days before the Marquette trial was to begin, DeRango stood drinking a beer at the end of the bar. An informant, Walter Cunningham, known as Fat Wally, walked in and started talking to DeRango about the case, asking a lot of pointed questions.

Fat Wally was quite solicitous and very concerned, so DeRango became suspicious almost at once, since Fat Wally had never expressed much concern about anything except his next fix.

DeRango noticed that Fat Wally kept reaching into his vest pocket. DeRango reached over, pulled Fat Wally's hand out of the pocket, and placed his own inside. He pulled out a transmitter, about the size of half a deck of cards.

"Wally, you're under arrest," DeRango started to say, but before he had finished, two FBI agents, a man and a woman, came in and grabbed Fat Wally. They were followed almost immediately by three other agents and Assistant U.S. Attorney Dan Reidy, one of the two men who originally had told Tom Sullivan about their suspicions of corruption in Chicago courts. Reidy had since become chief of special prosecutions and leader of a group of assistant U.S. attorneys assigned to Greylord.

DeRango, surrounded, asked who everybody was, and they told him. Standing with his hands on the bar, his right fist clenched around the transmitter, DeRango told the bartender to call the police. The feds told DeRango to give them the transmitter. DeRango refused. A beat officer, Philip Hanizel, arrived and asked what was going on.

"That officer is under indictment by a federal grand jury and has taken a piece of our equipment and won't return it to us," said the male agent who had arrived first, flashing a federal badge.

Reidy, a little less pompously, asked, "Would you ask officer DeRango to give us back our equipment?"

DeRango said he would not give it back unless ordered to do so by a supervisor. Hanizel summoned one.

Before the supervisor arrived, however, the phone behind the bar rang. The bartender who answered announced that it was DeRango's lawyer, Elliot M. Samuels, calling. Samuels wanted to speak to DeRango.

"No," said one of the agents, a pistol visible on his waist. "He can't move unless he hands over our equipment."

The place was crowded, and the people chewed pizza in silence, watching developments.

"Is he under arrest?" asked Hanizel.

"No, he's not under arrest," said the agent, "but he could be."

"If he's not under arrest, why can't he talk to his lawyer?"

"If he gives us our property he can talk to his attorney, but not until then," said the fed.

Samuels relayed a message to DeRango to call him when convenient and to get the names of the government people.

Lieutenant Robert Reilly, a police field supervisor, arrived. He suggested that everyone accompany him to the Marquette station, where the government agents could get their transmitter back.

Reidy declined the invitation and raised the stakes. He called Police Superintendent Richard J. Brzeczek at home. Brzeczek asked to speak to Lieutenant Reilly and told Reilly he was sending a deputy superintendent to the Home Run Inn.

Reidy sensed that the more the Chicago police became involved in the matter, the greater the likelihood of unwanted publicity. His call to Brzeczek, rather than facilitating a satisfactory solution, had escalated the problem.

"Look," said Reidy conciliatorily, "all this could be avoided if Officer DeRango would give us back our property. The thing costs thirty-four thousand dollars, and it is the responsibility of the agents. They don't want anything to happen to it."

Reidy guaranteed Reilly that DeRango would not be arrested if he turned over the transmitter. Reilly guaranteed Reidy's guarantee to DeRango, who turned over the transmitter, ending a ninety-minute standoff.

The government would have to try the case against the Marquette Ten without the benefit of the testimony of Fat Wally, who became just another in a long line of government undercover bunglers.

The trial started in the spring of 1982. The government claimed the cops were cozy with the drug dealers. The defense did not deny it.

In the twilight world of drugs, police and dealers live in murky symbiosis, feeding on one another. Cops trade confiscated heroin for information, overlook a sale in exchange for a promise of future cooperation, or let a seller they catch remain free if he promises to turn in some guns. The Marquette tac officers lived in wary coexistence with the drug overlords, neither side liking the other, but both sides keeping in touch. Some of the cops got their cars washed at a shop owned by Green Smith.

The defense claimed that a few tac officers could not guarantee protection for operations as sophisticated as Smith-Kelly's and Wilson's. The West Side was swarming with local and federal narcotics dicks, area detectives, beat patrolmen, and FBI agents who would have to be taken care of. Tac officers could offer only a small part of the protection the dealers would need. The only way the tac officers could have guaranteed protection would have been to pay the rest of the cops, laterally and vertically, perhaps as high as the district commander. But no other officers were accused of being involved with the tac cops.

Webb began to worry. He still didn't have any judges, and he was in danger of losing the case. One of the jurors especially worried him. The juror had begun to visibly react negatively to the prosecution witnesses. Webb wanted the juror dismissed.

"He offered us a deal," said defense attorney Bradley. "By that point in the trial, pretty late, I think Webb had come to believe that Schweitzer's simplistic domino theory—dealers to cops to lawyers to judges—was just wrong. Webb said he was willing to drop the charges on aiding a continuing criminal enterprise—the ones that carried mandatory ten-year minimum sentences—in exchange for our agreeing to dismiss the juror. I wanted to jump at the chance. It was a good offer, but by that time the cops were crazy. They were mad as hell and could not be reasoned with. They were not going to make any deals. They were going to fight everything all the way, and they wanted the juror kept."

In an ironic twist, that juror's father suffered a heart attack just as deliberations were about to begin. The juror was excused, and one of the alternate jurors took his place. In the end, the jury bought Webb's argument that sixty admitted junkies and drug dealers, murderers and rapists, perjurers and robbers, led by C.W. Wilson, couldn't be wrong.

Webb is an excellent trial lawyer with the boyish, toothy looks of Beaver Cleaver. He presented himself as a clean-cut, forthright, public-spirited prosecutor who would never put a bunch of degenerates on the stand and allow them to lie. There were a few touchy moments, though, especially when one of the street sellers, zonked out on smack, mumbled incoherently and began to nod off on the stand.

The turning point in the trial came when Gerald Werksman, defending tac officer Curtis Lowery, insisted upon having his client testify. Werksman assured the other defense lawyers that Lowery, the twice-wounded ex-Marine and holder of four hundred citations for outstanding police work, would make an excellent witness.

There was an FBI report dating from the early days of the investigation indicating that Lowery had told agents that he knew that cops had shaken down drug dealers in the Marquette District. The report could not have been used against the defendants if Lowery had not taken the stand. Werksman had seen the report, but had not shown it to the other defense attorneys. They heard of it for the first time when Lowery was cross-examined. Although Lowery denied the statement, Schweitzer cut him up with the FBI report. It was the one shred of evidence that seemed to back up some of the things the smaller dealers were saying—that the cops often shook them down. If the cops did that, the jury could reason, they could also take money on a continuing, conspiratorial basis.

When Lowery finished testifying, Billy Guide's lawyer, Jo-Anne Wolfson, was so angry that she lunged at Werksman in the courtroom, striking him with her fists and accusing him of being a government plant. She never spoke to Werksman again.

In his closing argument, Webb told the jury that the witnesses against the police had no incentive to lie. The little operatives, such as street sellers, had not been charged with anything, Webb explained. They had come forward on their own. The big operators like Wilson, Smith, and Kelly could not expect much either, Webb told the jurors. He said that he would inform the judges who sentenced Wilson, Kelly, and Smith about their cooperation, but he said that no deals had been struck, no guarantees made. Webb said he would have no control over what, if anything, the sentencing judges would do after he told them of the cooperation.

"Those dope peddlers that testified against these police officers are bad, evil people, and they ought to rot in jail, and as long as I am United States attorney I will do everything I can to see that is what happens to them," Webb told the jury.

It was a good speech, one the jury could easily take to mean that Wilson and Smith and Kelly were going to stay in prison for a long time, even if they did get a little time chipped off their sentences.

The Marquette Ten were found guilty on June 30, 1982. The following January all received a minimum of ten years without parole, some twice that much.

On March 8, 1983, Dan Webb appeared before Judge Charles Kocoras, one of his closest friends and the man who had sentenced C.W. Wilson. Webb was arguing for a sentence reduction.

"I have never worked with any witness who gave more full and complete cooperation than did C.W. Wilson," said Webb. "There are things that he did that were far beyond, I think, what anybody had expected that he would do. This man personally went out of his way to tell other people that they ought to give up the ghost and they ought to come in and start cooperating and expose the police corruption. Obviously, he was motivated by the hope that his cooperation would be pointed out to Your Honor, but I will tell you there were things that he did that he did not have to do. There were witnesses that he personally put himself on the line with by bringing them in here.

"I remember during the course of the investigation, as they were doing this, that his brother was murdered. He believes his brother was murdered by police officers. He did not stop. He continued forward. He has done that up until the current time.

"There is no question in his mind that dope peddlers who cooperate and testify against police substantially risk their lives. There is no question. There was evidence and testimony during the Marquette Ten trial that police officers out there threaten the lives of potential government witnesses."

Wilson's half brother, Rabbit Parker, was gunned down in the hallway of another dope dealer's apartment in November of 1981, just before the indictments of the Marquette Ten. Rock Calhoun later said that Wilson himself had ordered the killing because of a falling-out with Rabbit.

Eventually Kocoras reduced C.W.'s sentence from thirty-three years to the minimum ten. With good behavior Wilson had his sentence further reduced to six years and eight months. By certain meritorious activities, such as cooperating with the government, Wilson got another five months knocked off.

So C.W. Wilson, who the Marquette Ten jury probably thought would be in jail until the turn of the century, was released September 2, 1986. He had served his time at the federal minimum-security prison at Pleasanton, California, a campuslike farm where Patty Hearst served her time.

120

"I went in in a Cadillac and I'll come out in a Cadillac," Wilson once said. And he did. His brothers were waiting for him with his favorite Eldorado when he was released.

In March of 1985 the Marquette Ten began serving their time. They did not go to sunny campuses like Pleasanton, California. They went to places like Seagoville, Texas, and Danbury, Connecticut—big houses.

In December of 1985, his sentence cut in half at the request of James Schweitzer, Green Smith was released. He immediately resumed his position as the outside boss of the Avers Street operation, which he had continued to run from prison without interruption.

"The exact same location as before he went to prison," said Marquette District Sergeant Thomas Eichler. "The operation was exactly the same—the same methods, the exact same lookouts."

Eichler joined the tac unit just before the Marquette Ten were indicted; he supervised the eight officers who took the places of the ones who went to prison.

"Smith's family ran a smaller drug operation, waiting for him to get out. Smith was running the smaller operation by phone from the Metropolitan Correctional Center. Then the feds put him on work release during the day and never notified us. He was doing his drug business in the day and then going to the MCC at night. He wasn't out a week before he tried to take over the entire drug operation."

In the spring of 1986, four months after Smith was released from prison, Eichler saw him come out of a house on Avers Street with three other men. They had brown paper bags, which they tried to toss away when Eichler and two other plainclothesmen began to chase them. The police caught the men and recovered the brown bags, which contained a thousand tinfoil packets of heroin. A judge threw Smith back in jail.

When he had sentenced the Marquette Ten, Judge John F. Grady had said that the drug trade in the Marquette District could have been halted in a matter of weeks if the tac officers had made "good arrests," especially of customers. He ignored the fact that "good arrests" of drug dealers had never been made anywhere by tac officers. They are made by local and federal narcotics agents, who have the time, the equipment, and the money it takes to make undercover purchases—exactly the type of operations that brought about the indictments of Wilson and Smith-Kelly.

"Everything that the judge said should be done then is being done now," said Eichler. "Every contention that he and Dan Webb made has been shown to be wrong. I've harassed the dope dealers. I've locked them up. I've got them convicted. I think we've got ninety percent of the neighborhood over there under indictment. And yet they are still in business.

"The day we arrested Smith, I saw nine of the original seventeen people arrested in the conspiracy on the street. Nine of the seventeen names in the Smith-Kelly indictment were back at it. I went through there yesterday. They're still out there. They're still dealing. It's a never-ending thing. We just don't have the manpower. The animals are running the zoo."

Eichler said it was humiliating to go to Avers and Christiana Streets after the Marquette Ten were convicted.

"It was terrible, living with them out there. They would pull Schweitzer's card from their pocket, Webb's card from their pocket. They would tell you, 'You mess with us and we'll go down and see Dan Webb in the morning.' They did. It's a matter of record. They went down there and complained that the only reason they were being messed with was because they had testified. We were investigated over and over by the Office of Professional Standards."

But Dan Webb was delighted with the convictions. He said it was a breakthrough for corruption fighters. Before the Marquette Ten, it was almost impossible to convict policemen solely on the word of drug pushers, because the pushers were such unreliable witnesses. That gave the cops impunity to shake down drug dealers whenever they wanted.

He had to put a stop to that, Webb said.

6

Shady Dealings

☆

When the Marquette trial ended, and the prosecutor, Dan Webb, had accepted the congratulations of his friends and assistants, he was still faced with the fact that the convicted police officers had given him no judges.

The drug dealers had cooperated, testifying against the Marquette Ten, but, so far as Webb could prove, the bucks had stopped there.

In spite of the heavy sentences, the Marquette Ten did not talk. And the reason they did not, it was becoming apparent even to prosecutors, was because they had nothing to say. There was absolutely no evidence, through wired lawyers, bugged chambers, or squealing dope dealers, that the convicted cops were involved illegally with judges.

Webb began to look elsewhere to expand the Greylord sting, now more than two years old and somewhat of a

124

costly disappointment. The fancy electronics surveillance and undercover hugger-mugger had produced solid evidence against only a few judges, including the rather easy target of Warbling Wayne Olson. Even Olson had not been caught on tape actually accepting money from anyone.

The government felt it could present a fairly strong case against Olson, and perhaps a couple of judges in traffic court, but that was all so far.

Then one day Marlene Friedman appeared.

She said she had been dating an associate Circuit Court judge named Alan Lane, and she thought he might be kinky. Friedman told Charles B. Sklarsky, the assistant U.S. attorney who had been one of the original pushers for a court investigation, that Lane might be trying to blackmail her, that he might try to fix a case against her.

Her story was a bit shaky, but by that time Webb's assistants were willing to listen to anything. They wanted judges.

Friedman had originally gone to Jeffrey J. Kent, chief of the special prosecutions bureau of the Cook County state's attorney's office, which was cooperating with Webb's office in the Greylord investigation. Friedman surprised Kent, and later Sklarsky, by telling him she knew a big investigation of the courts was underway. This was May of 1983, and Greylord was supposed to be extremely secret, known to only an inner circle of investigators.

But in truth, there were many rumors starting to surface that the feds were probing the courts. Even careless Wayne Olson had been warned about it.

"Yeah, I heard," he said one day in 1982 to his partner in graft, James Costello. "But we're okay. I hear they're after Marquette cops."

Some of the Inspector Clouseau adventures of the FBI had also found their way into print, and it was getting harder to keep a lid on Greylord. Friedman knew lawyers.

She seemed to work her way into their circles. She knew prosecutors. She knew judges. Friedman apparently had heard some things.

On first meeting, Marlene Friedman could seem like a vital, interesting woman. Thirty-one years old, she was intelligent and attractive, with auburn hair, a full, sensuous face and dark, lively eyes. She was vivacious and artistically inclined. For a time she owned a doll store on Wells Street near Old Town, a neighborhood a couple of miles north of the Loop that had once, like several in lower Manhattan, been populated by artists and writers living on the cheap but long ago had been transformed into high-rent apartments near expensive shops and restaurants. The store was called Clones, and Friedman sold dolls that, for $150, were custom made to look like their owners. The store seemed like a gay diversion for Friedman, who didn't really have to work. Her father, who doted on her, was a wealthy manufacturer who had recently made her a present of a new Mercedes-Benz. She had grown up in the tony north suburbs and could vacation at her father's place in Florida. She had credit cards and liked expensive clothes— from Saks, I. Magnin, Neiman-Marcus, Bonwit Teller, Lord & Taylor, Gucci, Burberry.

But there was a dark side to Marlene Friedman. She had unpredictable mood swings and mysterious confrontations with the law. She had recently faced felony charges in Florida on some kind of swindle, and her father had come up with $50,000 for her to make restitution and get out of the state. Late in 1982 she had been accused of stealing a friend's credit cards—although she had her own— and using them at several Michigan Avenue stores. In December she was indicted on four counts of forgery and two of theft. Her case was scheduled before Judge Thomas J. Maloney.

Friedman said she didn't take the cards or use them.

She told friends she felt she would be acquitted. A test comparing her handwriting to that on the forged charge slips was negative, and she thought the witnesses placing her in the stores had made weak identifications.

In the spring of 1983 she went on a date with Lane, who was forty years old and single. She told him about her credit-card case. Lane told her that Maloney might send her to jail. Lane would explain later that he was merely warning her that Maloney was a prosecution-minded judge. But Friedman told a friend she thought Lane was suggesting he would fix the case against her if she didn't do something for him—perhaps something of a sexual nature. The friend, a lawyer, told her to report the threat to the special prosecutions bureau.

Although Friedman's story was thin and her personality unstable, the government was attentive when she started talking about Judge Lane and fixed cases. The prosecutors had heard his name before.

Lane had been linked with Arthur Zimmerman, a lawyer who had recently been indicted for soliciting $7,000 from a woman whose nephew had been charged with rape. Zimmerman told the woman he could fix the judge in the case. The judge was Lane. Sklarsky wanted to know, although he phrased it more delicately, how Friedman would feel about becoming a mole. The feds already had the Hillbilly Judge and the White Knight; now maybe they could have the Shady Lady (of Shady Lane).

Friedman apparently was not opposed to the idea, because that night Sklarsky visited her large apartment on Lakeview Avenue, an exclusive North Side street—in the manner of New York City's Central Park West—overlooking Lincoln Park. Sklarsky was accompanied by Jeffrey Kent from the state's attorney's office and two FBI agents, one a woman. They asked Friedman to find out if Lane could, indeed, influence Maloney in Friedman's case. The

FBI agents connected a tape-recorder to her phone. While everyone was still gathered, and Friedman was looking over her new undercover paraphernalia, the phone rang. It was Lane. As Marlene chatted, one of the feds scribbled a note.

"Ask him to help with your case," it said.

She asked.

Lane said he was preoccupied with a personal problem and didn't have time to get involved with her case. As an associate judge, Lane was subject to a quadrennial vote of the full judges in order to retain his seat. The vote was coming up in a few weeks. He was worried that the Zimmerman affair could get him knocked off the bench. But he told Friedman that, given the meager evidence against her, she probably did not need any help.

The lawyers and agents left at eleven o'clock that night, May 9. During the next two weeks Friedman met with the FBI and prosecutors several times. She has since claimed that they told her not to tell her lawyer in the credit-card case, Marvin C. Ashman, that she was cooperating with the government. In fact, she said, they told her to get a lawyer they picked for her—Tom Sullivan, the former U.S. attorney.

Sklarsky has claimed that no one from the government told Friedman to keep Ashman in the dark, and that the only reason he sent Friedman to Sullivan was that she said she wanted a new lawyer and asked for the names of some; he gave her Sullivan's name and some others.

In any case, Friedman met with Tom Sullivan on May 17, and three days later the two of them conferred with Sklarsky. Sullivan wanted to cut a deal for Friedman. In exchange for cooperation he wanted "consideration," as Sklarsky put it, "for her pending case." Sklarsky said he would check it out with the state's attorney's office. Until

Judge Wayne W. Olson: "I love people that take dough because you know exactly where you stand."

Judge Raymond C. Sodini, who ordered his clerks and deputies to stop squabbling about kickbacks: "You guys will have to work this out among yourselves. There's enough for everybody."

Judge Richard F. LeFevour, who fixed drunken-driving cases for $100 apiece: "Whatever comes in this office, stays in this office," he told a bagman. "You make yours out there."

Judge John J. "Dollars" Devine: "Thanks are nice, but they don't go very far. For those who help you, you should show your appreciation."

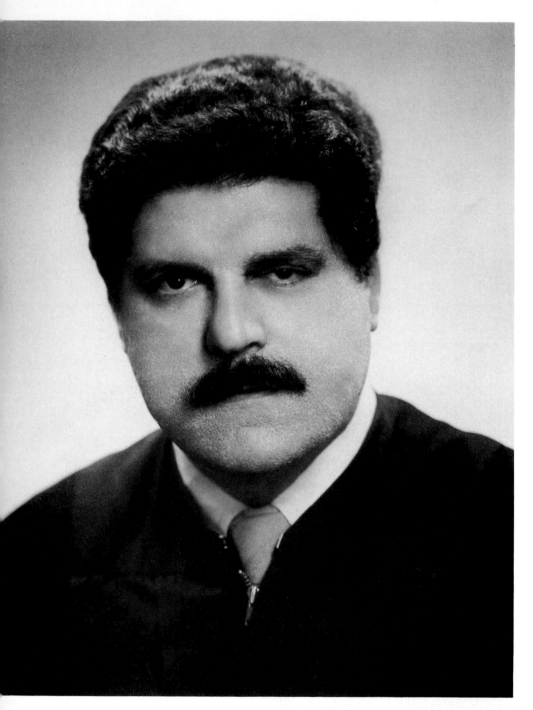

Judge Frank V. Salerno, who told his girlfriend she couldn't take back the mink coat he gave her for Christmas: it was stolen.

Brocton Lockwood, the "Hillbilly Judge,"
who wore a microphone in his cowboy boot.

Terrence Hake, "The White
Knight."

U.S. Attorney Dan K. Webb, who oversaw many of the Greylord prosecutions.

Vincent F. Davino, a hustler in action, in a branch courtroom at Central Police Headquarters. The photograph was taken by a hidden camera.

Marlene Friedman, the "Shady Lady" recruited by prosecutors to spy on her boyfriend, an associate judge suspected of corruption.

Judge Reginald J. Holzer, who liked to borrow money from the people who appeared before him—and then "neglect" to pay them back.

Judge Allen F. Rosin: He stood up behind the bench, spread his arms, and announced, "I am God."

they heard back, it was agreed, Friedman would keep her tape recorder on the pause button, so to speak.

On May 23, Lane called Friedman and said he heard she was working for the FBI. They met that afternoon at a North Side restaurant. She asked how he had found out. He said he heard it from a lawyer who heard it from a lawyer who heard it from a lawyer in the state's attorney's special prosecutions bureau. Her cover had been blown within three days of Sklarsky's contacting the bureau on Friedman's behalf. It might have been a record for spook ineptitude, not counting the agents who carried their FBI identification with them when they were trying to get the Chicago police to arrest them under assumed names.

After only two weeks in the spy business, Friedman was in out of the cold. But her romance with Lane heated up. They continued to date, minus her microphone. She told her friends she must have misconstrued Lane's intentions earlier. His comment about Judge Maloney's sending her to jail was not a "threat" but only a statement meant to convey Maloney's tough attitude toward defendants.

On a vote of the full judges in mid-June, Alan Lane did get thrown off the bench. A Chicago Bar Association report on Lane said he "does not have a good reputation for honesty and integrity. Attorneys, including fellow judges, feel that Judge Lane steers cases to particular attorneys and shows favoritism."

The report also accused Lane of using his position "to make after-hours advances on females, including an attorney for defendants." Shady Lane, indeed.

During this period, through June and July, Marlene Friedman was also seeing Sullivan socially. They went to a track meet together in early August. By that time, however, Friedman had hired another lawyer in the credit-card matter. She told friends she needed "a barracuda" who had never worked for the federal government. She was referred to Paul Bradley, the defender of the Billys in the Marquette Ten trial. Bradley, a former state appellate defender before he went into private practice, had certainly never been cozy with prosecutors.

Bradley was outraged by the behavior of the prosecution, both state and federal. He went to see Jeffrey Kent in the state's attorney's office. Bradley said the charges against Friedman should be dismissed, and if they were not, he would file a potentially embarrassing motion before Maloney. It would expose the state-federal attempt to use Friedman against Lane and Maloney and ask for a dismissal on the grounds that the actions of Sullivan and the prosecutors had deprived her of her Sixth Amendment right to effective assistance of counsel.

The state's attorney's office refused to drop the charges against Friedman, and on August 12, Bradley filed his motion. As might have been expected, it cooled whatever relationship was developing between Friedman and Sullivan. In a letter dated August 15, Sullivan resigned as Friedman's attorney, complaining, "I feel betrayed by you, and badly used by your attorneys."

While Bradley claimed the prosecutors had misused Marlene, the prosecutors claimed they had been ill-used by an unreliable and manipulative woman. However, since it had been the government's own idea to enlist Friedman in their network of slick undercover operatives—Fat Wally springs to mind—it really had little room for complaint.

On September 30, Judge Maloney denied the motion to dismiss Friedman's case. In a rather angry opinion, Maloney said Friedman took "naive" prosecutors on "some kind of waltz," and he lashed out at published reports about the case as "manipulated, contrived, distorted, and malevolent." Defense attorney Bradley could have asked for a different judge in the case, but he decided to stick

130

with Maloney, perhaps hoping the judge was more angry at the government for trying to find out if he was a crook than he was at Friedman for suggesting that he might be one in the first place.

After a quick, one-afternoon trial, the jurors began deliberations. They had been at it about two hours when they asked Maloney for clarification of his instructions to them. Under those circumstances, the law requires a judge to answer in writing, but Maloney called the jurors into the courtroom and answered them orally. He also sprang on them the fact that, if they didn't come to a decision within a half hour, he was going to make them spend the night in a hotel and bring them back in the morning. This was the first the jurors were told they might be sequestered. They came in with a verdict in ten minutes. Friedman was guilty of making three purchases totaling $1,350 from Saks Fifth Avenue with a stolen credit card.

The conviction was overturned on appeal because of Maloney's instructions and his "coercion" of the jury. The state never tried the case again, instead allowing Friedman to plea-bargain for a year's probation.

As for Arthur Zimmerman, the lawyer who admitted accepting $7,000 with the understanding that he would pass it on to Lane, he was acquitted in early 1985. The defense had taken a bench trial before Judge E. C. Johnson. Although Zimmerman had received the money, there was no evidence that a bribe had actually been paid. On a technical reading of the Illinois bribery statute, Johnson held that it applied only to public employees—not to intermediaries like Zimmerman.

State's Attorney Daley was furious about Johnson's decision. He immediately called a press conference to criticize the judge. Although Daley repeatedly bragged that his office won more than 90 percent of its cases, he often held press conferences to complain when he lost one. As a result

131

of Daley's criticism of the Zimmerman case, the Chicago Bar Association designated former U.S. District Court judge John Powers Crowley to review it, and Crowley issued a report describing the statute as ambiguous and calling on the General Assembly for clarification.

In sum, the case of the Shady Lady was not the finest hour of Greylord. No judges were indicted, and the prosecutors' bungling became a public spectacle.

Alan Lane went back into private practice. His name would come up on a recurring basis during Greylord. At least one lawyer and two bagmen testified they passed money to Lane when he was a judge.

Lane developed terminal cancer of the colon. When, in the summer of 1984, Dan Webb found out how sick Lane was, he decided to cut off any further investigation of him. Lane died in March 1985 at the age of forty-two.

As eager as federal prosecutors were to expand Greylord, they were just as eager to use Greylord as a linchpin for other investigations.

One such effort involved Chicago's most famous assistant federal prosecutor, Scott F. Turow.

Turow engaged in what a federal appellate court ultimately would hold to be "reprehensible" conduct. For a lawyer of Turow's stature—he would later write the best-selling novel *Presumed Innocent* and become a partner in a silk-stocking law firm—being criticized in a published appellate opinion is no slap on the wrist. It is an indelible blemish on one's reputation, remaining in the law books for one's biographers to contemplate.

What Turow did was use a sleazy criminal defense lawyer named Marvin Glass as an informant against his own client. The client, Ronald A. Ofshe, had hired Glass, a former assistant Cook County state's attorney, to represent him in a federal drug case in Florida. At the time, Glass was a target in Operation Greylord; the government had evidence he had solicited money from a client to bribe a Cook County Circuit Court judge in a drug case unrelated to the Florida case.

In the hope of escaping prosecution in the Greylord case, or at least getting leniency, Glass approached Turow in April of 1983. He offered to provide information on a conspiracy involving his client to sell "a ton of marijuana" and create a money-laundering operation. Turow relayed the offer to his boss, Dan Webb, who approved using Glass as an informant.

Webb's decision would have been questionable, at best, even if the offer had not raised the specter of invading the attorney-client relationship. Glass was a criminal lawyer in the literal sense—a criminal first, a lawyer second.

"He was an awful, awful human being, one of the most terrible people I have ever met," said a lawyer who once dealt with Glass. "He was like Lex Luthor—the ultimate criminal. There was nothing he wouldn't do."

Glass, thirty-eight years old in 1983, was only five three and had what another acquaintance called "something of a Napoleon complex." He wore silk suits, hand-sewn Italian shoes, monogrammed shirts, gold chains, and other heavy jewelry. He drove a yellow Rolls-Royce most of the time, but he also had a Porsche and a Mercedes-Benz. He collected antiques and hosted lavish parties at his suburban Northbrook home, including one at which he made a grand entrance atop a rented elephant.

The thing that really set Glass apart, however, was not his life-style but the criminality that financed it. He took legal fees without performing any services, and some of his clients wound up in jail as a result. The luckier clients, those who managed to keep out of jail, often entered into criminal partnerships with him. He became a business advisor for several clients who were drug dealers. He set

133

up a money-laundering scheme, involving Krugerrands, with a couple of clients. But when they left his office, he had arranged for them to be mugged and robbed of the satchel of Krugerrands they were carrying.

Violence was commonplace to Glass. It was best not to owe him money, as his former law partner learned. Glass claimed that the partner, Michael Pritzker, owed him a $50,000 gambling debt. Glass allegedly tried to hire a thug named Joseph DeCisco to break Pritzker's legs. DeCisco turned the job down because, he ultimately testified, he was afraid Pritzker would be able to identify him.

Glass went to another torpedo, Jack Kurnat, and gave him $2,500 to shoot Pritzker—not to kill him, just to maim him. On February 6, 1981, as Pritzker was jogging in Lincoln Park, his ear was shot off.

The shooting, of course, would have served no purpose unless Pritzker understood why he was shot. So, in a veiled way, Glass let it be known that an ear was the price one paid for not satisfying certain debts. Pritzker testified he confronted Glass two years later: "Marvin, you left me lying in the street for dead. You ruined my life. I thought half my head was gone. Every morning when I get up, I'm reminded of it."

Even if you didn't owe Glass money, it was dangerous to socialize with him. He was once invited to the home of wealthy neighbors for dinner. While enjoying their warmth and hospitality, he cased the place for a burglar-client, who had agreed to split the take with him.

When he approved making Glass an informant, Webb knew that Glass had been indicted twice in drug-related cases. The first was in 1973, the year Glass left the state's attorney's office, when a Cook County grand jury charged that he had accepted $750 from two clients to bribe Chicago cops in a marijuana case. The second was in 1982, when a federal grand jury charged him with conspiring to

134

defraud the Internal Revenue Service by helping a Champaign, Illinois, couple launder cocaine money. Glass was acquitted both times, but codefendants were convicted and sent to prison.

There were several civil suits pending against Glass when he went to work for the government. Two were for malpractice. One of these was filed by the Champaign cocaine couple, alleging that Glass took $72,000 in fees to represent them without telling them that he was also representing a man who wound up testifying against them. The other was filed by a suburban Chicago man who claimed that his widowed mother had paid Glass $112,500 to defend him in a drug case. Glass allegedly told the mother the son would spend "substantial time in prison" unless she paid the money. However, the man obtained another lawyer, pleaded guilty, and received only two years' probation.

Turow did not know at first that Glass was representing Ofshe in a drug case in Florida. Turow didn't even know who Ofshe was. All Turow knew was that Glass had obtained information about the "ton of marijuana" caper. However, on June 8, 1983, within a few weeks of their original conversation, Turow found out that Glass's source of information was Ofshe, that Ofshe was under indictment in Florida, and that Glass was one of two lawyers representing Ofshe.

Turow consulted with Webb. Two days later, without telling the U.S. attorney handling the Florida prosecution, Turow authorized Glass to wear a body wire during a conversation with Ofshe. Turow instructed FBI agents monitoring the conversation not to violate the attorney-client relationship, but only to record parts of the conversation relating to the ton-of-pot scam. When the surveillance was over, Glass gave his word he would withdraw as Ofshe's attorney.

Naturally, Glass, who had hardly ever been caught in the truth, did not keep his promise. He stayed in the case. In July 1983, Glass worked out a deal with federal prosecutors in Miami to drop the charges against Ofshe, promising that Ofshe would become an informant there. However, Ofshe had no knowledge of Glass's promise. Furthermore, he had no intention of becoming an informant. Two months later, the Miami U.S. attorney's office figured this out. The charges against Ofshe were reinstated in August 1983.

It was not until February 1984 that Turow finally told the federal judge handling the Ofshe case that one of Ofshe's lawyers was a government informant. Even then the disclosure was made secretly. The judge, Jose A. Gonzalez, Jr., permitted Glass to continue to represent Ofshe for two more months. When Gonzalez finally forced Glass to withdraw, the reason for the withdrawal was not given. Ofshe and his other lawyer were still in the dark.

It was another year—February 1985—before the Miami U.S. attorney's office informed Ofshe and the other lawyer, Melvin S. Black, that Glass had been a government informant. Black filed a motion to dismiss the case on the ground that the government had violated the attorney-client privilege, but the motion was denied. Ofshe then appealed the denial of the motion, but the Eleventh Circuit affirmed Gonzalez, saying that the surveillance produced no evidence against Ofshe. Besides, the court said, Ofshe had Black, who had "provided zealous representation at all times."

Nonetheless, the Eleventh Circuit condemned Turow's conduct, saying "we do not condone the government's use of criminal defense attorneys as informants against their clients." The zinger was in a footnote: "While we have not found the government's conduct sufficiently outrageous to warrant a dismissal of his [Ofshe's] indictment, we do believe that Glass's and Turow's conduct was reprehensible. Because the district judge [Gonzalez] is more familiar with the attorneys' conduct, we assume he will refer the matter to the Attorney Registration and Disciplinary Commission, 203 N. Wabash, Suite 1900, Chicago, Illinois 60601, for appropriate action."

Considering what a con man Marvin Glass was, it is probable that he was lying about the ton of marijuana and money-laundering conspiracy. No evidence of any such deal ever emerged publicly. Once again, it looked as if the government stinger got stung.

Meanwhile, Glass was indicted by a federal grand jury in Texas for participating in a $100 million drug ring, and by a federal grand jury in Illinois for extorting his former law partner, soliciting money from clients to bribe judges, and conspiring to distribute narcotics and launder the profits. Under plea-bargaining arrangements, he pleaded guilty in both jurisdictions and was sentenced to concurrent eight-year prison terms.

After his initial reprimand from the Eleventh Circuit, Turow probably should have left the matter where it stood. The Illinois Attorney Registration and Disciplinary Commission had never previously moved against a federal prosecutor, and there was no reason to think it would aggressively pursue him.

However, perhaps for the sake of his biographers, he filed a motion asking the Eleventh Circuit to delete the critical footnote from its opinion. The court did not take the suggestion kindly. Instead of deleting what it said, it strengthened it. In fact, it recommended that the Justice Department consider criminal prosecution of Turow for impeding the administration of justice.

The Justice Department, as might have been expected, rejected the suggestion. In May 1988, it issued a letter stating it had reviewed the facts and found that Turow "did not hinder or obstruct the administration of justice in any way."

Once again, the government's eager employment of sleazy characters and questionable tactics had led to public embarrassment and no accomplishment.

7

The Extravaganza

☆

Nnews accounts of Greylord paid little
attention to either the government's bungling or the eth-
ically questionable conduct.

Greylord was good copy. Its very name suggested something on a grand and noble scale—like Operation Over-
lord, the invasion of Normandy. No one wanted to clutter
up the coverage with anything that put the feds in a bad
light.

When Dan Webb called a press conference on December
14, 1983, to announce the first Greylord indictments, it
naturally was well attended. In fact, it was the biggest
press conference in years in the Dirksen Building—at least
since the 1969 Conspiracy Eight indictments. All the local
news organizations were present, and so were all the national organizations that had representatives in Chicago
and some that did not.

It was Wednesday afternoon at two o'clock, a good time for television—late enough that the camera crews had eaten lunch, early enough that tape could be readied for the five and six o'clock news. It was also good for the Chicago newspapers, both of which are published in the morning. They would have plenty of time to prepare stories for their home-delivery editions.

The public had long ago learned of Greylord. The previous August, Art Petacque of the *Chicago Sun-Times* had printed an accurate list of what and who were involved— and who would be named in the first indictments. But the preindictment publicity had not made the story stale. It had increased interest in the indictments.

The show opened like *Forty-second Street*.

The stage—a dais in the Everett McKinley Dirksen Federal Building—was crowded with performers, although not all of them had speaking parts.

Webb took care of the speaking.

What gave the event its boffo, Sol Hurok–style ambiance was the cast Webb had lined up for special appearances. Sharing the dais with Webb, the U.S. attorney, were Tom Sullivan, the former U.S. attorney; Rich Daley, the Cook County state's attorney; Fred Rice, the Chicago police superintendent; Dick Brzeczek, the former police superintendent; Ed Hegarty, the special agent in charge of the Chicago FBI office; Neil Hartigan, the Illinois attorney general; and James Zagel, Webb's successor as director of the Illinois Department of Law Enforcement. Even Douglas Roller, the head of the Chicago office of the federal Organized Crime Strike Force, was there, perhaps on the theory that he would be lonesome in the office with everyone else at the press conference. There were also various Webb assistants and FBI agents standing in the dais area. Webb made sure he mentioned those who were most involved in the investigation, including Dan Reidy, chief of special prosecutions, and Assistant U.S. Attorneys Chuck Sklarsky, Scott Lassar, John Podliska, and Candace Fabri.

There were far more cops and prosecutors on stage than there were indictees, there being only nine of them. Among them were Judge Wayne Olson, Associate Judge John Murphy, and former Associate Judge John Devine, who had been voted off the bench the previous June by the full judges amid reports he was under federal investigation.

Three lawyers were also indicted—James Costello, Olson's scam mate from Branch 57; Dean Wolfson, considered by most of his colleagues to be the most prolific of the lawyers who had cases fixed throughout the system; and Thomas G. Kangalos, a city attorney assigned to traffic court who was charged with operating a private racket of his own, similar to the one the LeFevours had going with the policemen who served warrants on citizens with multiple parking tickets.

Kangalos would take half price on overdue tickets, get the charges dismissed, and keep the money for himself. Sometime in September, when he found out his pal Brocton Lockwood, the hillbilly undercover judge, had more in his cowboy boots than his feet, Kangalos called in sick and never showed up for work again. He fled to Greece, the country of his birth.

Rounding out the list of indictees were three bagmen—Harold Conn, Ira Blackwood, and Allen Kaye, a bailiff who was charged with taking $10,000, ostensibly to pass on to unnamed judges in divorce court.

The indictments of three judges in a system of some 300 judges was hardly an amazing score, but Webb indicated that more indictments would be coming. "In my judgment, when the project is over and all the cases have been tried, I believe this will be viewed as one of the most comprehensive, intricate, and difficult undercover projects ever undertaken by a law enforcement agency," he said.

Indeed, more indictments were coming. But what Webb left unsaid was that only one more judge—Associate Judge John Laurie—would be indicted as a result of the actual sting operation. All of the other still-to-come indictments of judges would stem from conventional techniques. The most common of the conventional techniques was to find a hustler who had engaged in criminal activity, such as not reporting all of his cash bond refunds on his federal tax return, immunize him, and allow him to plead to reduced charges in exchange for his testimony against judges.

In an interview with *Chicago Lawyer* and WMAQ-TV back in August of 1983, a few days after the Greylord story broke, Webb had defined Greylord as "an FBI code name for a specific undercover operation that had now ended and had entered the grand jury phase." At the time, that definition served a purpose. It enabled Webb to deny that Marlene Friedman was related to Greylord; she was an embarrassment, and he didn't want her publicly associated with Greylord.

Now in December, however, that August definition no longer suited Webb. If he stuck by it, it would mean that Greylord—this comprehensive, intricate, and difficult project—was not much to brag about in contrast to, say, Abscam. Greylord, if Webb had stuck with the August definition, would have resulted in the indictments of only four judges, three of whom—Olson, Murphy, and Devine—were pathetic drunks who might have been more appropriately dealt with in an alcohol-abuse program.

Webb's solution was simply to redefine Greylord. With semantic sleight of hand, he began saying that Greylord consisted of two parts—the "undercover phase" and the "historical phase." This definition made Greylord look more impressive. It meant that Greylord ultimately could be credited with nailing more than a dozen crooked judges.

The day Webb made his hyped-up announcement of the

142

first indictments, the *Chicago Tribune* editorialized: "In order to ferret out venality, it was necessary to put hidden microphones in judges' chambers, to create phony cases defended by bogus lawyers, and even for FBI agents to commit make-believe crimes."

That became the conventional wisdom on Greylord— that the intrusive means employed by the government were justified because there was no other way to accomplish the ends of catching crooked judges. The conventional wisdom prevailed even though the so-called undercover phase would produce only half the number of indictments the historical phase would produce.

Greylord had few critics other than the targets of the investigation and the defense bar. One of the few, a thoughtful one, was Monroe H. Freedman, professor of law at Hofstra University in New York and a noted authority on legal ethics. At a symposium at IIT/Chicago-Kent College of Law in 1984, Freedman raised several objections to Greylord. His objections were different from those raised by the targets and their lawyers. In fact, said Freedman, the most frequent objections to Greylord were actually nonissues. He listed three.

"At the top of the list of nonissues," Freedman said, "is whether there is any problem with bugging a judge's chambers on a warrant obtained on probable cause." While the propriety of bugging generally might be debatable, he said, it is "preposterous" to suggest that judges are somehow entitled to be treated differently from others.

Freedman said entrapment was another nonissue. "One of the interesting spectacles of Greylord is judges suddenly discovering the Constitution," he said. "Judges who, in case after case, week after week, month after month, year after year, decade after decade, will tolerate police and prosecutor perjury, who will grant warrants in situations where there is not probable cause, or who will wink at

143

failures to honor people's rights, suddenly become outraged at the idea that such a thing should go on. As one judge said in one of the few opinions in this area, 'None of us is safe if these are the rules.' In the course of saying that, he distinguished doing the same thing in narcotics cases where you're really going after 'bad' people—not people who are corrupting the administration of justice, but 'bad' people. If there is anyone in our society who should not have the defense of entrapment—a defense I have argued with conviction in appropriate cases—it is a judge, who has sought out, not who has fallen upon, a position of unique honor and responsibility. For a person in such a position to say 'I couldn't say no' is inexcusable. That essentially, in this context, is what the entrapment defense is."

The third nonissue identified by Freedman was a series of technical violations of law in the staged cases. "It is said that the prosecutor who processes a sham case knowingly presents perjury. Yes, you can say that, in a mindless way, just as you can say that you should prosecute a fireman when he sets a backfire to prevent a forest fire from spreading. Whatever the elements of arson are, if you apply them in the same mindless way, I'm sure you can make out a case for arson. Yet I think we would all be shocked to find a fireman prosecuted for arson in such a situation. This conduct cannot be prejudicial to the administration of justice because the purpose is to ferret out corruption in the administration of justice."

Freedman then turned to what he called "real issues." Foremost among these, he said, was the chilling effect that the phony cases produce on the lawyer-client relationship. Knowledge that the government creates sham cases inevitably causes criminal defense lawyers to be wary of their clients. "Lawyers cannot be zealously and single-mindedly dedicated to their clients' concerns, but must always ask

144

themselves, 'Is this really a client or is this somebody with whom I must be on guard?' This concerns me greatly because the integrity of the relationship of trust and confidence between lawyer and client is central to the administration of justice.''

A second real issue, he said, was the danger that sting operations add to the power of prosecutors, "who already have enormous discretion to wield the extraordinary powers of government and who, all too frequently and too casually, abuse those powers with virtually no effort by any disciplinary body to take appropriate steps in particular cases of abuse.''

A final real issue mentioned by Freedman, although not unique to Greylord or to sting operations, was the publicity resulting from prosecutorial leaks and press conferences like Webb's extravaganza.

"It is inexcusable,'' Freedman said. "There is absolutely no justification for it. Unfortunately, this issue is ordinarily couched in terms of the prejudicial effect on the trial. That is not where we should be looking. The real evil is the direct impact on the accused. Anyone who has been close to a criminal prosecution knows that it is a punishing experience. Just to indict somebody is to punish that person severely. Then when you hype the adverse publicity by holding a press conference or going on television and saying, or clearly implying, as Dan Webb has done, that the defendants are guilty and that the government witnesses and informants are credible, it is among the most serious violations of professional responsibility.''

In newspaper stories about Greylord, there were repeated references to "sources close to the prosecution'' divulging information not contained in any indictment and therefore required by federal law to be kept confidential. In view of such references, Freedman said there was a sting operation he would like to see Webb conduct:

145

"I would like to see him run through some phony names of targets and then identify which people on his staff leak which names. Those people should be prosecuted for violating some of the most important responsibilities of the prosecutor."

Dan Webb did not act on the suggestion.

Matthias A. Lydon did not attend the press conference, although, in a sense, it was in his honor. Lydon had nothing to do with Greylord—not directly—but without a novel theory he had devised thirteen years earlier, much of Greylord could not have been.

In 1970, long before the government began running large-scale sting operations, Lydon was an assistant U.S. attorney in Chicago. He had been investigating a kickback scheme at Zenith Electronics Corporation. The company's purchasing agent was suspected of taking money from a man who sold television cabinets to Zenith.

It was not a particularly glamorous case, but Lydon proposed a new use of an old law—the mail fraud statute of 1872—to prosecute it. The statute was enacted by Congress, in the words of its sponsor, "to prevent the frauds which are mostly gotten up in the large cities . . . by thieves, forgers, and rapscallions generally, for the purpose of deceiving and fleecing the innocent people in the country." Traditionally, the law had been used to prosecute frauds that deprived victims of property—property meaning, usually, money.

In the Zenith case, however, Lydon proposed using the mail fraud statute in a case where the victim, Zenith, was not deprived of money. Zenith had been deprived, according to Lydon's theory, of the "faithful and loyal services" of its purchasing agent—an "intangible right."

Some of Lydon's fellow prosecutors thought the theory

146

was ridiculous. "One day we'll be prosecuting a husband who drops love letters to his mistress into the mailbox on charges of depriving his wife of his faithful and loyal services," said one.

Nonetheless, Lydon got approval for the indictment and won convictions in the case, known as *U.S.* v. *George*. In 1973, the U.S. Court of Appeals for the Seventh Circuit upheld the conviction. After the Supreme Court declined to review the case, federal prosecutors throughout the country began routinely using Lydon's theory to prosecute politicians and others under the mail fraud statute. Among those convicted under the theory were the former governor of Illinois, Otto Kerner, and a powerful Chicago alderman, Thomas E. Keane.

In the first round of Greylord indictments, four of the nine defendants—Olson, Devine, Costello, and Kaye—were charged with a total of seventy-nine counts of mail fraud. All of the counts involved intangible rights—defrauding the government of its right to the loyal, faithful, and honest services of its officials and employees. The "fraud" in each case involved cash bond refunds, which were mailed to lawyers after they fixed cases. Since the money belonged to the client, the state lost no money—no tangible property.

By the time of Greylord, Lydon was no longer so enamored of his intangible rights theory. He had since become a criminal defense lawyer and had been retained to represent one of the judges whose indictment Webb announced, John Murphy.

Murphy was not charged with mail fraud. But Lydon could take little solace in that. The intangible rights theory of mail fraud was a linchpin in a general trend of expanding federal jurisdiction in criminal cases that had traditionally been left to the states. The federal extortion statute under which Murphy was charged, for instance, was being broadly construed by the government to cover the passive acceptance of bribes.

Extortion, as applied in Greylord and earlier cases, including Abscam, is a violation of Title 18, Section 1951 of the United States Code, better known as the Hobbs Act. The Hobbs Act made it illegal to "obstruct, delay, or affect commerce or the movement of any article or commodity in commerce by robbery or extortion" or to attempt or conspire to do so. Every conceivable extortion violates the act, the theory goes, by depleting assets that would otherwise be available for the purchase of goods in commerce.

But how does accepting bribes constitute extortion? The Hobbs Act defines extortion as "the obtaining of property from another, with his consent, induced by wrongful use of actual or threatened force, violence, or fear, or under color of official right." In view of that definition, the courts have held, bribery and extortion are virtually indistinguishable.

In addition to mail fraud and extortion, several of the Greylord defendants—including Murphy—were charged with racketeering under Title 18, Section 1961 of the U.S. Code, also known as the Racketeer Influenced and Corrupt Organizations Act, or RICO.

RICO was enacted in 1970 to give federal prosecutors a weapon against organized crime. It is a complicated law that carries penalties of up to twenty years in jail and forfeiture of any ill-gotten property for criminals acting within an "enterprise." Congress specifically said that the law should be interpreted broadly; the courts have interpreted it so broadly that convictions are possible even if no crime has been committed. All prosecutors have to prove is that a defendant, acting within an "enterprise," agreed to commit two or more of a large number of offenses specified in the RICO act, including violation of state bribery laws. "Enterprise" has been defined broadly enough by the courts to include such entities as the Chicago Police Department and the Currency Exchange Association. In Greylord, the enterprise was the Cook County Circuit Court.

The expansion of federal criminal jurisdiction in the early 1970s was accompanied by an increase in the use of immunized-accomplice testimony. In a case against Cook County Clerk Edward J. Barrett, for instance, the government's star witness was an admitted criminal who had embezzled hundreds of thousands of dollars from his company. The witness was given not only immunity from criminal prosecution but also immunity from tax liability for every dollar he testified he paid in bribes to Barrett.

Civil libertarians warned of the dangers of both the expansion of federal prosecutorial power and the reckless use of immunity. A leading critic of the trend was George Anastaplo, who served as a sort of conscience for the legal profession in Chicago. Anastaplo was not a lawyer, although he had graduated first in his class at the University of Chicago Law School in 1951. At the time, applicants for admission to the bar were asked whether they were or ever had been members of the Communist Party. As a matter of principle, Anastaplo refused to answer. He was denied admission to the bar and, remaining true to his principles, refused to reapply. He went into academia, teaching variously at the University of Chicago, Rosary College, and Loyola University.

Writing in the *Chicago Tribune* of April 22, 1973, Anastaplo warned that, as bad as political corruption was, the trends in federal prosecution might be worse. "Of course, 'cleaning up' corruption can contribute to the restoration of public confidence in the administration of justice in this country," he wrote. "But recklessness in such matters may be promoted whenever a prosecuting attorney is left free to exploit the courts for his or his party's political advantage. . . . [T]he deliberate exploitation of government power for political gain, even to expose and jail crooks, may ultimately do more damage to the vital public opinion central to our regime than the crooks themselves whose greed all too often gives politicians a bad name."

The practice of immunizing accomplices, Anastaplo said, was particularly dangerous in cases where their testimony was the principal, if not the only, evidence against a defendant, as it would be years later in both Marquette Ten and Greylord. To safeguard against perjury by such witnesses, Anastaplo recommended that all accomplice witnesses be tried and sentenced before they were permitted to testify against others. "That is, the prosecution should have no further hold over an accomplice, except for whatever perjury he might commit when he does testify."

But of even more concern to Anastaplo was what he saw as a growing reliance on the federal government to supervise the conduct of local officials. "Do we really want, for instance, a comprehensive criminal code intruding more and more into our everyday lives?" he asked rhetorically. "That is, dare we permit the centralization of power that a growing dependence upon Washington moves us toward?"

Anastaplo's answer, of course, was no. He said that there was probably—in the early 1970s—less corruption in Illinois than there had been a generation earlier. "But however that may be," he continued, "some—perhaps even a good deal of—discreet corruption may be preferable to further open encroachments by the federal government upon the dwindling prerogatives of our local communities. Such encroachments are especially to be guarded against whenever an outraged sense of justice is likely to be transformed by the promptings of ambition, first into self-righteousness and then into ruthlessness."

*　　*　　*

Of the approximately 25,800 members of the Cook County bar who were not targets of Greylord, few were as interested in Webb's extravaganza as were Patrick A. Tuite and Edward M. Genson. They watched the live television coverage, sending assistants to monitor the press conference. Then they conferred by telephone.

Tuite and Genson were defense lawyers, and Greylord would be keeping them quite busy over the next several years. For Genson, involvement began on August 5, 1983, the day the *Chicago Sun-Times* first broke the story that there was an undercover investigation of the courts. The *Sun-Times* did not even know how to spell Greylord; in early editions, it was "Graylord." While the paper was still trying to confirm the spelling, Genson and Tuite were getting their first calls from potential clients.

Tuite fielded calls at his La Salle Street office, but Genson was not so easy to reach. He was in London, acting as a solicitor in an armed-robbery case involving two Chicago men. They were accused of sticking up Graff Diamonds Ltd. and escaping with the Marlborough diamond, a big rock whose theft had the London papers aflutter. Genson was bored. He had taken the case with the understanding that he would be authorized by the court to function as an assistant barrister. After arriving in London, however, he was informed he would be regarded as a solicitor, meaning that he would not help try the case. With the barrister, who Genson did not think was particularly good, making all the decisions, Genson had nothing much to do. Then the calls started coming. The first was from Wayne Olson.

In August, no one outside the government knew the scope of the Greylord investigation, and many lawyers were extremely nervous. It was a common practice in Cook County for lawyers who otherwise engaged in no illegal activity

151

to routinely give clerks money—as little as a couple of bucks—to have their cases called promptly. If the federal prosecutors had been interested in corruption at that level, they could have obtained thousands of indictments.

Those worried about Greylord most often turned to one or the other, Tuite or Genson. Between them, they would eventually represent about fifty Greylord clients, some indicted on that first day, some later, some who would never be indicted but were under investigation.

One of the reasons clients flocked to Tuite and Genson was that they, in addition to being among the best criminal defense lawyers in the city, were regarded as the best among the few who split their practices between state and federal courts. Most defense lawyers practiced pretty much in one or the other. The judges and lawyers under investigation in Greylord had experience with Tuite and Genson from state court, knew they were good there, and assumed they were good in federal court as well.

Tuite and Genson also had reputations for taking many cases to trial. Many other practitioners in federal court did mostly plea-bargaining and little trial work. A businessman is often willing to plead guilty in exchange for probation. But lawyers and judges are unwilling to plea-bargain because a guilty plea results in automatic disbarment.

In an immigrant-rich city like Chicago, Tuite's and Genson's backgrounds had many similarities. Tuite's father was born in Ireland, Genson's in Russia. Tuite's family settled on the North Side, where Patrick was born in 1937. His father got into the electricians union, where the Irish had some influence. Genson's family settled on the Jewish West Side, where Ed was born in 1941. His father was a precinct captain and worked a number of different city jobs.

Neither Genson's nor Tuite's parents had gone to college, but they were determined that their sons would. Tuite went to the University of Illinois, where he received a degree in liberal arts. Genson went to Northwestern University, where he received a degree in political science.

Genson's father, a bailbondsman, was in awe of the power and prestige of the law, and more than anything he wanted his son to be a lawyer.

"Dad was a criminal-lawyer groupie," said Genson. "He dragged me into courtrooms. That's all he ever wanted me to be. This is all I ever wanted to be. He supposed that if he exposed me to the law books, I'd be a lawyer. Lawyers would throw out a book, a supplement that would be out of date, and he would bring it home. I recall specifically a 1943 *Illinois Revised Statutes* sitting in the living room for years and his asking me to read it. He felt that this would give me a step up in law school. I was about eleven at the time. I would read it page by page.

"He wanted me to go to DePaul University, because all of the lawyers he knew went there. Then my grandfather found out it was a Catholic school and laid the law down that I was going to go to Northwestern."

While at Northwestern University School of Law—and even before, while he was in high school and college— Genson would sometimes go to a branch court where the judge, Saul Epton, let him sit behind the bench and watch the proceedings. It was in Epton's court that Genson first saw Tuite, four years ahead of Genson in school, trying cases as a young prosecutor. "My initial impression was that he was a good lawyer," said Genson. "And I was right."

Tuite's original goal was journalism. He was sports editor of his high school newspaper—also a baseball star— and he wrote sports in college. But newspaper jobs were hard to find, didn't pay well, and Tuite's father, tempered by the struggles of the Depression, had never encouraged his son in journalism. "He always said, 'You'll never make any money at that' and 'They're all drunks,' " said Tuite. "I took an aptitude test, and they said I'd be a good lawyer. My father said, 'Hey, why don't you give law school a try?' So I did."

Tuite developed a strong interest in labor law and, after graduating from the University of Illinois School of Law, tried to get a job with the National Labor Relations Board. He was told he had to have a political sponsor, so in 1961 he met with Senator Paul H. Douglas of Illinois.

"His administrative aide said, 'Are you pro-labor or pro-management?' " said Tuite. "I said, 'I'm pro-labor.' He said, 'That's good. Do you belong to any unions?' I said, 'Yes, I carry a card in the electricians union. I worked my way through law school as an electrician's apprentice.' And he said, 'Forget it.' The year before, when Douglas ran for reelection, the local electricians union backed his opponent."

Tuite went to several labor law firms, but they all told him to get experience at the NLRB. Tuite was married, had a baby, and needed a job. With the help of a politically connected uncle, he got one in the state's attorney's office. Tuite stayed in the office seven years, rising to chief of the criminal division before going into private practice in 1968.

When Genson got out of law school in 1965, he considered trying for a job in the state's attorney's office, too, but he did not have the clout. His father had died while he was in law school. "He died just at the beginning of my last year," said Genson. "He never saw me try a case. That would have fulfilled him. I was his son the lawyer. I was in the top quarter of my class, but in those days it didn't make a difference. I couldn't get into the state's attorney's office because I didn't have a political sponsor. Grades in those days were irrelevant. If you didn't have a political sponsor, you didn't get a job. It's changed now, but that's how it was in those days."

Genson went out on his own almost immediately, taking whatever criminal cases he could get. His first big case came in 1969, when the Reverend Jesse L. Jackson arranged representation for a group of West Side civil rights leaders who had been arrested. Genson was part of a defense team that included some of the best lawyers in the city. The team, which was led by R. Eugene Pincham, the city's leading black defense lawyer, won the case. That was a state case, and about a year later Genson had his first big federal case, getting an acquittal for a well-known syndicate figure, Jimmy "The Bomber" Catuara.

The Catuara case set Genson on an exceptionally successful trial career in federal court. At the time the Greylord investigation became public, he was on a two-year winning streak. Some of the cases had involved co-defenses with Tuite. The two had differences in style, but they got along well together.

Although Genson has sophisticated tastes in art and antiques, he does not care much about clothes. A heavyset man with reddish hair, a bit disheveled, he is sometimes abrasive toward witnesses and condescending toward prosecutors. He would have been out of place—physically, not mentally—in that Queen's courtroom in London. Tuite, on the other hand, would have blended in quite well in England. Tall and handsome, his black hair graying at the temples, Tuite wears conservative suits with a fashionable flair—such as a double-breasted gray herringbone. He wears wide, spread collars that are often plaincolored while the shirt is striped. His ties are silk and subdued.

Tuite speaks softly, politely, and if angry at a witness on cross-examination, he is more likely to use sarcasm than volume. Genson is loud, outraged, and can be grating. The contrast in styles serves both of them well when they try cases together.

Genson suffers from a neurological problem called dystonia, which attacks certain muscle groups. "The one that affects the leg, which is what I've got, is an Eastern European Jewish congenital thing," he once explained. "It's linearly progressive, where it gets a little worse each year. If they don't develop a cure, I'm eventually not going to be able to walk very well."

A smile sneaked across Genson's round face.

"Boy, I'm waiting for that," he said. "Can you imagine? I take my wheelchair—not a motorized one—and approach the witness with the exhibits in my teeth. Slowly and with labor. 'Would you look at this, please?' I say. I'll never lose a jury trial."

Until the day of the press conference, defense lawyer Thomas J. Royce had an intense interest in Greylord as well, but, as things turned out, he didn't stick around for the extravaganza. He had a brief meeting in the federal building and then left. His client didn't need him anymore.

Royce's client was Roger D. Murphy, a Chicago police sergeant assigned to the courtrooms at Belmont and Western. The two courtrooms there had once been part of Judge LeFevour's hustling empire. In Branch 29, the misdemeanor court, Judge John Murphy, no relation to Roger, presided. In Branch 42, the felony preliminary-hearing court, Black Jack Reynolds presided. Eventually those judges were transferred, but Sergeant Murphy stayed. His job was to coordinate the appearances of the police officers who were scheduled to testify each day.

At age fifty-three, Murphy was a thirty-year veteran of the police department. A large, quiet man, he and his wife, Marianne, were the parents of six children, whom they raised on the Northwest Side. To make ends meet, Murphy had a number of part-time jobs through the years, including his most recent one as a security guard at a neighborhood savings and loan association. His life seemed to revolve around his family. He drank infrequently and with moderation. He seldom had, or needed, more than a few dollars walking-around money.

According to those who worked with him, he was easygoing and friendly. "He always counseled the younger cops," said one of the policemen in the Nineteenth District, which is headquartered in the same complex as the Belmont and Western branch courts. "He was like Sergeant Esterhaus on *Hill Street Blues*."

Royce was a close personal friend of Murphy's. They lived in the same neighborhood. Royce's kids, when they were younger, went over to the Murphys to swim in a little plastic pool in the backyard. Along the way, Murphy bought a cottage on Lake Delavan, just over the state line in Wisconsin. The family vacationed there, and, in 1981, after the kids were grown, Murphy sold the house in Chicago, and Marianne moved permanently to the cottage. Murphy went up there on weekends. During the week he stayed in an apartment with their daughter, Susan, recently divorced, and her baby.

About once a week Royce would pick up coffee and rolls and stop by the courthouse at Belmont and Western and take a break with Murphy. In late November 1983, just after Thanksgiving, Murphy told Royce that he had been handed a subpoena by a former assistant state's attorney named David Grossman, who had been working undercover with the FBI during the Greylord investigation. The subpoena ordered Murphy to appear before a federal grand jury on Wednesday, December 14, the day of the press conference.

"You're on your way down, Roger," said Grossman, according to Murphy.

The harsh language had frightened Murphy, a simple, unsophisticated man.

Royce was angry about what Grossman had said. There

157

were a lot of reasons why the federal government might want to talk to Murphy, since so much hustling had taken place in the courtrooms where he worked. But Royce was convinced of Murphy's personal integrity.

Royce checked with Assistant U.S. Attorney Candace Fabri, who was conducting the grand jury investigation. He learned that, indeed, Fabri did not consider Murphy a target, she merely wanted him to testify about the routine in the courtrooms—which lawyers had access to the judge's chambers and generally how things worked there.

Royce told Murphy he had nothing to worry about, but Murphy worried anyway. He repeated again and again that Grossman had said they were going to put him in prison. Murphy was convinced that in the federal system, innocent people went to jail. He knew Royce had defended a Marquette Ten defendant, Thomas Ambrose, who had gone to jail, even though both Royce and Murphy had thought he was innocent.

Many of those who work in the state system—policemen, court personnel, even some lawyers—have an almost morbid fear of the federal system, according to Royce. This fear sometimes extends to the federal building itself. They don't like to get near it. They would never eat at the Berghoff, for instance, one of the most famous restaurants in Chicago, because it is next door to the federal building. That fear is one of the reasons lawyers flocked to Ed Genson and Pat Tuite as soon as they read about an investigation in the paper. "It's like a snake or a tarantula," said Royce. "You don't want to get close to it."

Murphy was such a person. He was afraid to testify. He and Royce talked about the possibility of taking the Fifth Amendment. But when Royce became certain that Murphy had nothing to hide, they agreed that he would testify. Royce said he would go with Murphy. Although lawyers cannot accompany witnesses into the grand jury room, Royce assured Murphy he would be right outside. If Murphy had any question about how he should answer a question, he could come out and consult. He had nothing to hide. All he had to do was tell the truth.

Still, Murphy was frightened, more than he had ever been in his life. He told Royce he was afraid of elevators. He would have to take one at the federal building, where the grand jury sits on the fifteenth floor.

By Tuesday, December 13, Royce was worried. Murphy was so depressed that Royce was afraid Murphy might try to commit suicide. That night there was a birthday party for Royce's niece, the daughter of his brother. Royce's brother was a cop and also a friend of Murphy's. Royce invited Murphy to the party. Murphy drove to the house, but he did not go in. Instead, Royce went out and rode around with him for a half hour.

"You're not going to go to jail," said Royce. "You're just going to go in and tell the truth. Don't worry."

Royce could tell Murphy had been drinking, which was unusual.

"You got a gun, you son of a bitch," said Royce. "Give me your goddamn gun. I need it for a couple of days."

Murphy gave him his service revolver. Royce knew Murphy probably had another gun—every big-city cop has more than one—but Murphy said he didn't.

Royce got home around 11 P.M. and received a phone call from Murphy's daughter, Susan, who was also worried.

Royce went over and talked to Murphy, then went home. But at about 2:30 A.M., Susan called again. She said her father had gone out.

Royce went looking for him, driving around the neighborhood, searching for Murphy's black Pontiac outside bars.

He went to Resurrection Hospital. He called the police and asked if there had been any accidents or suicides. Finally, he went home.

In the meantime, so did Murphy. But he didn't stay long. He went into Susan's bedroom, kissed her and the baby, and said he was going out again.

At 6:30 A.M. Royce received another call from Susan.

"He did it! He did it!" she cried.

Royce went over to Susan's apartment. She said she did not hear a shot, but a few minutes after her father had kissed her, she looked in the vestibule outside the front door, in the area where the mailboxes were. He lay there, dead, his other gun at his side.

Royce did what he could to comfort Susan. He went home, showered, shaved, dressed, and went to the Dirksen Federal Building. He took the elevator to the fifteenth floor—the ride that had so frightened Murphy.

He was numb, emotionally and physically, from shock and from lack of sleep. He found Candace Fabri. Too tired to go into detail, he kept his message succinct.

"Your witness will not appear," he said. "He killed himself this morning."

At the press conference that afternoon, Webb was asked about Roger Murphy, whether he was a target of the Greylord investigation, perhaps to have been indicted that very morning.

Webb said Murphy's death was a "tragic event."

"I personally believe it's something that should just be left behind," Webb said. "I'm not in any way implying any misconduct on Mr. Murphy's part whatsoever. We deeply regret that this occurred."

The reporters did leave it behind, moving on to questions about technique and secrecy and the Hillbilly Judge and the White Knight.

160

Standing in the back of the long, second-floor room used for the press conference, and wryly amused by the opening-day flavor of it all, was a large man in a dark suit, white shirt, and tie. He went unrecognized by the reporters in the room, except for those few who covered the courts and the state's attorney's office on a regular basis. He was William F. Kunkle, Jr., the first assistant Cook County state's attorney, the number two man in the office behind Rich Daley.

Kunkle, a Republican, had entered the state's attorney's office in 1973, shortly after Bernie Carey had been elected. By 1979, Kunkle had become Carey's chief deputy, the number three spot in the office. When Carey, trying for a third term, was defeated in November 1980, it was widely assumed that Kunkle, who had campaigned openly for Carey, would have to leave office. But Kunkle's reputation was so good—he was regarded as one of the best prosecutors in the county—that Daley not only kept him but eventually promoted him.

Kunkle was one of a half-dozen or so people in the state's attorney's office who knew about Greylord. He had, in fact, been involved in it from its inception. He had helped select Terry Hake, and he was the man in the office who participated most in the day-to-day decisions concerning tactics.

"Basically, I was the contact with the feds," said Kunkle some years later, after he had left the state's attorney's office. "Dan Reidy and I used to meet on a regular basis, and if they needed a phony case run through somewhere, and they needed an assistant not to screw it up, I usually took care of that sort of thing."

Kunkle said he would merely tell the assistant state's attorney assigned to a courtroom where the case would be heard, something to the effect: "Go ahead and give the defense their eighth continuance" or "Go ahead and drop the charges."

As the press conference broke up, someone who knew something of the leak-prone nature of the county prosecutor's office spotted Kunkle.

"Bill, was Greylord the best-kept secret in the history of the state's attorney's office?" he asked.

"Not only was it that," answered Kunkle. "It was the *only* kept secret in the history of the state's attorney's office."

8

All Rise

☆

The trials began with Harold Conn because the government wanted to start small.

Conn was deputy clerk in traffic court, one of the dependable bagmen. He was charged with taking $1,610 in bribes, ranging from $20 to $370, from Terry Hake and David Ries, both of whom were wired during the transactions. The money was to be passed to judges to fix seven different traffic cases.

Conn went on trial before Judge John A. Nordberg in U.S. District Court on March 5, 1984, a Monday. After jury selection and opening statements, the public got its first look at Hake on Wednesday. The courtroom was packed for the debut of the White Knight.

This, essentially, was why Conn was tried first—so that the government could test the credibility of its moles, Hake and Ries, and the Greylord methods—phony cases and surreptitious recordings.

Hake was the star. Everyone wanted to size him up. Ed Genson and Pat Tuite stopped by to look, as did other defense lawyers. Prosecutors were in and out, including Dan Webb.

Hake was good. On the stand for most of two days, he looked wholesome and sounded sincere. He was patient and polite.

On the first day, Hake told how he passed money to Conn to fix traffic cases before Judge Devine, including the drunken-driving case in which Devine left his own courtroom and heard Hake's case in Judge Laurie's courtroom.

The jury also listened to tapes Hake made, including one from July 7, 1981, which Hake said was the first time he ever passed out money in his role as a crooked defense lawyer. On that tape, Conn said Devine was willing to accept $150 from Hake for a drunken-driving fix—instead of Devine's usual $200 price—because Hake was new to private practice. The quality of the recordings was poor, but the government provided the jurors with transcripts.

On the second day, Hake said he passed money to Conn in December 1981 to fix a case before Laurie for an FBI agent charged with shoplifting candle snuffers from Marshall Field and Company. By the time of that case, Laurie had been transferred to a branch court at Eleventh and State. This was the first time Laurie's name had been mentioned as having been directly involved in any wrongdoing. He had not been indicted, although he had long ago retained Tuite. According to Hake, Conn said he had telephoned the judge about the upcoming shoplifting case. On December 17, the day the case was to be heard, Hake, wearing a wire, went into Laurie's chambers.

"Is your man up today?" Laurie asked. "Your friend called."

"Oh, okay," Hake replied. "I don't know if he told you, but I do need an NG [not guilty], if that's okay."

"We'll see," said Laurie—according to both the transcript and Hake's testimony based on his independent recollection.

Then Laurie gave Hake some advice on how to present the case in the light most favorable to the defendant.

Next the jury heard a tape recording of Hake paying Conn money in an illuminating scene of hallway venality. Since no price had been established before the trial, Conn told Hake that another bagman, James Trunzo, had called Laurie to find out how much he wanted. The jurors and spectators sat fascinated as the tape was played.

"Well, Trunzo called him and, you know, he said it's worth a deuce, you know what I mean?" said Conn.

"Okay, so a deuce for John and then, then I'll just give you and Trunzo whatever you want, huh?" said Hake.

Hake said he had a wad of $20 bills, but did not want to count them in the open corridor. Conn directed him to a nearby pillar.

"You can stand behind there," said Conn. "They can't see you behind there."

Hake moved behind the pillar. The rustle of paper could be heard on the recording.

"Here's a hundred, then, and here's another hundred," said Hake. "That's two hundred for Laurie."

Conn said he and Trunzo would take whatever Hake thought proper and "split it down the middle."

Hake testified he peeled off four more $20 bills and gave them to Conn.

Conn was charged with nine counts of extortion—taking money from Hake and Ries to fix cases—plus one count of racketeering—arranging a fix as part of a criminal enterprise.

Conn could not deny that he had taken money. The tapes

showed he had. However, through his defense attorney, Sheldon Sorosky, he denied that his conduct amounted to either extortion or racketeering.

Sorosky contended there was no evidence that Conn either fixed cases or demanded money. Hake and Ries simply gave him money because they were naive—not because they were extorted. Conn was experienced enough that he could tell when a case could be won on its merits. He didn't have to pass money to a judge; he could keep it all himself. As for the racketeering count, Sorosky contended, even if the jury believed Conn gave money to judges, it did not necessarily follow that this was part of an enterprise—the necessary element under the RICO statute. He might have been acting just as a courier. In another line of defense, Sorosky contended that the whole Greylord investigation was illegal and should be thrown out of court.

Sorosky cross-examined Hake for three hours, contending that, by posing as a crooked lawyer, Hake had broken state laws and violated the canons of ethics. Hake was composed and answered in his best altar boy manner.

"I knew that my conduct was proper and was ethical," he said. "It was lawful because it was a federal investigation of federal law violations." Fake cases were not a fraud on the courts. He told some untruths, not lies. "A lie is something you do for personal benefit."

Hake was followed to the stand by Ries, who had already been an FBI agent when the Greylord investigation was launched. For Ries, Greylord was only an assignment. For Hake, it was a career change; even more, it would change the way he would live the rest of his life.

Ries testified that he had paid Conn $850 in connection with six cases and introduced the names of four additional unindicted judges into the proceeding—Daniel J. O'Brien, Michael E. McNulty, Arthur A. Ellis, and John H. Mc-Collom. On tape, Ries was heard passing money to Conn, who said he would pass it to O'Brien and McNulty for drunken-driving cases, and to Ellis for a property-damage case. Ries testified that Conn told him McCollom had acted as an intermediary in the case before Ellis.

The judge in the Conn case, John Nordberg, was a Republican former Cook County Circuit Court judge from the northwest suburbs who had been appointed to the federal bench by President Reagan in 1982. Generally considered intelligent and fair-minded, Nordberg had a reputation for dawdling a bit before making decisions. In this case, he would be asked to make one that could make or break Greylord.

Before final arguments, Sorosky made a motion for dismissal based on the argument that the investigation was illegal. In support of his argument, Sorosky placed Professor Melvin Lewis on the stand. Lewis, who taught a class in professional responsibility at John Marshall Law School, said the Greylord tactics of phony cases and false testimony are "prohibited by the Illinois code of ethics for lawyers and also fall outside the American Bar Association code."

If Nordberg ruled against the government, and if he were affirmed on appeal, Greylord would fall apart. Further prosecutions would not proceed. Nordberg said he would give his ruling the next day, a Wednesday, when closing arguments were to begin. The next day, he said he would delay the ruling until Thursday.

"This is one of the first cases of its kind in the federal courts," said Nordberg. "We are sailing in uncharted water."

And then, on Thursday, Nordberg denied the motion. He said the investigations did not violate the constitutional rights of its targets or violate the canons of ethics. He reasoned, in essence, that the ends justified the means.

"In this case we are dealing with alleged bribery and extortion by a court clerk," he said. "While the vast number of judges and court personnel are hard-working . . . underpaid, there are a few bad apples in the barrel. Apparently, some have been able to conduct their nefarious business unscathed. It may be that the only effective way to root out this corruption is a sting operation like that used in these cases."

The motion had been heard and the decision delivered outside the presence of the jury, which, after closing arguments, took less than four hours to find Conn guilty on all counts.

Dan Webb held a press conference and was obviously buoyed by the verdict. "There's no question that the verdict tonight by the jury is one we're exceptionally pleased with," he said.

Now he was ready to take on a judge.

A week after Conn was found guilty, the grand jury returned a second wave of Greylord indictments, including that of Judge John Laurie, whose name had been so prominently mentioned at the Conn trial.

The government also reindicted John Murphy and John Devine, adding additional charges to those made when they were originally indicted the previous December. Included in the new charges were allegations that Terry Hake and David Ries had passed money to the judges by way of Jimmy LeFevour.

Jimmy and his first cousin, Judge Richard LeFevour, had been under investigation for a long time. When the new indictments against Murphy and Devine came out, Jimmy and his lawyer, William J. Harte, began to consider the evidence against him. It was much like the evidence against Conn, who was facing a stiff prison sentence because he was refusing to cooperate with the government.

One day in late March, to the surprise of the government, Harte offered to make a deal. Jimmy would become

168

a government witness in exchange for being allowed to escape prosecution for felonies. He would plead guilty to misdemeanor income tax charges, allowing him to keep his police pension.

Dan Webb was happy to make a deal. Jimmy would be the most important witness the government had flipped. He not only knew many of the secrets of traffic court, he also knew a lot about corruption throughout the First Municipal District, over which his cousin was the presiding judge.

On April 19, 1984, Conn was sentenced to six years in prison and fined $2,000. The next day, based on information supplied by Jimmy LeFevour, Judge Murphy was indicted for a third time. On May 29, 1984, Murphy went on trial.

Webb prosecuted the case personally, assisted by Scott Lassar. Murphy was defended by Matthias Lydon, the former assistant U.S. attorney who had used the mail fraud statute so ingeniously thirteen years before. Lydon and Webb had been assistants together when James Thompson was the U.S. attorney.

U.S. District Court Judge Charles P. Kocoras, who presided over the Murphy case, was also a former assistant U.S. attorney from the Thompson era. As a matter of fact, Kocoras and Webb had started working at the U.S. attorney's office on the same day. They were close friends.

Murphy, who did not know that his prosecutor and his judge were so close, was charged with one count of racketeering, nine of extortion, and seventeen of mail fraud. It was alleged that he had accepted some $2,000 in bribes from Hake, Ries, and Art Cirignani, Hake's old buddy who, when he found out Hake had bugged him, became a government witness.

The government again used Hake and Ries as witnesses and played tapes that, as in the Conn trial, were sometimes muffled and were augmented by transcripts that the jury could read. The testimony and the tapes contained more adventures of greed and squalor in the corridors and seedy back rooms of the Chicago courts. Spectators in the packed courtroom loved it.

On one tape Murphy and Hake were sitting in the judge's chambers at Belmont and Western talking about a case that Murphy would hear that day. Hake told him his client was accused of battery, but the complaining witness had waited two months before filing charges.

"Two months later?" asked Murphy.

"Yeah, after the incident," said Hake.

"Don't worry about it," said Murphy. "They wanna go to trial two months later, I'll throw the fucker out the window."

In another case, Murphy was heard to tell Hake a way to present a criminal-damage-to-property case so Murphy could give him a not guilty. Then Murphy added, "I think your guy is guilty, anyway."

Hake said he arranged two favorable rulings from Murphy through Jimmy LeFevour in May of 1983. To make payment, Hake and LeFevour went into the men's room off the hallway outside the courtroom. Hake had $600 for LeFevour, but as they entered the washroom they saw other men. Hake stood in front of the mirror and fussed with his hair as LeFevour walked directly to a toilet stall. The men lingered, and as Hake combed his hair he saw the reflected face of LeFevour peering over the top of the stall, scoping the situation. When the men left, Hake walked to the stall and gave LeFevour the $600.

Although Hake was a leading man in the prosecution's case, LeFevour was the star of the show. The spectators wanted to see and hear the man who was willing to turn in his first cousin and lifelong patron to save his pension. Once again, Genson, Tuite, and other defense attorneys

170

dropped by to take the measure of the enemy. Prosecutors also slipped in side doors to see how LeFevour presented himself.

Webb broadened LeFevour's testimony to include more than payoffs to Murphy. He outlined the whole legal feudalism Judge LeFevour had set up, first in traffic court and then in the First District branch courts. LeFevour said he paid $100 a case to Murphy on ten to fifteen different occasions to fix cases. On a larger scale, he said he arranged fixes with Murphy for Judge LeFevour. This happened hundreds of times.

When he gave money to Murphy, LeFevour said he was acting as bagman on behalf of interested attorneys. When he arranged the fixes on behalf of LeFevour, no money was paid to Murphy. Instead, Richard LeFevour received the money—$100 a case—and kept it. Then he had the cases assigned to Murphy, who fixed them. That was the deal. Murphy was allowed to make all the money he could on his own, but in exchange he had to fix—free—any cases Judge LeFevour sent.

Several other judges had the same deal. They were given fiefs of courtrooms in return for servicing Judge LeFevour. Jimmy Lefevour said he fixed at least one drunken-driving case on behalf of his cousin every day from 1975 to 1981. He estimated the fixes generated a minimum of $150,000 in bribes for Judge LeFevour.

For the first time in public, Jimmy LeFevour explained how the "hustlers' bribery club" worked. Five lawyers each paid $500 a month for the privilege of working the hallways. Jimmy kept $500 for himself and gave the rest to Judge LeFevour.

After Jimmy's testimony reporters rushed to Judge LeFevour, still presiding judge of the First Municipal District, for comments. He had not yet been indicted—nor had Jimmy.

"I guess I would call it trial by media," Judge LeFevour said. "I'm innocent. Not guilty. I haven't had a chance to defend myself, but I will. I'm confident. I'm not worried about it."

Meanwhile, Murphy was defending himself, although not too well. He was the only witness in his own defense, except for five character witnesses, including a former U.S. attorney, Edward V. Hanrahan.

Putting Murphy on the stand was a calculated risk for the defense. Doing so exposed him to the skillful cross-examination of Webb. On the other hand, Matt Lydon thought there could be a dividend in having Murphy take the stand. He reasoned that, although the public might be wary of judicial integrity on the whole, a judge on an individual basis still carried considerable prestige.

Given anything close to an even case, Lydon felt, a jury would side with a judge against moles, and certainly against informers like Jimmy LeFevour. Against both informers and agents, it might be a jump ball, and worth the chance. So Judge Murphy, with a hush fallen over the courtroom, took the witness stand.

He was his own worst enemy.

Wearing a blue suit, white shirt, and striped tie, his gut bulging against his single-breasted suit coat, Murphy, with his white hair, flushed face, and double chins, looked like Paddy the Irish Ward Boss. His manner on direct testimony was poised enough. Genteelly led through a series of questions by Lydon, Murphy smiled frequently and, when appropriate, looked at the jury with sincerity. He punctuated his answers with "sir."

"Every case I saw I ruled on according to the evidence I heard before me," Murphy said.

"Did money ever play any part in your rulings?" Lydon asked.

"No, sir," Murphy answered.

"Did you ever accept money to rule on cases?" Lydon asked.

"Never," said Murphy, and looked at the jury.

But during four hours of cross-examination over two days, Murphy's carefully presented manners deserted him. Murphy had been a judge for more than a decade and had obviously become accustomed to the autocratic authority of the bench. Webb sensed Murphy's arrogance and began probing, trying to break Murphy's protective layer of geniality. It wasn't hard. Within an hour, Webb had Murphy shouting and pounding his fist on the railing of the witness box.

"I never fixed a case for any human being alive or dead!" he shouted at one point, thumping the railing.

Murphy leaned against the back of his chair and folded his arms defiantly across his chest, his jaw locked, Mussolini-style.

"Did lawyers ever offer you a bribe?" asked Webb.

"If they had, I would have had them indicted," answered Murphy. "No case I heard was corruptly disposed of."

When he wasn't being combative, Murphy was evasive. Sometimes he had to be reminded to speak louder, other times he was told by Kocoras to avoid giving a speech and to answer Webb's questions directly. He was forced to admit "it was possible" he met with Jimmy LeFevour and discussed a couple of cases of interest to Terry Hake—the cases in which LeFevour did the Kilroy over the toilet stall while waiting for his dough.

"Mr. LeFevour told me that Hake was his friend and asked me to help him," said Murphy.

"What business does a bagman like LeFevour have talking to a judge?" Webb asked over the shouted objection of Lydon. The objection was sustained.

In answer to another question, Murphy said he thought LeFevour was "trying to curry favor with me, but it went

173

in one ear and out the other. It did not affect my rulings."

The tapes the government played for the jury had caught Murphy swearing frequently, but he balked when Webb asked him to read the transcript containing his "I'll-throw-the-fucker-out-the-window" remark. Murphy turned to the jury and said innocently, "I don't normally use that kind of language, except in chambers and private conversations."

"Read it," Webb said.

Murphy looked at Webb defiantly.

"Do we have that understanding, Mr. Webb?" he asked.

Webb glared at Murphy.

"Read it!" he growled.

Kocoras intoned, "Judge Murphy, just read the transcript."

Murphy did.

At another point Webb showed Murphy the transcript of another meeting with Hake in chambers, where Hake said if the judge needed "something extra," Hake would "see" Jimmy LeFevour. Webb wanted to know what Hake was referring to by "something extra."

"Do you think he's talking about carrots there?" Webb asked.

"I don't care what he's talking about," Murphy said petulantly.

"Did you think he was talking about money?" asked Webb.

"Absolutely not," said Murphy.

Murphy's memory often failed him. For instance, he couldn't remember the time he dismissed a woman on a drunken-driving charge, even though she had admitted under oath she was drunk. The prosecutor in that case remembered, though, and testified about it.

In closing arguments, Lydon claimed that Murphy was merely a defense-minded judge and that the government moles, in their zeal to get a judge, had misunderstood his intentions. He also argued that the bagmen who testified against Murphy—Jimmy LeFevour and Joe Trunzo—couldn't be trusted because they had been given deals by the government. He also criticized the undercover methods used by the government.

In his instructions to the jury, Kocoras, taking his lead from Judge Nordberg in the Conn case, said the techniques used in Greylord were legal and appropriate and that those methods should play no role in their deliberations.

The jury was out fourteen hours over two days and came back with a guilty verdict on all counts except one of mail fraud and two of extortion. The counts on which he was acquitted involved payments David Ries had made to Ira Blackwood, supposedly to pass to Murphy. Blackwood did not testify, and Ries could not say from firsthand knowledge that Murphy actually got the money.

Jurors said in interviews that Murphy hurt himself by taking the stand. "Most of us thought he was lying and evasive," said one juror. Another said, "Initially I thought he was not guilty because he was a judge, but listening to the evidence changed that. Especially the way he never answered Webb's questions directly."

Several jurors said they became convinced Murphy was insincere after he resisted reading the transcript because it contained foul language. They had already heard it on the tapes.

The jury believed Jimmy LeFevour. "We figured if he did perjure himself, he would be in even more trouble," one juror said. "What reason would he have to lie?"

An obviously pleased Webb, with Scott Lassar at his side, talked to reporters in the lobby of the federal building.

"There is no question that I consider the trial to be a statement on behalf of the court as well as the jury that the Greylord project had developed reliable and accurate witnesses and evidence," said Webb.

"There is no question the jury said they believed Jimmy LeFevour. They convicted Judge Murphy on every single count of the indictment in which Jimmy was a witness, including certain counts in which Jimmy was the only witness who testified against Judge Murphy.

"There is no question that for the first judge in the history of the state of Illinois to be convicted of crimes relating to the performance of his judicial duties is a very important verdict," Webb said.

The jury reached its verdict at 4:45 P.M. Within an hour, Chief Judge Harry Comerford announced that Judge Richard LeFevour, mentioned so unfavorably throughout the trial, would be relieved of all duties "until his name is cleared."

Years later, after he had returned to private practice, Webb would say that if he had lost the Murphy case there would have been no more Greylord indictments.

Kocoras set Murphy's sentencing for August 31. While Murphy prepared an appeal, based primarily on the undercover methods used by the government, Kocoras notified the defense that he was moving the sentencing up to August 8.

When Murphy appeared for sentencing, arrogant and defiant, he read a statement. "I cannot plead with you to be lenient in imposing punishment for a crime I did not commit. I can show no remorse when I've done nothing to be remorseful for."

Dan Webb, arguing for a heavy sentence, said Murphy was, among other despicable things, a liar. "The jury said you are a liar, you are a perjurer, you are a hardened criminal."

Murphy got ten years and a harsh lecture from Kocoras,

who called Murphy an "infidel to the cause of justice." "The overwhelming evidence of your corruption, Judge Murphy, and the specter of the institutional origins of it have stained us all," said Kocoras. "Honest and dishonest judges as well have been brought into disrepute."

Murphy was allowed to remain free while his appeal was pending. And then it was discovered why Kocoras had moved up the sentencing date. He was going on vacation—with Dan Webb.

Two weeks after the Murphy sentencing, a television reporter, Peter Nolan of WMAQ-TV, the NBC-owned station in Chicago, received a tip that Kocoras and Webb were vacationing together in Georgia. Nolan made a few calls and found that the Webbs and Kocorases were registered at Callaway Gardens, a resort near Pine Mountain, seventy miles south of Atlanta.

Nolan called the Webb cabin. Webb answered and, although he had been critical of Murphy's alleged lies, commenced lying himself. He told Nolan the families were not vacationing together, that the Webbs were staying in a remote area quite some distance away from the Kocorases. Webb said he had seen the judge only once, when he had run into him one day in town.

Nolan took a camera crew and flew down to Callaway Gardens. Nolan discovered, and showed on the air, that Kocoras and Webb had cabins side by side, numbers 829 and 830. Webb had left a few hours before Nolan arrived, but Kocoras was there, and Nolan talked to him. According to Nolan, Kocoras said his friendship with Webb was well known, especially to Matt Lydon, who was a friend of both the judge's and the prosecutor's.

On camera Kocoras, dressed in a polo shirt, with pines whispering in the background, said: "The fact is that you do try cases and sometimes the people who are before you are lawyers who are known to you and sometimes fall into the category of friends, but that's the nature of the judge business."

Nolan also talked to Murphy. "Now one of the things Mr. Webb made a great deal of fuss about during the trial was that I had *ex parte* communications with lawyers," said Murphy. (*Ex parte* communications are meetings between a judge and counsel or a litigant from one side in a case without the other side being present. They are unethical.) "I don't know how Judge Kocoras could change the sentencing date unless he had some kind of conference or communication with Mr. Webb, the U.S. attorney."

Murphy also said he felt Kocoras had "violated the canons of judicial ethics when he did not recuse [disqualify] himself from my case. And I feel that Mr. Dan Webb, by personally prosecuting me, placed his integrity on the line and in jeopardy."

The U.S. Court of Appeals agreed—up to a point. In July of 1985 it handed down a ruling, written by Judge Frank H. Easterbrook, criticizing Kocoras and Webb for not putting their friendship on the record before the trial. Had they done so, said Easterbrook, Murphy would have been entitled to a different judge.

"The statute places on the judge a personal duty to disclose on the record any circumstances that may give rise to a reasonable question about his impartiality," Easterbrook wrote. "We conclude that an objective observer reasonably would doubt the ability of a judge to act with utter disinterest and aloofness when he was such a close friend of the prosecutor that the families of both were just about to take a joint vacation. A social relationship of this sort implies extensive personal contacts between judge and prosecutor, perhaps a special willingness of the judge to accept and rely on the prosecutor's representations.

"The U.S. attorney lays his own prestige, and that of his

office, on the line when he elects to try a case himself. It is a particular blow for the U.S. attorney personally to try a highly publicized case such as this and lose. A judge could be concerned about handing his friend a galling defeat on the eve of a joint vacation. A defendant especially might perceive partiality on learning of such close ties between prosecutor and judge."

As bad as Easterbrook made all that sound, however, he said it did not warrant reversal of the conviction because there was a difference between an appearance of impropriety and an actual impropriety.

"It is important to the administration of justice that judges both be and appear to be impartial," wrote Easterbrook. "When a question about impartiality reasonably arises, the judge must stand aside in order to preserve public confidence in the courts. But this does not imply that a judge who is a close friend of counsel will provide an unjust disposition; if it implied that, the question would be one of actual impropriety rather than the 'appearance' of impropriety."

Easterbrook said Kocoras gave Murphy a fair trial; there was no showing that there had been actual improprieties on the part of the judge. Therefore, whether or not there had been an appearance of impropriety prior to the trial no longer mattered. In addition, he said, it was too late for Murphy to bring up the relationship between Webb and Kocoras. Even though Murphy claimed he did not know that Webb and Kocoras were such close friends, his trial lawyer, Lydon, not only had been in the U.S. attorney's office with both of them but had later been in private practice with Webb. Lydon had known about the friendship, and if he hadn't elected to bring it up before trial, that was a choice with which Murphy was stuck.

Of course, as defense lawyers quickly pointed out, judges make rulings on close legal questions in every trial. Whichever way they are decided, it is hard to detect prejudice on the part of the judge. On decisions that are not close, a judge would not jeopardize himself by making an obviously incorrect decision on behalf of the side he favored. The reason for prohibiting behavior that creates the appearance of impropriety is that actual impropriety is virtually impossible to detect.

The difficulty of proving judicial impropriety, in fact, was the whole rationale given by the government for using the undercover methods of Greylord. Part of Murphy's defense was that the phony cases the government tried in front of him—cases that the government moles said were fixed—were of such a nature that any judge could have favored the defendant. On cross-examination, Hake admitted that was true.

"We made them close cases because we know judges don't like to stick their necks out in overwhelmingly guilty cases," said Hake.

Murphy's appeals lawyer, former U.S. Attorney Hanrahan, asked for a rehearing on the matter in front of all the judges of the Seventh Circuit.

The rehearing was denied.

The government had slipped a tackle, but it was about to be thrown for a loss.

Although Wayne Olson and John Devine, who were in the first wave of Greylord indictments, had not yet been tried, the trial of Associate Judge John Laurie, who was in the second wave, began in July 1984.

Getting Laurie to trial as quickly as possible was part of the defense strategy.

Laurie had hired Pat Tuite as his main trial lawyer, but he also had the full-time services of his brother-in-law, Robert Egan, a capable lawyer. Laurie was regarded as a good lawyer himself, and since he was relieved of his judicial duties the day after his indictment, he devoted full time to his defense.

One of the things the three decided was that the quicker the case could get before a jury, the better. They wanted to take advantage of the fact that few Greylord defendants had yet been tried. They wanted Laurie to have his day in court before the public—potential jurors—grew used to judges being on trial and convicted.

Laurie, it was decided early by the defense, would take the stand on his own behalf. He was no Murphy.

Only thirty-eight years old when he was indicted, Laurie was handsome and well mannered. The son of a wealthy owner of a North Side pizzeria and liquor store, Laurie had been in private practice for eleven years before being appointed to the bench through his family's connection to Illinois Attorney General Neil Hartigan, a political boss on the North Side, where the Laurie family businesses were located.

Laurie's youth and Italian good looks made him a kind of judicial version of Terry Hake, against whom he would be matched on the stand. Tuite was eager for the confrontation.

"Probably no lawyer in the city could have defended Laurie as well," said Ed Genson, who stopped in to watch some of the trial. "Pat was in his element here. Laurie was a nice kid, and nobody can project the humanity of his client as well as Pat. That's his forte."

The judge was Prentice H. Marshall, a former University of Illinois law professor and, before that, a partner in Jenner & Block. Although a Democrat, Marshall was appointed to the federal bench in 1973 by President Nixon. The appointment was recommended by Charles H. Percy, the Illinois Republican senator, who had set up a nonpartisan screening procedure for federal judicial appointees in Illinois. The Percy-era appointees were high-class in general, but Marshall was regarded as the head of the class. The defense was pleased to have him; there would be no vacations with a prosecutor for Marshall.

Laurie was charged with accepting $3,000 in bribes, $400 of it from Hake, who was the first witness for the prosecution. On direct examination by Scott Lassar, Hake said he twice gave bagmen Harold Conn and James Trunzo $200 to give to Laurie to influence cases.

The government played tapes secretly recorded by Hake of two conversations he had with Laurie, one in his chambers and one in the hallway outside his courtroom at Eleventh and State. The conversation in the chambers was the same one the jury had heard in the Conn trial, where Hake wanted a favorable ruling in the candlesnuffer shoplifting case.

"Did you ask Laurie for a particular verdict?" Lassar asked.

"Yes," answered Hake, "I asked him for an NG."

"What did Laurie say?" asked Lassar.

"He said, 'Sure,'" answered Hake.

Tuite, dressed in a tailored blue suit with double-vented jacket, couldn't wait to get at Hake on cross-examination. This was to be no timid exercise. Tuite attacked Hake's motivations and techniques and even, in a subtle way, his character. He pointed out, for instance, that Hake, the White Knight, had once referred to Trunzo as a "slimy dago." But the thing Tuite most wanted to get to was Hake's truthfulness.

In the Conn trial Hake had testified that, when he had asked Laurie for a not-guilty verdict, Laurie had replied "We'll see"—not "Sure."

Tuite went back to the beginning. On the day of the conversation with Laurie, Hake had returned to the FBI office and made a report. When Hake asked for the NG, said that report, "Laurie said that he would see."

"Is there anything in that report, in any fashion whatsoever, that Judge Laurie said, 'Sure'?" asked Tuite.

"No, nothing," answered Hake.

A few days later, Hake reviewed a typed transcript of the Laurie conversation. That transcript also quoted Laurie as having said, "We'll see."

Hake reviewed that transcript shortly after it was typed and made another report saying that he "found the transcript to accurately reflect the pertinent information that is recorded on the tape."

In view of that, Tuite asked: "And the transcript reflected the words 'We'll see,' didn't it?"

"The script said 'We'll see,' yes," Hake answered.

"You didn't change it at that time, did you?" Tuite continued.

"No, because I thought I heard 'We'll see' on the tape," Hake admitted.

Tuite then called Hake's attention to the Conn trial, in which Hake had testified that Laurie had said, "We'll see."

"Do you remember that?" Tuite asked.

"I remember that, yes," Hake said.

Tuite then returned to the day of the conversation. "When you left those chambers that day, and you went out to try the McClain case, you did not have a feeling of certainty that the judge would find your client not guilty, did you?"

"I did because he said 'Sure,' " Hake answered.

Tuite gave Hake—and the jury—his best incredulous look.

"Well, wait a minute," he said. "You made the report that day that he said, 'We'll see.' "

"Yes," said Hake.

"Well, if you left the room thinking he said 'Sure,' why did you put in your report, 'We'll see'?"

Hake's answer was evasive. He said he understood Laurie to mean that an acquittal would be forthcoming. Tuite

kept pressing sarcasm-laden questions, and Hake continued to be vague and unresponsive.

Hake did have an explanation for his change in testimony—how "We'll see" had become "Sure" between the
Conn and Laurie trials.

Just before Laurie's trial began, Hake said, he took the
tape of the Laurie conversation to FBI headquarters in
Washington to have it "enhanced." After the enhancement,
Hake claimed, he could then hear what Laurie really said
was "Sure."

Enhanced or not, the quality of the recording was poor.
Tuite said he definitely could hear two syllables. Judge
Marshall said he couldn't tell what Laurie said. He ordered
that the transcript given to the jury to follow while the
tape was played contain both versions—"Sure" and, in
parentheses, "We'll see."

Hake was followed to the stand by Trunzo, who said he
passed bribes to five judges over the years, including Laurie. But, under Tuite's rapid-fire cross-examination, Trunzo
admitted he sometimes took money from attorneys and
kept it himself, never passing it on to judges. He said this
was not the case with Laurie, who Trunzo said received
his money for the shoplifting case.

Martin Schachter, one of the lawyers who was allowed
to hustle in the hallways and courtrooms of Eleventh and
State, then testified that he dropped $100 payments to
Laurie once every couple of weeks for a year—whenever
he had accumulated $1,000 in hustled fees. He said he left
the money in the judge's desk drawer or in the pockets of
his suit coat as it hung in the closet. He said, however,
that Laurie never asked him for any money, or accepted
any directly.

Finally, the government put on Jimmy LeFevour, who
related more dark tales about his cousin, Richard Le-
Fevour, the prince of payoffs. Jimmy said that in 1982 his

cousin had decided to organize corruption in the newly opened gun court, where weapons misdemeanors were heard and where Laurie was sitting.

"Judge LeFevour instructed me that he wanted a weekly payoff from the lawyers who were hustling cases in gun court, and he would split it fifty-fifty with Judge Laurie," said Jimmy LeFevour.

Jimmy said Laurie agreed. For three weeks, Jimmy said, he left between $150 and $200 in Laurie's desk drawer. But he admitted under cross-examination that Laurie told him to stop the payments after that.

Tuite attacked LeFevour relentlessly on cross-examination, bringing out his disreputable background, which had gone largely unnoted during the Murphy trial. He pointed out that the pension he was trying to save by cooperating with the government was no small thing; it would be worth $250,000 by the time LeFevour was seventy-two.

LeFevour admitted he went on long binges for several days at a time over a quarter of a century. Some days he drank a case of beer a day, mixed with some whiskey. He had been hospitalized four times for alcoholism during the last year and a half.

Tuite suggested that LeFevour, under such conditions, might be prone to forget, to get his facts scrambled.

"There is nothing wrong with my memory, Mr. Tuite," said LeFevour. "I'm sorry to disappoint you."

Thereupon, referring to LeFevour's most recent hospitalization, five months earlier, Tuite asked: "Do you remember telling the doctors you drank for nine days straight?"

"I don't remember," answered LeFevour.

After the government rested its case, Tuite put on his defense, which was Laurie.

Laurie testified for four hours. At the time of the trial Laurie had only been a judge for three years; at the time of some of the crimes he was accused of, he had been a judge for only a few months. Laurie said he had been thrust into a high-volume courtroom, dilapidated and dirty, staffed by entrenched regulars, where it was hard to keep track of where everyone was.

He created a credible picture of an inexperienced but honest judge, working amid noisy confusion, trying to arrive at fair decisions. He never accepted any money, he said, and when he found out Jimmy LeFevour had left money in his chambers—$200—he immediately returned it. He said he tried to get rid of the hustlers in his courtroom, but all it got him was a demotion from Judge LeFevour, who banished him to the West Side. On cross-examination, he was calm and polite, his story consistent; Scott Lassar was unable to confuse or anger him, as Webb had Murphy.

In his final argument, Tuite knew his strongest point would be Hake's inconsistency. He also knew he did not want to call Hake an out-and-out liar. He didn't want the jury to feel he was condemning Hake, since he knew most people regarded him as a hero. So he said Hake was merely overzealous. He said Hake was like a knight on a white charger who, with his armored mask obscuring his vision, lances the wrong person, an innocent bystander.

He reminded the jury of Hake's reports and previous testimony quoting Laurie as saying "We'll see" in the candlesnuffer case.

"Then, lo and behold, miracle of miracles—it will probably go down with the parting of the sea and the burning bush—it changes," said Tuite. "On the Friday before we're going to start trial on Monday morning, it becomes 'Sure.'

"I'm going to use Hake to go with me to singles bars so that when I ask a lady if she'll go out with me and she says, 'We'll see,' Hake will tell me she said 'Sure.' "

The jurors laughed.

They acquitted Laurie on all counts.

Laurie, entering into a stipulation with the Judicial Inquiry Board, accepted a one-month suspension without pay. Then he was restored to full judicial duties by Chief Judge Comerford.

After the acquittal, each member of the defense team received a gift from Laurie—an engraved candlesnuffer.

On one side the engraving read "We'll see."

The other side, "Sure."

The mood in the U.S. attorney's office was glum. After the Laurie acquittal, the upcoming trial of former Associate Judge John Devine, due to start the following month, assumed tremendous importance.

"The prosecutors' fear after the Laurie acquittal was that, if Devine got acquitted, that was going to be the end of it," said former U.S. District Court Judge Susan Getzendanner, who was the judge in the case. "There was a deep sense of pessimism, and everybody just assumed that Devine was going to be the make-or-break of their investigation."

Dan Webb agreed, in an assessment that was a bit more earthy.

"I question whether any prosecutor, after getting kicked in the balls, would have come back for more," he said.

The Laurie trial had shown that juries would still give the benefit of the doubt to judges if credible doubt could be created by the defense. An attorney and two bagmen had testified in the Laurie case that they had dropped off money for Laurie, but none could say the money was actually placed in his hands. Neither could the man generally considered to be the most credible of the government witnesses, Hake, the altar boy. Hake, in fact, had been caught in such inconsistency of testimony that it looked as if he might have been lying.

The Devine case was different. Hake would be able to testify that he placed $100 in the hands of Devine. The incident had taken place on February 3, 1983, in Devine's chambers in traffic court where he had been reassigned after receiving some bad publicity for allowing hustling at Eleventh and State.

Devine had discharged Hake's fake client on a drunken driving charge when Hake, wired for sound, walked in.

"Listen, I can be fair with you?" said Hake.

"Whatever you want," said Devine.

"Okay, good," said Hake. "Is one okay?"

"Yeah, sure," said Devine.

Hake testified that Devine took the money and put it in his left pocket. It was the first—and it would turn out the only—time Hake could testify that he gave money directly to a judge. Not even Warbling Wayne Olson, the boisterous bribe master, had been caught on tape taking money from Hake.

And, when the trial was stripped to its essence, that payoff became the government's case.

The Devine trial started on September 12 in front of Getzendanner, the first woman ever to serve on the U.S. District Court for the Northern District of Illinois. She had been appointed by President Carter in 1980 and served for seven years before returning to private practice.

Devine, whose smelly reputation had resulted in his removal from the bench by the full judges in June 1983, was charged with twenty-seven counts of extortion, twenty-one of mail fraud, and one of racketeering.

He was defended by Ed Genson. The prosecutors were Charles Sklarsky, one of the government people involved in Greylord since its inception, and Sheldon Zenner, who had a special knack for negotiations—talking defendants into pleading guilty.

Zenner and Sklarsky had lined up three lawyers who

had flipped to testify against Devine, as well as bagman Joe Trunzo, one of the double-dealing Trunzo twins, whose mirror-image brother had testified against Laurie. Cynical courtroom observers were never sure which Trunzo they were looking at. Maybe, they suggested, the government put on whichever brother was handy. Like Rosencrantz and Guildenstern, their roles seemed to be interchangeable.

In the three previous trials in which he had testified, Hake had always led off the government's cases. This time the government set things up by putting on two of the attorneys who had begun cooperating, Martin Schachter and Art Cirignani.

The lawyers told tales of insatiable greed by Devine, who was unbending in his insistence that those who wanted to win cases before him "pay the price."

After a day of direct testimony by Hake, Genson went to work. The cross-examination lasted three days.

It was Hake's fourth trial in five months. Cross-examination is one of the most mentally draining experiences a human being can undergo. To be subject to it so many times, for such long stretches, in so short a time span could cause a complete emotional collapse in many people. He had been labeled a zealot, an opportunist, a liar, a suborner of perjury, a violater of legal ethics, and a sneak. Except for a stretch of fumbling and evasiveness in the Laurie trial, he had held up impressively.

Now Genson went after him as a Judas, a man who would sell out his best friend, Cirignani, for the price of a government job. Genson, disgusted and abrasive, brought out many of the details of the Hake-Cirignani relationship—how they became friends, shared secrets. All the time, Genson said, Hake was pushing his friend to incriminate himself and others. Hake destroyed the best friend he had. For what? A crummy job in the FBI.

Hake withstood it. Then, on redirect, questioned by Sklarsky, he said that he once suggested to Cirignani that he try cases without fixing them. Cirignani dismissed the suggestion, he said.

"What did you do?" Sklarsky wanted to know.

"I went home and cried to my mother," said Hake, and his voice began to crack.

"Because Cirignani was your friend?" asked Sklarsky.

"Yes," said Hake, beginning to cry.

The courtroom was silent except for his sobs.

Getzendanner called a recess.

Genson did not put Devine on the stand. A grouchy, irascible man whom people did not take to, the defense was afraid Devine would lose his cool—if he had any—on the stand, à la Judge Murphy.

The jury found Devine guilty on all counts except two of extortion.

Dan Webb was attending a conference in San Diego when the verdict came in. Reached by phone, he bubbled with good spirits.

"Simply a resounding verdict on the entire Greylord project," he said.

Zenner and Sklarsky said the Devine verdict "reaffirms the integrity" of Terry Hake.

When Devine came up for sentencing before Judge Getzendanner on December 18, 1984, she was brief.

"I'm not going to make any speech," she said. "Your crime was despicable."

She gave him fifteen years.

In an interview after she left the bench, Getzendanner credited Hake with winning the case. "Flipping the hustlers didn't make a difference," she said. "That jury would have acquitted. It was Hake. His personal credibility to the jury. That is certainly how the prosecutor, Sklarsky, argued the case. He put it to them—'If you don't believe

Terry Hake, acquit him.' The case came down to that."

In fact, said Getzendanner, the balance of the Greylord investigation probably hinged on Hake in the Devine trial.

"I always had the view that Greylord gained credibility through those early convictions, making it a lot easier to flip people," she said. "Without those early convictions, which were based on Hake, Greylord would have died because witnesses would have become more self-confident and they wouldn't have been making deals with the prosecutor's office.

"My guess is, just from watching the jury in Devine and hearing about other cases and the Laurie acquittal, that unless Terry Hake could put money in judges' hands you weren't going to get a conviction.

"Now, in later cases they did get convictions just on the testimony of flipped lawyers. But I think by that time everybody knew there were convictions in Greylord cases. I think every juror knew that. They were more willing to accept the idea that judges take money.

"And now, of course, we have the judges pleading guilty. A couple of years ago, you wouldn't have predicted that any judge would plead.

"I think Hake is a saint, and I think a lot of people share that view."

After Devine, other members of the colorful old traffic court gang fell one by one—LeFevour, Olson, Reynolds, Sodini, McCollom, Salerno, McNulty, Oakey—and prosecutors turned their attention to new frontiers.

The investigation took a step up the social ladder to the chancery and divorce courts, where the participants, while not the crème de la crème of society, were far removed from the branch court hustlers who dominated the previous Greylord cases.

Likewise, the techniques employed by the government in the chancery and divorce courts were far removed from

191

the Greylord techniques, as outlined by Webb in August 1983. ‹

There would be no stings, no phony cases, no agents pretending to be crooked lawyers or defendants, no concealed microphones.

But the results would be dramatic.

9

The Judge Has Got the Shorts

☆

Bernard S. Neistein—first his cigar, then his 250-pound hulk attached to it—walked into Irvin Richman's office and plopped himself into a chair, smoke swirling around his head.

Neistein and Richman were partners in the law firm of Bilandic, Neistein, Richman, Hauslinger and Young, the Bilandic being Michael A., the former mayor of Chicago, who succeeded Richard J. Daley. Neistein was a former state senator and Democratic committeeman.

The politically connected law firm had a lot of cases in the Chancery Division of the Cook County Circuit Court, where many major business disputes were settled. The judges there were considered the most able in the system. All chancery matters are decided without juries, and a chancery assignment carries a great deal of prestige for a judge.

One of these judges was Reginald J. Holzer, about whom Bernie Neistein, on this day in June 1980, was about to speak. "I saw Judge Holzer and he's got the shorts," said Neistein in his best Chicagoese, meaning that Holzer could not make payments on a $10,000 loan from a bank in which Neistein and Richman owned stock.

Neistein had just made one of the greatest understatements of his life.

At the time, Judge Holzer was more than $550,000 in debt. He was spending more than $100,000 a year on a salary of $43,500. To make up the difference, he borrowed from lawyers and others who appeared in front of him and from banks he had been referred to by those appearing in his court.

Holzer kept a list of creditors—at least those he could remember. He had borrowed from more than fifty banks in the Chicago area, as many as twenty at a time. Every other month or so, he would take out a yellow legal pad and begin writing. Names of relatives, friends, *real* friends, and pals (those who didn't charge interest), and banks. All had numbers after their names. He would subtotal the various columns. Finally he would write a figure in the corner of the front page. That was how much he owed. In 1972, when he was making $29,000 as a judge, the figure was $274,750. In 1976, it was $377,165. In 1980, it had become $556,965. In 1984, it would climb to $667,500. Then federal prosecutors, the FBI, and the IRS started looking into his finances and the yellow sheets stopped.

Chancery court has jurisdiction over, among other things, business foreclosures. In each foreclosure, a receiver is appointed to collect the rents and pay the bills for the foreclosed property. Being a receiver can be highly lucrative, and the chancery judge has absolute discretion as to whom he appoints. Holzer appointed as receivers people he had borrowed money from and, when they collected their receivers' fees, he considered his debts paid and crossed their names off his yellow sheets. Although he was in effect getting kickbacks, Holzer never called them that. He just told lawyers or receivers what bad financial straits he was in and asked if he could borrow, say $10,000. Then he would stiff them.

There was very little Holzer wouldn't stoop to. He was known to sell the art on his walls to lawyers for high prices, a slick practice known to purchasing agents in some fields. Holzer's wife, Estelle, sold insurance and he often recommended that a lawyer with a case before him, or a man looking for a receivership, buy some term life—say a million dollars' worth. Estelle sold so much insurance that she became a star of the Prudential Insurance Company of America, consistently earning more than Holzer.

Still, Holzer fell further behind. He could not deny anything to the women in his life, Estelle and their daughters, Audrey and Bambi. Clothes, cars, trips, parties, lessons, fancy schools. He wanted to be a judge and also to be rich, but the two aspirations didn't mesh. So he stole. It was the least he could do for Estelle and the girls.

Estelle, a teacher, had started selling insurance in 1972, at a time when the sum of her husband's salary and shakedowns could not pay for the family's life-style. Eight years later, in a paperback book on her success in the business, she wrote: "It's hard to reduce your standard of living. It's hard to replace your cashmeres with polyester, your Cadillac with a Chevy. And why should a judge's family eat hamburger when a lawyer's family eats steak? Our daughters were soon to enter Yale and Northwestern universities—the dollar signs in red ink loomed large. Yes, we needed money. More than I could earn as a teacher."

Neither the judge nor Estelle had ethical qualms about using his position to solicit business for her. "Whoever said 'It's not what you know, it's who you know that counts' was probably a successful life insurance agent," she said in the book, which was titled *Success Comes in Cans.*

The Holzers, unscrupulous and driven, were a matched set. They could not remember not knowing one another. Reggie Holzer met Estelle Starkman in 1931, when he was four and she was two. Their parents were friends and they lived in adjoining West Side neighborhoods, he in Logan Square, she in Humboldt Park, to the south.

Reggie was the youngest of four children. He was fourteen years younger than his only brother, Lou, who was to become a wealthy businessman in Hollywood. Some friends of the Holzers felt that it was Lou's financial success that was behind Reggie's drive.

His ambition showed itself early. At Roosevelt High School during the Second World War, Holzer, short and straight with neatly combed red hair, was active in student affairs and the ROTC. In his senior year, he was class president and battalion commander. Some fellow students recall him as a bit arrogant, some as somewhat sanctimonious, all as ambitious. He had a walk that was part strut that he would carry into adulthood.

Holzer was a political anomaly—a big-city child of the Depression who was also a Republican. In law school he became friends with other young Republicans with political ambitions—Richard B. Ogilvie, who would become governor of Illinois twenty years later, and William J. Scott, who would become state treasurer and attorney general, and who would precede Holzer to prison when he was caught spending campaign funds for personal purposes without paying income tax on the money. Holzer graduated from Chicago-Kent College of Law in 1951 and went into solo practice.

In the meantime, Estelle Starkman had graduated from Roosevelt High in 1947. She was a straight-A student and valedictorian. She attended Chicago Teachers College, and she and Holzer began a romance that led to their marriage in 1950. He called her Dimpy, because she had big dimples, and one day she would drive a Cadillac with DIMPY license plates.

The Holzers moved to a brick ranch-style home in Lincolnwood, a suburb just over the northwest border of the city. Besides his law practice, he worked part-time as a hearing officer for the Illinois Commerce Commission.

In 1962, Ogilvie was elected sheriff of Cook County, and he hired Holzer as his legal advisor, a full-time position. Holzer kept his part-time job at the Commerce Commission, kept up a private practice, and did some venturing.

Holzer was briefly connected with a movie company. Among his legal clients at the time were Michael and Bernice Acosta, who, according to a lawsuit they later filed, he conned into investing in a movie called *Two Before Zero*, starring Basil Rathbone. It was an anticommunist picture. Holzer said it couldn't miss and that many important people in Hollywood wanted a piece of the action.

The Acostas had just lost most of their life savings in an unrelated venture, but Holzer helped them to arrange a second mortgage on their home and refinance their cars. They raised $100,000 and gave it to Holzer. "I guarantee you will triple your money," he said.

Two Before Zero bombed and the Acostas lost their home, their cars, and their life savings. Holzer, who stood to make money if the movie did well but risked nothing of his own, eventually settled the suit for $6,000.

Holzer had another show business dalliance while he was on Ogilvie's staff. He was a partner in Gemini Records with Richard Cain, a top Ogilvie aide. Gemini Records had one property—the alleged vocal talent of Cain's girlfriend, Harriet Blake, who had once won a local talent contest, the Harvest Moon Festival.

Cain was one of the more colorful figures of the era. His

grandfather, whose name was Scully, originally Scalzetti, had agreed to testify against some crime syndicate goons involved in the kidnaping of a ten-year-old boy. The night before he was to testify, Scully and several companions stopped by a restaurant. Five gunmen entered, herded Scully's party into a back room, and, as Scully ran for the door, shot him in the head and back. They beat him with baseball bats and left him dead. That was in 1928.

Because of the execution of his grandfather, Cain professed a deep hatred of organized crime. That is what motivated him to go into law enforcement, or so he said in the early 1950s when he became an informant for a Justice Department special prosecutions unit headed by Richard Ogilvie, then an assistant U.S. attorney. Several years later, it turned out that in spite of the ugly demise of his grandfather, Cain had been working for the crime syndicate at the same time that he had been an informant for Ogilvie.

While he supplied Ogilvie with trivial details about the mob, he supplied the mob with not-so-trivial details about the federal investigation. Cain told the mob that three businessmen were revealing their underworld connections to prosecutors. The businessmen all turned up murdered during a nine-month period in 1959–60.

Then Cain became a contact man between mob boss Sam ("Momo") Giancana and the Kennedy administration's efforts to disrupt the regime of Cuban Premier Fidel Castro. He helped train Cuban exiles in 1961 for the Bay of Pigs invasion, and he said the CIA paid his salary.

In 1962, Cain approached newly elected Sheriff Ogilvie and professed, "I know the hoods, I am not afraid of the hoods, and I hate the hoods." Ogilvie hired him as his chief investigator.

Cain, thirty-eight years old, was still double-dipping for the mob. He used his connections to get nightclub gigs for Harriet. The next step supposedly was to record Harriet on the Gemini label and prevail upon his connections to get good positions on jukeboxes controlled by the mob, but before the plan came to fruition Cain got into a scrape that cost him his job.

In 1964, Cain staged a spectacular raid on a suburban motel and claimed to have found drugs worth $42,000. But prosecutors claimed, and produced persuasive evidence to back it up, that Cain planted the drugs in the motel and then staged the raid to make himself look good. The drugs were a small fraction of the loot that had been taken in a burglary three months earlier. Ogilvie fired Cain.

In 1968 Cain was sentenced to four years in prison for bank robbery. When he was paroled, in 1971, he and Sam Giancana went to Mexico. There Cain was Momo's chauffeur, interpreter, and goodwill ambassador to Caribbean countries where gambling casinos were being set up.

Cain made frequent trips back to Chicago. During one of them, on December 20, 1973, he sat talking at a table with four men at Rose's Sandwich Shop on Grand Avenue, in a little Italian enclave on the Northwest Side. The four men left. Cain sat alone for a few minutes, and then two men wearing ski masks entered, one carrying a shotgun and the other a handgun.

"Up against the wall, motherfucker," said one of the gunmen to Cain. Four other customers were also ordered to stand against the wall and not to turn around. Cain stood facing the men. The one with the shotgun fired twice into Cain's face, and he crumpled to the floor. Forty-five years almost to the day after his grandfather was killed, another Scalzetti, in another restaurant, for another reason, lay dead on a floor with his face destroyed, a victim of the same organization.

Holzer's business dealings with Cain had to end when Ogilvie dumped Cain in 1964, but by then Holzer had a better scam: He was going to become a judge. Ogilvie got him slated by the Cook County Republican Central Committee for a Circuit Court vacancy in 1966. Timothy P. Sheehan, the Republican county chairman, knew about Holzer's questionable dealings with the Acostas and with Cain, but Holzer's "Chinaman," the Chicago parlance for political sponsor, was too strong to be denied. In the same election in which Holzer was elected a full judge of the Circuit Court, Ogilvie was elected president of the Cook County Board of Commissioners, a springboard to his election as governor two years later.

On the bench, early on, Holzer displayed fine legal abilities mixed with arrogance and pomposity—traits not dissimilar from those of the strutting ROTC officer. In his first assignment—the criminal courts—he lectured jurors on how to dress to show proper respect for the law: dresses for the women, coats and ties for the men.

Holzer himself was clothes conscious. His suits were conservative, in a pinky ring kind of way. His pinstripes, for example, were not the thin, widely spaced kind they have at Brooks Brothers. They were broad and set close together, in the style of Prohibition gangsters or ward politicians dressing up. The suits came from Hart, Schaffner and Marx. He wore wing-tip shoes with thick soles from Florsheim. He got them shined every day—with a free ticket his sister-in-law arranged for him at a shoeshine parlor across from the Daley Center. He looked neither very good nor very bad in his clothes. He was about five feet six inches tall, pudgy faced, and stocky. He had the pale, freckled complexion of a redhead and long strands of hair that flapped over the top of his head.

He wore broadcloth shirts with spread collars and ties of materials that had a little too much sheen, and he tied large Windsor knots. In the winter he favored Tyrolean hats with saucy bristles sticking out of the bands. He wore camel hair overcoats, fashionable in the legal profession, but his always seemed to have a stylistic quirk, like a flap breast pocket. Somehow, one had the impression that Judge Holzer got a deal on his clothes.

Estelle had more expensive tastes. Between 1978 and 1983, she charged more than $125,000 worth of clothes at such stores as Saks Fifth Avenue, Gucci, Bonwit Teller, and I. Magnin. "I like nice clothes," she said.

While requiring public deference to the law and to himself, Holzer was pimping from the beginning. Soon after he was assigned to the criminal courts, rumors began to circulate that he could be reached.

He was suspected of taking a payoff in a sensational 1968 murder trial. The murder victim was Donna Brown, a member of one of Chicago's most prominent black families. Her father and uncle were lawyers and businessmen, and her first cousin, Oscar Brown, Jr., was a well-known entertainer. Donna, age forty-one, was strangled and shot repeatedly in the utility room of her South Side home three days before Christmas in 1967.

Police had no leads, but were under pressure to solve the crime. The city's black newspaper, the *Chicago Daily Defender*, demanded action with a month-long campaign of editorials and cartoons accusing the police of not caring about black crime victims. Finally, the victim's husband, Dr. John M. Branion, Jr., a physician, was arrested and charged with the crime.

The case against Branion was weak. There was no physical evidence linking him to the killing, nor was he shown to have a credible motive. Moreover, he had an unimpeachable alibi. A nurse, a hospital administrator, a pharmacist, a laboratory technician, fourteen patients, and two other witnesses could account for every minute of his time during the period in which the crime occurred.

Nonetheless, a jury of eleven whites and one black found Branion guilty. After the trial, the defense made a motion for acquittal notwithstanding the verdict. The motion contended that the evidence had been insufficient to prove Branion guilty beyond a reasonable doubt. Such motions are common after criminal trials, but they are rarely granted. In the Branion case, however, a rumor emanated from Holzer's courtroom personnel that the motion would be granted.

The prosecutor, Pat Tuite, heard the rumor and went to see Holzer alone in his chambers, which was improper but common in the Circuit Court in those days. Holzer confirmed that he intended to grant the motion, according to an affidavit filed years later by Tuite in a federal habeas corpus proceeding. "I asked Judge Holzer to let the Appellate Court decide the case," Tuite's affidavit said. "Judge Holzer said that he didn't want Branion to be in custody awaiting an appellate decision. I left, feeling that Judge Holzer would rule against the prosecution."

Although such a ruling seemed justified, Holzer was not motivated by justice. He was, according to another affidavit filed in the habeas corpus proceeding, being paid off by Branion's brother-in-law, Nelson Brown, an attorney. Although Branion was accused of killing Brown's sister, Brown believed Branion was innocent. An affidavit filed by William L. Hooks III, a friend of Branion and Brown, tells that part of the story. "After Dr. Branion was convicted, and while Judge Holzer was deciding what to do about the defense motion for a judgment notwithstanding the verdict, Nelson Brown came to me and said that Judge Holzer was looking for a bribe, and Nelson asked if I had any money. I said that I did not."

Brown went looking elsewhere, but he needed more time. It would have looked bad to outsiders if the defense asked for a delay in the case at that point, so Holzer decided to get the prosecution to ask for one. He called Tuite at home.

"Pat, this is Reggie," Holzer said, according to Tuite's

affidavit. Holzer asked Tuite to ask for a one-week continuance. He did not explain why. Tuite responded that he did not want a continuance. "I told Judge Holzer that I was ready to proceed," said the affidavit. Then, to Tuite's great surprise, Holzer said he would deny Branion's motion, and Tuite agreed to ask for the continuance.

Holzer had been busy scheming. He had backed away from his plan to overturn the jury's verdict, but still intended to make money. The next day in court, as Holzer had requested, Tuite asked for the continuance. Holzer feigned anger and granted only a two-day delay—a subterfuge to make it appear that he did not want a delay but was reluctantly acceding to the prosecution's request.

Later, according to the Hooks affidavit, Holzer met at a Holiday Inn with Nelson Brown, who by now had raised $20,000 from other friends of Branion. "They had imposed a condition that $10,000 be paid to Judge Holzer in advance and the remaining $10,000 be paid as soon as John Branion was freed," said the Hooks affidavit. "At that meeting, $10,000 was passed to Judge Holzer."

Two days later, just before the case was to come up in court again, Holzer gave Nelson Brown the bad news that, as he had previously told Tuite, he wasn't going to overturn the jury's decision. Holzer gave Brown an elaborate cover story, according to the Hooks affidavit. "Judge Holzer said that he could not accept the remaining $10,000 because the state's attorney had somehow gotten wind of the meeting in the Holiday Inn and threatened to arrest anyone concerned and to lock up the judge, too, if the judge reversed the jury's verdict," the affidavit said. "Judge Holzer said he would, however, release John Branion on bail in return for the $10,000 that was paid."

Holzer, in court shortly afterward, let the jury verdict stand and sentenced Branion to twenty years in prison. He set an appeal bond of only $50,000, allowing him to remain free pending appeal by posting only $5,000 cash. Holzer also allowed Branion to move to Cheyenne, Wyoming, pending appeal.

When the United States Supreme Court affirmed the conviction in 1971, Branion jumped bail and went to Africa. He wound up in Uganda, where dictator Idi Amin put him in charge of a rural clinic. After Amin was overturned in a *coup d' état* the Ugandan government turned Branion over to the Cook County sheriff's police. He was returned to Illinois to begin serving his prison sentence in November of 1983. Branion then petitioned the U.S. District Court in Chicago for a writ of habeas corpus, and the story of the alleged Holzer bribe emerged through the Tuite and Hooks affidavits. The person with direct knowledge of the incident, Nelson Brown, was by that time dead. Branion claimed he knew nothing of the bribe attempt, and Holzer, on advice of counsel, would not discuss it. The writ of habeas corpus was denied in 1987 by U.S. District Court Judge Susan Getzendanner, who held that Holzer's alleged corruption had not been prejudicial to Branion.

As the Branion case showed, there was plenty of opportunity to make money in the criminal courts, but it was important to be careful, to be subtle. Criminal cases have a tendency to attract attention. There are reporters permanently assigned to the Criminal Courts Building and a press room is located there. Holzer, in the view of many former prosecutors as well as some judges, developed a system of intentionally introducing reversible error into cases so defendants who paid off could win on appeal.

"Holzer always had the reputation of being somewhat kinky," said Tuite, who was chief of the criminal division of the state's attorney's office when Holzer was in the criminal courts. "It seemed obvious to people in the state's attorney's office that he was on one hand giving a guy a conviction and a sentence for the purposes of the press, but on the other hand basically giving the guy a free ride on appeal. He was really giving a hollow victory to the state."

Holzer's apparent intentional introduction of reversible error became a running gag among judges of the Illinois Appellate Court. In 1968, a man named Mark Kroll was charged with twenty-four counts of theft and three counts of conspiracy for draining funds from an insurance company. Kroll took a bench trial before Holzer, but the case was so strong that Holzer could not justify an acquittal. There was a drawn-out trial, in which more than five thousand pages of testimony were recorded, but Kroll did not testify himself.

Several weeks later, Holzer issued a written opinion dismissing all of the theft counts but finding Kroll guilty of the conspiracy counts. In his opinion, however, Holzer stated that the guilty finding was based partly on Kroll's failure to take the stand in his own defense. "The defense's failure to present denial testimony, which only it could offer, leads this court to the conclusion that it must resolve the issues in this case in favor of the prosecution," Holzer wrote.

The statement was a thinly veiled invitation for the Appellate Court to reverse the conviction. There are few points in law any clearer than a criminal defendant's right to remain silent. Failure to testify cannot be construed as evidence of guilt. But Holzer's trick was just a little too obvious.

The Appellate Court affirmed the conviction in 1972, saying that Holzer "was merely commenting on the uncontradicted nature of the state's case." The author of the opinion, Judge Joseph J. Drucker, personally delivered a copy of the opinion to Holzer.

"Congratulations, Judge," said Drucker. "You were just affirmed in the Kroll case. I wanted to present you with a copy of the opinion personally."

Kroll still got a good deal. Holzer had sentenced him to only a year in prison. If he had been convicted of the theft counts that Holzer threw out, his sentence probably would have been three to five times that long.

Holzer spent several years in the Law Division before being assigned to the Chancery Division in 1978. Holzer was always aggressive about getting assignments that were considered prestigious. He tried to get on the Appellate Court himself, losing a countywide election in 1974. Two years later, he ran unsuccessfully for the Illinois Supreme Court. After Ronald Reagan became president, Holzer's name appeared several times on lists of candidates under consideration for a federal judicial appointment. If he was not a serious contender, at least his name was in newspaper or television reports as someone "under consideration." From a distance Holzer looked impressive. But the closer you got, the uglier he became.

Estelle was not pretty in action, either. When Howard Orloff, a wealthy automobile dealer, wanted to get his son into law school he asked advice from his lawyer, Jerrold Morris. Morris talked to Holzer, who wrote a letter on the son's behalf. Almost immediately, Orloff received a call from Estelle. She succeeded in selling him $100,000 worth of life insurance. Estelle was achieving the social status she wanted. The Holzers moved from one home in Lincolnwood to a bigger one with a swimming pool. They had large and frequent parties, but they never seemed gay or spontaneous. They were those structured, ostentatious affairs more associated with rich socialites than with suburban social climbers. Estelle even had a society interior decorator, William Phillips. At one party with a Wild West theme, two cowboys on horseback patrolled the front yard, greeting guests and chewing up the lawn.

But Estelle had something more than Lincolnwood in mind for herself. East Lake Shore Drive in Chicago—now, there was a place for a distinguished jurist and his socially prominent wife to live. East Lake Shore Drive is a one-block stretch of magnificent apartments and hotels over-looking miles of beaches and parks. That single block is home—or *pied-à-terre*—to some of Chicago's oldest money. It would make a fine address. It is also close to everything, including the finest restaurants in the city. That was im-portant to Estelle, since she didn't cook. Never had, even when the girls, Audrey and Bambi, were little. They ate out. Mrs. Starkman hadn't raised a short-order cook.

In 1976, the Holzers bought an apartment at 179 East Lake Shore Drive. Since it was a cooperative, the apart-ment only cost $75,000, but assessment and taxes, plus payments on a personal loan they took out to buy the place, ran the Holzers' housing expenses up to $3,400 a month. And Estelle immediately put her decorator to work. It cost $50,000 to make the apartment suitable. Holzer's salary at the time was $35,000. He owed $366,000. When Audrey got married, the Holzers spent $21,000 for a wedding next door at the Drake Hotel.

Estelle, who likes to gamble, engaged in Saturday night poker and frequent visits to Las Vegas gaming tables. To feed social habits like those took money. If you were Reg-inald Holzer, chancery court was a good place to get it.

A lot of cases involving big money were heard in the Chancery Division, and a lot of high-priced lawyers prac-ticed there. Many would be eager to do a favor for a judge who asked for one. The judges also appointed receivers to manage property involved in disputes. Receivers could be lawyers or businessmen—or just about anyone the judge saw fit to appoint. There was a great deal of chumminess in chancery, with lawyers and real estate types continually courting the judges to get business. Someone like Holzer, who always needed money for something, could be expected to find a willing benefactor in chancery court. In fact, it was not always clear who was doing what to whom in chancery. Was it extortion or bribery? Did people give money to Holzer because there was an implied threat that he would rule against them if they didn't pay? That would be extortion. Or did they simply lend him money with no *quid pro quo* real or implied? That might be dumb, but not illegal.

Certainly it would be hard to picture Bernie Neistein as a victim. As he sat in Irv Richman's office that day in June 1980, Neistein was sixty-three years old and as stubby as the butt of his cigar. He had white hair that was mostly gone on top, and thick black eyebrows that contrasted markedly with his silver sideburns.

Neistein, who has seldom been seen inside a courtroom, was known as "the master of ceremonies" by his law partners. He was the business-getter, always walking around with a thick wad of $100 bills in his pockets, thicker if he was going to the track, which he did whenever he got the chance. Neistein was familiar with racetracks. As an Illinois state senator in 1971, he was indicted for illegally concealing on his financial disclosure form his ownership of stock in the Fox Valley Trotting Association, which was dependent on a state agency for racing dates. Although not convicted, Neistein quit the senate the next year, after serving for eight terms. He was the first senator ever indicted under the Illinois Legislative Ethics Act, an appropriate distinction.

While in the Senate, Neistein was a leading member of what was called the "West Side Bloc," a group of Chicago legislators who voted for bills that were thought to be good for organized crime interests, such as legalized gambling. A 1971 Chicago Crime Commission report called Neistein "the crime syndicate's man in the Senate." In 1960 he was elected Democratic committeeman of the Twenty-ninth Ward and kept that post until 1976, long after the ward had gone black. The ward's changing racial makeup didn't bother Neistein. He hadn't lived there for years. He lived in a condominium in the swank Carlyle Apartments, on Lake Shore Drive almost kitty-corner from the building the Holzers would move into.

Neistein's reputation as a fixer predated Holzer's as a fixee. If anybody was going to come in contact with a chancery judge looking for money, it was Neistein. In December of 1979, Neistein arranged for a $10,000 loan for Holzer. The two disagreed later on who made the first contact. Holzer claimed it was Neistein, on the private judges' elevator in the Daley Center.

According to Holzer's version, Neistein asked him, "Judge, the rumor is you're in financial trouble."

"I'm sorry to hear there is such a rumor, but it's true," Holzer said he answered.

"Well, I know some guys at a bank," said Neistein.

"I could use some help," said Holzer.

Neistein claimed Holzer made the first approach, either in the building or on the phone. He asked Neistein to drop by his chambers, where money was first discussed.

"I didn't do too much talking," said Neistein. "He said he was in a bind and needed a loan of $10,000. I said, 'I'll have to get back to you.'"

The next day Neistein met with his partner, Richman, and they agreed to get Holzer an unsecured loan from the Republic Bank, in which they owned a one-quarter interest. Holzer was supposed to repay $1,000 a month. Six months later, when Holzer hadn't made a single payment, Neistein and Richman met again in Richman's office, and they agreed to repay the loan themselves in $1,000 monthly installments.

Each month, Holzer would receive a slip from the bank saying that a payment was due. He would then call Neistein, who would pick up the slip and make a payment.

"The whole thing took a matter of two minutes," said Neistein. "I'd walk in and say, 'Hello. How are you?' He gave me a white slip and I'd be on my way."

Asked why he made the payments, Neistein said:

"He was a judge. A power. A king in his courtroom. My philosophy has always been, don't rock the boat. Don't make no waves. A public official asks you to do something, you do it."

In December of 1982 the Holzers were going to Las Vegas so Estelle could do a little gambling. The day before they were to leave, Holzer called Arnold Karzov, a lawyer who practiced in the Chancery Division. Holzer asked Karzov to come to his chambers immediately. When Karzov, whose office was across the street, arrived a short time later, Holzer was conducting a trial. Karzov walked through the courtroom and went to Holzer's chambers. Holzer recessed the trial and joined Karzov in chambers.

"We exchanged pleasantries," Karzov would testify later. "He said he was going on vacation the next day. He said he was short of funds and could I loan him a thousand dollars."

Karzov said he didn't have that kind of money on him. Holzer suggested he go right over to the bank and get it. Karzov, who had a case pending before Holzer and knew he would have more, decided it would be "prudent" to get the money.

Karzov went to the bank and Holzer went back on the bench. A little while later, Karzov returned with the $1,000 in an envelope, walked through the courtroom again, and waited in Holzer's chambers. The same trial was on, and Holzer recessed it again. He hopped off the bench, walked quickly into his office, and, quite chipper, took the envelope and told Karzov he would pay him back after the New Year. He didn't.

Two years later, in November 1984, after Holzer found out he was under investigation, he sent Karzov $500, with a promise to pay him the other $500 "shortly." He never paid. The government claimed the only reason Holzer paid the $500 was to make it look as if the money had indeed been a loan and not a shakedown.

In 1977, Holzer borrowed $2,500 from Fred Lane, uncle of Judge Alan Lane, a personal injury lawyer who had many cases in front of Holzer in the Law Division. Holzer never paid it back. When the loan became publicly known after Holzer was indicted, it was just one small debt among $650,000 worth for Holzer. It was a bigger deal for Lane. He was by that time president of the Illinois State Bar Association.

Whether borrowing money directly or asking someone to arrange a loan through a bank, Holzer consistently ignored payments. In February of 1978, Russell Topper had a case before Holzer involving $2 million in damages. If Topper won, he stood to collect $200,000 in legal fees. One day the phone in Topper's office rang.

"This is Reggie Holzer," said the caller, according to Topper's court testimony. "I'd like to talk to you about something important."

"What about tomorrow?" asked Topper.

"O.K. I'll see you after my call."

The next day in his chambers Holzer said, "Russ, I know about you and your reputation among chancery lawyers. I know you're reliable. I'm deeply in debt. My wife has gone to work as an insurance agent. My daughters are

211

going to universities. This judgeship doesn't pay much. I need help. I know you represent banks and bankers. Can you help me get a loan?"

"I don't represent banks and bankers," Topper answered. "I know one. I'll see what I can do."

"Do the best you can," said Holzer.

"How much are you looking for?"

"Ten thousand dollars. I'll pay it back the best I can."

"I'll see what I can do."

Topper said he talked to a banker he knew who refused to give a loan without security, so Topper drew $10,000 of his own money out of a bank and had a cashier's check made out to Holzer. He brought it to the courtroom, where Holzer was on the bench again. When he spotted Topper he recessed the court. They went into Holzer's chambers.

"Judge, I've got that loan for you," said Topper. He reached across the desk and handed an envelope to Holzer, who walked to a corner, pulled out the cashier's check, and walked back to the desk.

"You're a great guy, Russ. I'll pay you back," said Holzer. He never did.

Shortly after Holzer moved to chancery, he was called upon by Ernest Worsek, a businessman who had been getting receiverships from Holzer's predecessor, Judge Sheldon Brown. Worsek, who years earlier had been active with Holzer in the Niles Township Republican organization, said he would like to continue as a receiver. Holzer let Worsek keep the receiverships he had and awarded him a few new ones in the next few months. Then, in September of 1978, Holzer summoned Worsek to his chambers.

"He mentioned that his wife was in the insurance business and was in a sales contest," Worsek said later. "He asked if I would take out a life insurance policy for a million dollars. I said I was uninsurable because of high blood pressure and diabetes."

"Do you know anyone else who may be in a position to buy a policy?" asked Holzer.

"Let me think about it and get back to you," said Worsek, who sent his son-in-law to see Estelle. She sold him a $500,000 policy, which Worsek paid for. Worsek began making $800-a-month payments to Prudential, but his troubles were only beginning. In December 1978, Holzer put the bite on him for a $15,000 loan, in May 1979 for $10,000 more, and in February 1983 for another $10,000. Worsek came up with the cash each time by borrowing from a friend and then paying her back at interest. Beset by payments, Worsek took $20,000 from a receivership account and transferred it, illegally, into his personal account. To pay back the receivership, he sold his home. Along the way Holzer had Worsek transfer $62,000 in receivership funds from one bank to another, where Holzer had an account. By arranging the transfer, Holzer hoped to make himself look good.

Finally, Worsek said he couldn't afford to keep up the payments to his friend, and he asked Holzer to make them. Holzer didn't make the payments, and he cut off Worsek's receiverships.

When Estelle became an insurance agent in 1972, chancery practitioners were struck with a sudden realization of their own mortality. Estelle started by contacting six hundred friends on her Christmas-card list. Charles Swibel, a big real estate developer, bought a $1 million policy. Swibel was also head of the Chicago Housing Authority, the agency that oversaw Chicago public housing, which was occupied almost exclusively by blacks. After Jane Byrne was elected mayor in 1979, Swibel was put in charge of her fund-raising. Estelle was a big supporter of Byrne. One day Holzer put the arm on Stanley Lieberman, a real estate executive who had previously bought $400,000 in insurance from Estelle, to guarantee a $150,000 loan to the

Byrne reelection campaign. A few months later, Byrne appointed Estelle and two other white women to the housing authority's board of directors, replacing three blacks. This alienated many black voters who had supported Byrne in her first election. It no doubt helped Harold Washington defeat Byrne in the 1983 Democratic primary election and go on to become Chicago's first black mayor.

In March of 1984, Worsek was visited by the FBI. By then Holzer's finances were under close investigation, touched off, ironically, when he had pushed himself for a federal judgeship. Worsek called Holzer.

"I think we should talk about it," said Holzer. They met the next day in Holzer's chambers. But they didn't talk. Holzer motioned Worsek to be quiet. Then he scribbled a note to Worsek: "I think we should communicate in writing."

Holzer wrote questions: "What happened with the FBI? What did you say?"

Worsek wrote answers. Holzer scrawled that Worsek should get a lawyer. When the meeting was over, Holzer took the crumpled notes and flushed them down the toilet in his chambers.

Worsek and Holzer had three or four meetings over the next several months, so furtive that Holzer, afraid of bugs, would have them meet in jury rooms instead of his chambers. They would sit and pass notes back and forth. "I do hope you'll work with me, that you won't testify," Holzer wrote.

After each meeting Holzer would flush the notes down the toilet.

The conferences did Holzer little good. After Holzer was indicted in May 1985 on thirty-three counts of mail fraud, extortion, and racketeering, Worsek turned government witness.

*   *   *

214

At the trial, Worsek, Neistein, and six other witnesses testified that they made loans to Holzer, feeling that if they did not it would jeopardize their cases or receivership appointments. None of the witnesses could say that Holzer actually threatened them in any way, but the lead prosecutor, Scott Turow, argued that there was an implied threat, constituting extortion and bribery.

Throughout the trial, before Judge Prentice Marshall, which spanned six weeks of early 1986, the Holzers presented a united front. Estelle testified for the defense. The girls, Audrey and Bambi, were there every day: Audrey, a lawyer, lending legal support; Bambi, a Los Angeles stock broker, offering encouragement, sitting close to her mother, pouring water at the defense table for her father and his lawyers.

The defense was led by a brilliant trial lawyer, Edward L. Foote, the head of litigation at the law firm of Winston and Strawn. Foote was reputed to be working for free, Holzer being more than half a million dollars in debt. Foote argued that Holzer was merely a deadbeat, that he borrowed money meaning to pay it back, but his finances were such a scrambled mess that he never could.

In the end, it was the yellow sheets that destroyed Holzer—the legal pads on which he had totaled his debts. Turow, in a crisp and agile cross-examination of Holzer, was able to show a link between what Holzer borrowed and the receiverships he awarded. Holzer testified that it had been his custom, whenever he paid off a loan on his list, to draw a line through the amount due opposite the lender's name. But Turow was able to show that sometimes there would be a line drawn through an amount when no payment had been made. Turow suggested it was more than coincidence, in these cases, that Holzer had invariably just awarded the lender a big legal fee or receivership. The cross-examination left Holzer a mumbling, hoarse, self-contradicting, sometimes petulant wreck on the stand.

"He turned his official position into a cash station," Turow said in his closing argument to the jury. Privately, Foote could not disagree. "I think Scott made points with the cash station remark," Foote said while the jury was deliberating. "That's what he was running. It's hard to answer. There is no answer."

The jury got the case on Valentine's Day, deliberated over a long weekend, and came in with a guilty verdict on twenty-seven counts—twenty-three mail fraud counts, three extortion counts, and a racketeering count.

Judge Marshall dismissed the jury, expressed admiration for the way the lawyers conducted the case, and left the bench.

As the spectators filed slowly out of the courtroom, Holzer stood alone for a few moments at the lectern in front of the bench. Estelle walked slowly up to him. There, in the center of the crowded but practically silent courtroom, they embraced.

They embraced with the understanding of two people who have done so many times through a lot of happiness and a lot of sadness, and they embraced for a very long time, occasionally patting each other on the back.

Estelle went over to Foote and they hugged each other for a few moments. Then Estelle walked back to the front row of spectator seats, where Audrey and Bambi stood. The trial was not easy on the Holzer women, who came out looking like free spenders who kept Holzer—not a particularly high liver—busy scurrying up funds.

Estelle hugged both daughters.

The spectators were leaving but the courtroom remained almost silent.

Audrey walked up to her father, still standing in the

216

center of the courtroom, and for a long time they embraced, wordlessly, tightly.

Finally, the courtoom was empty of all but the Holzers— Reginald Holzer and the three women for whom he had done so much, so much of whatever it was he had done.

They all left together.

Three months later, Holzer was sentenced to eighteen years in prison, the stiffest sentence handed out to a Greylord defendant.

10

I Am God

☆

Sheldon T. Zenner, an assistant U.S. attorney, walked briskly toward the Jackson Boulevard entrance to the Dirksen Federal Building. It was Saturday and Zenner was dressed in shorts and a T-shirt. He often worked on Saturdays, but on this warm June morning in 1987, Zenner was in a race against time.

Zenner showed his identification to a security guard at the door of the stark, Mies-designed building, which was closed to the public for the weekend. He walked quickly across the empty lobby and took an elevator to the fifteenth-floor offices of the U.S. attorney for the Northern District of Illinois.

In his own small office along the east wall, Zenner began writing. He was drawing up an indictment that he would present to the grand jury, and time was important because the statute of limitations on the alleged crimes was going to run out in four days.

"UNITED STATES OF AMERICA v. ALLEN F. ROSIN," the document began. Zenner worked on the indictment the rest of the day and into the evening. When he finished, he was pleased, not so much that the indictment represented an accomplishment—it was the culmination of a three-year investigation—but at what he hoped it would accomplish.

Allen Rosin was a former Circuit Court judge. He had been on the bench for twenty-one years before being turned out by the voters in November 1986. He had been named as a bribe-taker in three Greylord trials, and this bad publicity had led to his ultimate defeat at the polls, where a 60 percent approval vote is required for retention.

Rosin's name was first mentioned in June 1984 by Jimmy LeFevour, the master bagman of the First Municipal District, in the trial of John Murphy. LeFevour said that Rosin had been on the take when he was assigned to traffic court during the 1970s. At the 1985 trial of his cousin, Judge Richard LeFevour, Jimmy had testified that Rosin was among ten crooked insiders in the system of corruption Judge LeFevour had established. Finally, in May 1987, eight lawyers who testified against another former traffic court judge, John McCollom, also said they had paid bribes to Rosin in the old days.

The old days in traffic court had ended for Rosin in 1980, when he had been transferred to the Domestic Relations Division, commonly called divorce court.

Zenner had been negotiating with Rosin's attorney, John L. Sullivan, in an effort to get Rosin to plead guilty and cooperate in the investigation of other divorce judges and lawyers. Rosin had considered pleading guilty but decided against it. During the negotiations, he had given the government a waiver of the seven-year statute of limitations. Zenner had sought a second waiver, in the hope of persuading Rosin to cooperate, but Rosin wouldn't agree to it. The clock resumed running on the statute of limitations. It would expire on Wednesday, June 22, which was why Zenner had to hurry to present the indictment to the grand jury.

The indictment would charge Rosin with racketeering, mail fraud, and tax violations. Although most of the alleged violations occurred in traffic court, it wasn't traffic court crimes that the government was most interested in. Greylord had nearly obliterated the traffic court crooks from the LeFevour days. By now ten judges had been nailed for activities there. The government hoped the Rosin indictment would carry Greylord into divorce court.

Zenner was an excellent negotiator. His specialty was getting defendants to admit to crimes and, in exchange for leniency, to cooperate in future investigations. Lawyers, even potential defendants, seemed to like Zenner, as opposed to the way they felt about James Schweitzer. Zenner was blond, of average height, with pleasant, even features and, his shorts and T-shirt showed, a muscular body. He had a friendly, polite manner. When he talked to the various felons connected with Greylord, he was understanding, familiar. He came on as someone who wanted to do what was best for the defendant. It was Zenner who persuaded Martin Schachter to plead guilty and become a government witness. Schachter was the first, and possibly the most important, of the branch court hustlers to flip.

"Zenner can get anyone to come over," said Ed Genson. "If the defendant is Jewish, he gives him the old neighborhood stuff. 'I remember your mom from the restaurant,' he'll say, or something like that."

There had been rumors about divorce court for about ten years, horror stories about the proceedings in some courtrooms there. Zenner and a partner, Assistant U.S. Attorney Thomas M. Durkin, had been working on Rosin and also on a lawyer who had practiced before Rosin in divorce court. Zenner felt he was close to getting the lawyer to cooperate. In addition, on Wednesday, the grand jury would return the Rosin indictment, further pressuring that lawyer.

In the old days, when Daley was mayor, the divorce court was considered by many attorneys to be relatively free of corruption, at least in cases involving children. The family and everything connected with it was said to be sacred to Daley; a political underling could get into more trouble with the mayor by indiscreet philandering than by discreet larceny. Divorce judges might not have been great scholars during Daley's time, some may have been incompetent, but they were not venal.

Then Daley died. Soon thereafter, the chief judge of the Circuit Court, John S. Boyle, was voted out of office. There had been no major scandal during Boyle's tenure, but there was disenchantment in some quarters with his style. He was very much a Machine creature. Both a liberal bar association, the Chicago Council of Lawyers, and the conservative *Chicago Tribune* opposed Boyle's retention in 1978, and the voters dispatched him.

The new chief judge, Harry Comerford, began to use divorce court as a dumping ground for judges who had become *persona non grata* in other venues, usually because their reputations for stealing had become thunderous. Rosin was transferred there from traffic court. Later Black Jack Reynolds and Wayne Olson would end up there, too. Rosin almost immediately began to smell up the place.

Divorce court had some built-in problems. It was structured to drag out cases over long periods of time, greatly inflating legal fees, especially those of the steady group of practitioners there. These lawyers became familiar with the new judges, knew their idiosyncrasies and propensities for the bribe, and could arrange to get just about any case assigned to any judge they wanted. The division operated on a "master calendar system." Two judges handled only preliminary motions, others only trials, and others only postdecree matters. Until a case made it to the final stage, it could be lateraled from one judge to another for years.

The court also had jurisdiction over fees, which was almost a scandal in itself. In any other civil matter, a litigant enters into a fee agreement with the lawyer. If the lawyer is not paid, he can sue the client. But in divorce cases, the judges award fees. That made it possible for some divorce lawyers to charge $250 an hour and up—as much as senior partners in major law firms charge corporate clients. Sometimes, just to keep up appearances, judges would somewhat decrease the fees lawyers requested.

The combination of the case-lateraling from judge to judge and the friendly fee-fixing produced incidents in which the lawyers got more than the people who were dividing the assets. In one case that began in 1979, three years after Daley's death, a man and woman were disputing the division of $450,000. By 1988, the case was still going on. The legal fees had reached $300,000.

The delaying of cases was bad when money was involved but worse when children were involved. Many custody cases dragged on so long without a decision being made that the issues became moot: The children involved reached majority age. The process was so emotionally and financially draining that some lawyers were not surprised when Hutchie Moore, an ex-cop confined to a wheelchair, pushed himself into a semistanding position in divorce court one day and opened fire with a pistol. He killed his ex-wife's lawyer and a judge, Henry A. Gentile. After that, an elaborate system was established to find hidden guns, but nothing was done to improve divorce court procedures.

In 1984, David W. Thompson, a management consultant who had been divorced in Cook County, made some interesting criticisms of the system. Thompson, a psychologist, said the system was a laboratory in which lawyers were conditioned like Pavlov's dogs. The positive reinforcement was profit, as in business. However, in business, profit usually flowed from efficiency. In divorce court, the opposite was true. Profit flowed from inefficiency—the longer cases dragged on, the higher the legal fees.

The divorce bar, said Thompson, had modified Parkinson's Law: "Work expands to fill the maximum billable hours."

Thompson noted that there was such a clique of regular lawyers practicing in the divorce court that even honest judges had a strong identification with them. This clubbiness stemmed from the common backgrounds of the lawyers and judges, which superseded any identification with, or concern for, those outside the system—that is, the litigants.

Certainly, there was an impression gained by anyone who had experience in the divorce court that some lawyers, once they got their cases assigned to the judges they wanted, were shown favoritism. Once he arrived on the scene, the principal favor-dispenser was Judge Allen Rosin.

Rosin was a 100 percent Chicago product—born there, entirely educated there, his whole career there. His attitudes and mores had been shaped by the city's precinct politics, and he had never had a job that wasn't connected to politics. Except for a distinguished hitch in the Marine Corps, where he was badly wounded, Rosin had never ventured much beyond the wards of the city by the time he became a judge.

223

After his release from the Marines, Rosin became a juvenile officer in the Cook County sheriff's office, under the sponsorship of Seventh Ward committeeman James Ronan, a powerful Democrat. Rosin attended John Marshall Law School on the side, graduating in 1958. Along the way he got married. He and his wife, Marlene, had a daughter, Andrea, in 1957 and another, Marcey, four years later.

In the early 1960s, Rosin ran for alderman of the Seventh Ward, but lost. In 1965, Ronan got him appointed a Cook County magistrate. In 1970, under the new Illinois constitution, all magistrates were automatically elevated to associate judges. He was assigned to traffic court.

According to testimony in ensuing trials, Rosin became a dependable member of Richard LeFevour's bribery club, taking care of LeFevour, taking care of himself. Rosin was consistently assigned to the major courtrooms, where he would take care of drunken-driving cases and whatever else needed fixing. Decorum was not a requisite for the outback that was LeFevour's traffic court, and certainly, there was not much decorum in Rosin's courtroom. Boisterous and self-important, he alternately scolded, joked, laughed, and cajoled. He could be courteous or rude, depending on his mood, and he never seemed to question his own behavior.

When Rosin wasn't throwing his weight around on the bench, he was a man of some wit and hearty good humor. He was good with kids, a man's man, a karate expert, a softball player, and a keen follower of Chicago's professional teams. He was a war hero who suffered pain without complaint. He was bright and, with his street smarts, had the qualities that could have made him a good trial court judge.

But, like a lot of the other Greylord judges, Rosin had grown up in a political atmosphere that, as frequently as not, encouraged corruption. Even when it was not encouraged, it was passively condoned: You may choose to be honest yourself, but don't condemn others for being dishonest. Most of the men of Greylord were shaped to believe that if one did not grab some graft, while others all around were grabbing, one was a sucker. A man like Rosin, the ex-Marine and jock, was always going to be one of the boys on the inside, not some sissified, do-gooding outsider, and certainly never a sucker.

So the money came in for Rosin, and for someone who had been a judge since he was thirty-four years old, he and his family lived well. He was an expensive dresser in a mobster kind of way, with white-on-white shirts, pearl-gray ties, and black mohair suits. His clothes were carefully tailored and he wore them well. He was perpetually tanned, of average height, young-looking into his fifties, with a short nose and elongated upper lip, making him resemble Jackie Cooper. He wore his dark hair in a razor cut and had tinted, aviator-style glasses. The Rosins lived in a twelfth-floor condo on Astor Street, one of the classiest addresses in town, just east of the Ambassador Hotels on the Near North Side.

Rosin rode horses, and during the 1970s he began to enter some amateur rodeos. He eventually bought a few acres in Arizona that he called a ranch. One of his most prized possessions was a pair of hand-sewn black leather cowboy boots. After he was transferred to divorce court in 1979, he wore them, spit-shined Marine-style to a high gloss, with his mohair suits beneath his robes.

The presiding judge of divorce court, Charles J. Fleck, assigned Rosin, with his dubious reputation from traffic court, to hear postdecree custody matters—arguments after divorces are granted over who gets custody of the children. There was plenty of opportunity for corruption there— parents would do almost anything to get their kids.

Almost immediately, Rosin established a close relationship with a group of regular divorce practitioners who were the Domestic Relations Division's equivalent to the traffic court's miracle workers. These included Stuart N. Litwin, Martin Tuchow, Sanford Kirsh, and Arthur M. Berman.* Kirsh and Berman were law partners, and Litwin and Tuchow shared office space on La Salle Street.

Tuchow was a Democratic Party insider, the committeeman from the North Side's Forty-eighth Ward and a member of the powerful Cook County Board of Commissioners. Elections in the Forty-eighth Ward, which included some high-class lakefront neighborhoods as well as the city's largest skid row area, had become infamous under Tuchow for questionable practices and charges of fraud. In a variation of an old Chicago tradition, Tuchow's precinct workers would offer winos cigarettes to get them to vote.

As a county commissioner in 1980, Tuchow had arranged for a friend of his to get a contract to lease $934,170 worth of snow-removal equipment to the county. It was later revealed that the company the friend operated didn't even exist when Tuchow arranged the deal. The company came into being only after the contract with the county was signed. Armed with the contract, the friend was able to borrow enough money from a bank to buy the equipment that he in turn rented to the county for $25,000 a month. Tuchow's various finaglings eventually caught up with him and in 1985 he went to prison for accepting kickbacks on county contracts.

But, before he left for his stay in the iron-bar hotel, as they say, Tuchow was a power around Rosin's courtroom. He and the other members of the inner circle—Litwin, Berman, and Kirsh—would meet each morning in Ro-

*Not to be confused with Arthur L. Berman, a Chicago lawyer and Democratic state senator.

sin's chambers for coffee and sweet rolls, provided by the judge.

Rosin was proud of his chambers in the Daley Center, several blocks and a complete lifestyle away from the grimy offices of traffic court. Rosin's chambers, on the fifteenth floor, had a panoramic view of the Lake Michigan basin, and on clear mornings, Rosin and his guests could see the Indiana Dunes and the Michigan shoreline fifty miles across the water. Rosin had decorated his chambers with Western art and cowboy memorabilia, including antique spurs and photographs of himself riding in a roundup and competing in rodeos.

As much as his new chambers were an improvement over his old quarters in traffic court, Rosin's behavior on the bench was not. He still possessed the same lack of judicial demeanor, and decorum was as hard to come by as a fair hearing in his courtroom. He was loud, sarcastic, and talky, almost to the point of prattling. He gave rambling speeches at the start of his call. He once talked for forty-five minutes about being too busy to hear any emergency motions. Other mornings, he talked of his military deeds, particularly being wounded in action. He talked fast normally but slowed down somewhat when making self-aggrandizing statements. He sometimes banged his fist and made other gestures that belittled lawyers and litigants who were unfamiliar with the procedures in his courtroom. He made it clear to those not in his inner circle that they were indeed outsiders. He sometimes stood up behind the bench, spread his arms, and announced, "I am God!"

One day in 1982, a man began hitting his wife's lawyer. Rosin, robes flying, vaulted over the bench, alighted in the well of the court, and gave the man a karate punch, flooring him.

The insiders did not have to behave any more decorously

227

than the judge. On one occasion, Arthur Berman was testifying in support of his petition to have Rosin award him a huge fee in a divorce case—a fee run up at the rate of $250 an hour. Berman leaned back in the witness chair, his feet propped up on the railing that enclosed the witness box, and popped little pieces of candy into his mouth as he testified. It was a vivid picture of arrogance and disrespect. As was the custom, Rosin awarded Berman his fee, but somewhat less than he had asked for.

Outsiders marveled at how often insiders prevailed in causes of questionable merit before Rosin. In fact, clients of lawyers with the right connections rarely seemed to lose.

Tuchow, incidentally, was not the only Democratic politician who fared well before Rosin. The law firm of Edward R. Vrdolyak, a powerful committeeman who eventually was elected to Daley's old post of Cook County Democratic chairman, once represented a doctor who wanted custody of his four-year-old child. Against virtually all of the evidence brought out in the case, Rosin granted the doctor custody. The Appellate Court reversed his decision, saying it was "contrary to the welfare and best interests of the child" and awarded custody to the mother. In another case, Rosin ordered that child-maintenance payments, instead of going to a mother, be given to her lawyer to satisfy his fee. The lawyer was a Democratic state senator, William A. Marovitz. The Appellate Court reversed that ruling, too.

Shortly after Rosin moved to the divorce court, Stuart Litwin represented a man named George Stratigakes, who was seeking custody of his son. George's wife, Mary Catherine, already had custody of two daughters. Litwin cross-examined Mrs. Stratigakes and began to humiliate her on the stand. Over objections, Rosin allowed the humiliation to continue. After eliciting from Mrs. Stratigakes that she had borrowed money from a boyfriend, Litwin asked:

"Mrs. Stratigakes, could you please define 'whore'?"

She answered, "A whore is someone who is paid for sex."

"Isn't it true, Mrs. Stratigakes, that you're a whore?"

"Objection!" her lawyer shouted.

Rosin only smiled and did not sustain the objection.

"Mrs. Stratigakes," Litwin resumed, "could you please define 'fellatio'?"

Rosin let things continue on this plane for a while longer, mildly amused, before he put a stop to it. He awarded custody to Litwin's client.

Mrs. Stratigakes later filed a complaint with the Illinois Judicial Inquiry Board, claiming that her husband told her Rosin had been fixed in the case.

Allegations of fixes were made publicly against Rosin from time to time. He appeared unperturbed, claiming they were the slanderous ravings of disgruntled losers.

"They would criticize God," he said.

Visitors to his courtroom knew who Rosin thought God was.

One of the more tragic cases Rosin became embroiled in was that of Barbara and Michael Friedler, who had been divorced in 1977. Michael was a well-to-do stockbroker, capable of paying substantial legal fees, which in the end came to well over $100,000.

Barbara originally had been awarded custody of their two children, Lisa, seven, and Lane, four, but when Barbara remarried the following year, the children indicated they wanted to live with Michael. Barbara agreed, and Michael obtained a court order giving him "physical possession" of the children—meaning that Barbara couldn't get them back without a hearing.

Soon, however, Barbara changed her mind. She filed a petition to change possession. Michael contested the petition, claiming that Barbara was an unfit mother. Two court-appointed psychologists and a court-appointed psychiatrist agreed with Michael, and it appeared that Barbara's petition would be denied.

While the matter was pending, however, Barbara continued to be allowed visitation. One day she picked the children up at Michael's home and did not bring them back. She took them to Louisiana, where she and her husband had secretly moved. She promptly started a custody proceeding there, without disclosing to the Louisiana court that the matter was pending in Chicago.

After a hearing in Louisiana, the children were returned to Michael. When the Chicago judge handling the case, John J. Crown, was told what had happened, he was livid at Barbara and her lawyer, Stuart H. Wolf. Declaring that the Louisiana action had been instituted "in derogation of the jurisdiction of this court," Crown ordered both Barbara and Wolf to appear before him five days later to show cause why they should not be held in contempt of court. He warned that their conduct "might lead to disbarment and maybe incarceration, depending on the facts."

Before the hearing, one of the court-appointed psychologists, Norma Nissenson, wrote Judge Crown a letter. Nissenson had appeared as a witness in Louisiana, and had observed Barbara at that time. On that basis, she said in the letter, she had determined that Barbara was not "sufficiently stable to consider the best interests" of the children. "Her behavior, in this respect, has been unpredictable at best and potentially volatile," said the letter. Nissenson recommended that Barbara not even be allowed to visit the children without someone else present.

Once again, things did not appear to be going well for Barbara. But at the appointed hour for the show-cause hearing, a new lawyer appeared on her behalf—Stuart Litwin.

Litwin asked Crown to disqualify himself on the ground that the remark he had made five days earlier about disbarment and incarceration indicated he was prejudiced. Crown refused—at first—saying he was not prejudiced.

At Litwin's request, however, Crown agreed to go into his chambers to discuss the matter further with lawyers for both sides. Because no court reporter was present, there was no record of what was said. Afterwards, the lawyers refused to discuss what happened. Michael's lawyer, Jerome Berkson, would not even tell him. But whatever was said must have been persuasive. When Crown emerged from the meeting, he granted the request he had denied just a few minutes earlier.

Although Crown refused to say what had made him change his mind, he was obviously angry. In an interview with *Chicago Lawyer* a few days later, he lashed out at Litwin and his law partner, Bernard Kaufman. "They will very seldom try a case before me," said Crown, "because they know I'll try it on the facts and the law. They don't want to work with the facts and the law."

Crown made it clear what his attitude had been up to the point he disqualified himself. "I thought the mother belonged in jail and the lawyer should be disbarred," he said. "With the mother in jail and the lawyer disbarred, I guess I would have to have awarded custody to the father."

The case went back to Presiding Judge Fleck for reassignment to another judge. But Fleck did not reassign the case. He kept it himself—which was highly unusual.

A few months later, Litwin requested a hearing to present new evidence that Barbara should have custody. At that hearing Nissenson, the court-appointed psychologist, came up with a new report that said Barbara should get the children. Asked what caused her flip-flop, Nissenson testified that "a miracle happened." She claimed that Lisa, now ten years old, had pleaded with her—this is the supposed miracle—"Norma, Norma, I can tell you the truth, please help me go back to my mother."

231

After hearing Nissenson's recommendation, Fleck announced he was immediately sending both children to Louisiana, where they would stay with their mother until there was a final disposition of the case.

At that point, Helen Friedler, Michael's new wife, asked Fleck to delay this decision until he could hear a University of Chicago psychiatrist named Robert Galatzer-Levy, who had treated the son, Lane, in twenty-three sessions. Helen said it was Galatzer-Levy's opinion that Lane would commit suicide if he had to go back to Louisiana. Fleck agreed to a one-day delay. The next day, Galatzer-Levy testified.

"I think it's urgent that Lane remain in the custody of the Friedlers," he said.

"Why?" asked Michael's lawyer.

"Because I think he's at risk of killing himself if he is out of their custody."

"Is the child suffering from severe depression?"

"Yes, he is."

"Does he have a fixation or suicidal ideation?"

"He has a suicidal ideation."

"Now, how strongly do you believe that this child may attempt to kill himself?"

"I think it's likely. I think without proper treatment, that under sufficient stress this child is likely to attempt to kill himself."

Fleck decided to let the Friedlers keep Lane but ordered Lisa to Louisiana, another unusual move. Splitting custody of young children is considered wise only in the rarest of circumstances. If one child was a danger to the other, that would be grounds to split them. That was hardly the case with the Friedler children, although Fleck tried to say it was.

"When I talked to the two kids," Fleck said, "the kids didn't get along. I asked Lisa, 'How are you getting along with your brother?'

"She told me, 'He bugs me.' "

When Fleck asked the same question of Lane, he said, "She bugs me."

So Fleck split the children, even though the day before he had been willing to send them both to Louisiana, regardless of what they thought of one another.

After *Chicago Lawyer* carried a story about the strange goings-on, Fleck took himself out of the case. He went on vacation, leaving instructions that the case was to be assigned to Rosin.

The fight was still on for permanent custody of the children, and Michael Friedler wanted Lisa back. Several lawyers told Friedler he did not have a chance against Litwin in front of Rosin.

In a sworn statement that he gave to Assistant U.S. Attorney Dan Reidy, Friedler said one lawyer went so far as to suggest that he consider fleeing the country with Lane, because he would never get a fair trial before Rosin. The lawyer, Sheldon Kirshner, said Rosin threatened, off the record in his chambers, to take Lane away from Friedler unless he agreed to give up Lisa, according to Friedler's FBI statement.

As a result, Friedler dropped the fight for custody of Lisa. Friedler did get Rosin to put in an order that Barbara should provide psychiatric care for Lisa. But Friedler told the FBI that Kirshner warned him not to push Rosin on the enforcement of the psychiatric treatment provision. To anger Rosin, Kirshner was quoted as saying, would be to jeopardize the entire agreement and Friedler's custody of Lane.

Thus, the temporary split in custody was de facto permanent.

Both Friedler children later displayed severe behavior problems—problems that Michael blamed directly on Rosin and Fleck. In 1988, looking back on the whole custody battle, Friedler said he might have done things differently.

"I might have played the game in Chicago," he said. "I might have gone to a lawyer and said, 'Here's thirty thousand dollars; let's fix the case.' Maybe that was not possible. Maybe Rosin was already committed to the other side. But, whatever the options, I would certainly not assume the system would be honest."

Another divorce litigant, Sidney J. Goldberg, a social worker, became so frustrated with Rosin in 1982 that he took a desperate and what appeared to be a foolish gamble.

Goldberg was fighting to prevent his ex-wife from moving their two young sons to Detroit. The ex-wife was the daughter of a wealthy mattress manufacturer, and her father had obtained the services of Rosin insiders Arthur Berman and Sanford Kirsh. Rosin was indicating he was going to let the woman leave town with the boys when Goldberg wrote a letter to Rosin.

"Most attorneys familiar with the situation believe that Mr. Kirsh and Mr. Berman have you in the bag," said the letter, which was delivered to Rosin's courtroom. Rosin wasn't there when the letter arrived, and one of his aides, thinking he would be helpful, took it downstairs to the sheriff's office, where Rosin's mother worked. Lillian Rosin read the letter before passing it on to her son.

Rosin thought Goldberg had sent the letter to his mother, and he was infuriated by that, more so than by the accusation. He summoned Goldberg to court. When Goldberg appeared, Rosin launched into a tirade.

"I've been a judge for eighteen years and a policeman for five years before that," said Rosin. "You think you get hard-boiled, but nobody gets hard-boiled when they have to look at their mother's face being presented a letter like this. Thank you very much. Special messenger, hand-delivered to my mother. Proud. I hope you're proud." Rosin let this sad message register for a moment and then continued.

"I couldn't wait to enlist in the Marine Corps and volunteer to go to Korea, where I was wounded and came back with half a leg. I fought for my country."

It was all getting to be too much for Rosin.

"I don't want to look at this man again. He committed Hitlerism in the pure sense of the word when he sent that letter. And that's the word I am using, Nazism, Hitlerism."

Goldberg, an Orthodox Jew who was wearing a yarmulke, was flabbergasted.

"I never sent that letter to his mother," Goldberg said. "I don't even know if he has a mother. This man is absolutely crazy."

At the same time of the Rosin letter, Goldberg had sent a second letter, this one to the Judicial Inquiry Board. The letter made the same points, that "Judge Rosin is known not to consider the evidence of the case but to rule in favor of his friends and to be influenced by money."

As foolhardy as it seemed Goldberg was in sending the letters, they accomplished their purposes. The resulting publicity left Rosin with no option but to surrender the case to another judge. After a hearing, the new judge decided that if the ex-wife wanted to move to Detroit, she would have to relinquish custody to Goldberg.

The state's attorney's office charged Goldberg with criminal contempt of court for sending the letter but it subsequently dropped the charges after Goldberg wrote a letter apologizing for having sent it. However, Goldberg did not retract the allegation that Rosin was corrupt.

In 1983, Goldberg, Friedler, and a group of other litigants who had lost in front of Rosin banded together. Calling themselves "Victims of Al," they demanded that the U.S. attorney's office, the FBI, and the Judicial Inquiry Board investigate Rosin.

They couldn't have known it at the time, but the investigation was already on. The relationship between Rosin and his chums handling divorce matters was becoming well known, even in divisions outside of domestic relations. Some of the insiders even joked about it. One day in 1983, Berman was headed into Rosin's chambers to get a signature on an order. He looked over at the opposing lawyer, threw up his hands, palms open, and quipped: "See, no bribe!"

In December 1983, the first Greylord indictments were returned, and in the spring of the following year, Rosin's name was first mentioned at the Murphy trial. By 1986, he was in some trouble, and he knew it, at least so far as his reelection was concerned. For the first time, Rosin began to display some caution in his judicial behavior. He began ruling against the insiders, even turning against Stuart Litwin. In one case he ruled against Litwin so lopsidedly that the Appellate Court reversed him. He began to lobby bar groups for favorable recommendations in the November election. He had his friends write to newspapers, urging that they endorse him.

None of it worked. All the major bar groups and both major newspapers recommended that Rosin not be returned, and he wasn't.

Sheldon Zenner finished his work on that Saturday in June 1987 and went home.

The coming week would be busy. There was the indictment before the grand jury on Wednesday, and sometime during the week he wanted to talk to the divorce lawyer who was close to turning. Zenner, the specialist in such matters, knew when he was getting close. The Rosin indictment might just do it. And once he could get one lawyer to flip, experience had shown Zenner, others would soon

236

come tumbling after. The criminal secrets of the divorce court were about to be exposed.

Rosin did not work that weekend. Since being turned out of office the previous November, he did not have a lot to do. Some days he donated time to Chicago Volunteer Legal Services, which provided free representation to the poor. Other days he rode horses. Sometimes he went fishing.

And he worried. He knew his indictment was imminent. A conviction would mean he would lose his generous judicial pension. Even if he made a deal with the government and copped a plea, he would lose his pension. One day in May, walking on Michigan Avenue, he saw Art Petacque, Pulitzer Prize-winning reporter for the *Chicago Sun-Times*. Petacque and Rosin had gone to Lowell grammar school together. Petacque told Rosin to come out and visit him sometime at his home in Lincolnwood. Rosin did.

Sitting in Petacque's recreation room, Rosin said he was the subject of vicious rumors by lawyers he had ruled against or otherwise offended. Petacque told Rosin he was comparatively young, at fifty-six, and even if he were convicted, he would have time to establish a good life for himself.

"Yeah, I guess you're right," Rosin said, without much conviction. He looked out the window.

"Sometimes I find myself looking out the window and thinking about killing myself," he said.

He said the feds were after him to make a deal and that, if he didn't agree, prosecutors threatened to subpoena his mother, who was then eighty-three years old, and his daughters, who were then thirty and twenty-six.

But what really worried Rosin was that if he didn't make a deal it would be revealed in court that he had been romantically involved for years with a female judge. The

IRS and FBI were doing a complete financial examination of his records, as they had done with Judge Holzer, trying to show that he was spending much more money than he was declaring he earned. Some of the expenditures pertained to living arrangements for his lady friend. The expenditures were bound to be revealed in a trial, and Rosin was mortified at the thought of the public embarrassment to his children.

On Monday, June 21, Sheldon Zenner went to his office in the federal building. The news on the radio that morning was about Fred Astaire, who had just died in Los Angeles. Zenner reviewed his work of Saturday, the indictment of Rosin.

Rosin had a racquetball game scheduled for noon that day. After he left the bench, Rosin had become a member of the McClurg Court Sports Center, located near the CBS studios east of Michigan Avenue. When he wasn't riding or fishing, Rosin played racquetball.

He arrived quite a bit early for the racquetball game, about 9:45. He was dressed in slacks, a sport shirt, and a sport coat. He idled about, then left the club for a few minutes and returned. He took some items out of his locker and went to a curtain-draped tanning booth. He drew the curtain and sat down on the stool.

Wearing his spit-shined cowboy boots and his Marine Corps dog tags, he placed the items he had removed from the locker on the floor in front of him. There were photographs of his wife, Marlene, and his daughters, Andrea and Marcey. There was a Father's Day card they had given him the day before, which was also the first day of summer. There were his military medals. And there was a .38-caliber, snub-nosed revolver.

Then, surrounded by the things he loved most in the world, Allen Rosin picked up the pistol and shot himself in the right temple. He slumped to the floor, dead.

11

Reform, Chicago Style

☆

Perhaps it was inevitable that W. Jason Mitan would become involved in Greylord, however indirectly.

His credentials were perfect.

Mitan first became entangled with the justice system in 1960, when he was twenty-two. He had been selling Cadillacs in the northern suburbs, but authorities discovered that he did not have titles to the cars he was selling. He pleaded guilty to running a confidence game and was placed on three years probation.

He next opened a used car lot in the western suburbs, but fell behind in his rent on the lot. The landlady, a rich widow named Eva Brennan, came to collect. Mitan, an extremely handsome, dark-haired man with a smooth style around women, immediately charmed her. Then he romanced her. Then, in June 1961, he married her. She was fifty-eight, he twenty-three.

They lived in splendid style in her big home in Geneva, Illinois, in those days a horsey, exurbanite community west of Chicago. He opened an automobile body shop in Chicago. He drove the toll road between Chicago and Geneva every day. He lived in high style, spending his wife's money, hitting Rush Street night spots, tipping the waitresses big.

But he was a chiseler at heart. He put slugs in the expressway toll baskets. He was caught when the state police, seeing a pattern, stationed a man with a walkie-talkie inside one of the coin receptacles. The officer crouched there, quarters, dimes, and nickels bouncing off his head, until the slugs arrived. Then he notified another cop in a squad car who arrested Mitan.

The body-repair business brought Mitan into contact with the ambulance-chasing business, an unethical pursuit that naturally attracted him. He decided to go to law school and enrolled at DePaul in 1969.

In a closed-book examination his first year, he provided so many citations—not just the name of the case, but also the volume and page number—that the professor concluded that Mitan had obtained a copy of the exam in advance. At a hearing into the cheating charge, Mitan defended himself by saying he had taken a memory course.

Mitan stayed in school, but he never did as well on a test again, the effects of the memory course apparently having diminished. They were not revitalized after graduation in 1972, either. He had to take the bar examination four times before finally passing it in 1974.

During law school, no longer in need of the former Eva Brennan—then well into her sixties—Mitan divorced her in Haiti. He married a much younger woman in January 1972.

In May 1972, three months before he took his first bar

exam, Mitan, who up until then was known as James W. Mitan, had his name officially changed to W. Jason Mitan, an affectation he thought gave him an elegance his behavior did not.

When he filled out the questionnaire that accompanies the application for a law license, Mitan may have set a record for lying. He even outdid C.W. Wilson, the drug dealer in the Marquette Ten case who once admitted he lied under oath about everything but his name. Mitan lied about his name, saying he had never changed it. He also lied about his age—knocking off five years—where he had lived, and where he had worked. He denied ever being arrested or convicted and having been divorced. He even, for no apparent reason except that it was his style, made up a military career for himself, saying he had been in the Naval Reserve for five years. He had never been in any branch of the service.

When he finally passed the bar exam in 1974, he set up his ambulance-chasing business. He paid chasers who would bring in accident victims, and employed a man to coach the victims on how to exaggerate their injuries. He then farmed out the cases to lawyers who had the skills to litigate or settle the cases—skills Mitan never bothered to develop.

Mitan continued to play king of Rush Street nightlife. He wore mink coats and gold necklaces, tipped big, drove expensive cars, and gambled in Las Vegas. He also borrowed big.

In 1977, he was being pressured to pay back $150,000 he owed a bank. The lawyer for the bank, Fred L. Drucker, started searching for Mitan's assets. He discovered, among other things, that Mitan had a $60,000 loan from another bank that had been secured by a woman named Janice McDaniels, who worked as Mitan's office receptionist.

McDaniels's husband had died. She had gone to Mitan

to settle the estate, gone to work for him, and gone to bed with him. She was pregnant by him. When Drucker told McDaniels that Mitan already had a wife and family out in the suburbs, she was surprised and upset.

All in all, Drucker was making life uncomfortable for Mitan. So Mitan's main assistant, Fred Harvey, hired a man to kill Drucker. Harvey was a long-time crook who was almost as old as Mitan's first wife. He had an arrest record dating back to the Depression. When Harvey was twelve, his father had been killed in a shoot-out with police in Little Rock, Arkansas. Harvey picked up his father's gun and shot two policemen, and had battled authority ever since.

"You hit this guy," Harvey told the hit man, a small-time thief named Michael Filimoniuk. "You shoot him in the head. You shoot him in the heart to make sure. You kill anybody else in the office."

Filimoniuk never pulled the job off. Instead, he told Drucker about the plot. Drucker called the police, who had Filimoniuk wear a wire and go back to Harvey to further discuss the murder. Filimoniuk did, and Harvey, a tough old bird who was then almost seventy, became suspicious. He whipped out a knife and had Filimoniuk pinned to the floor before the police crashed in and saved him.

Harvey was sentenced to four to fifteen years for solicitation to commit murder, but refused to implicate Mitan in the plot. "I've always hated squealers and I won't become one at this late date," Harvey told prosecutors.

All this captured the attention of the Attorney Registration and Disciplinary Commission, which for some time had been looking into ambulance chasers generally and Mitan specifically. Eventually, the commission persuaded the Illinois Courts Commission that the lies Mitan told on his application for admission to the bar were enough to have him disbarred, without going into the details of his law practice and related activities.

Mitan was disbarred in January 1980, but, according to allegations in disciplinary commission files, continued to run his ambulance-chasing operation after his disbarment, with a succession of licensed attorneys fronting for him.

In 1985, unaware of the materials in the commission's files, Mitan retained Daniel M. Pierce to represent him in an effort to get his license back. Pierce was mayor of Highland Park, one of Chicago's ritziest suburbs, and a former Democratic state legislator. Pierce decided that, as a first step, Mitan should get a pardon for his confidence-game conviction, and arranged a pardon hearing before the Illinois Prisoner Review Board in October 1985.

At the hearing, Pierce failed to disclose that Mitan had been disbarred, although it was pointed out that he had graduated from law school. When asked specifically by a member of the board if he had taken the bar exam, Mitan gave a false answer: "I would need the pardon here." Pierce said nothing to correct the record, and the board recommended a pardon, which Governor Thompson granted in April 1986.

Mitan then brought a lawyer named Jerold S. Solovy into the case to help him get reinstated. That's where the paths of Mitan and Greylord crossed.

In the summer of 1984, the chief judge of the Cook County Circuit Court, Harry Comerford, spurred by the Greylord revelations, appointed a commission to look into the courts. It was called the Special Commission on the Administration of Justice in Cook County, and it was a classic blue-ribbon committee.

Blue-ribbon committees are a fine Chicago tradition. Mayor Daley had been a master at them. Any time a scandal threatened the Democratic Party's vise-grip on an upcoming election, he appointed a blue-ribbon committee to investigate and prepare a report. Blue-ribbon committees always have businessmen on them. Businessmen tend to be Republicans and give a committee a nice bipartisan flavor.

Blue-ribbon committees are announced at press conferences called by the mayor or other appropriate official. Then the committee members go to work and into oblivion. Some months later their report—a recapitulation of the problem and some generalized recommendations on what to do about it—is announced at another press conference. Sometimes the recommendations are leaked in advance, but the press conference always makes headlines. The mayor responds with heartfelt thanks for the committee's hard work and promises to consider all of the recommendations in the report.

Then the report is burned, or locked in a vault, but in any case ignored.

Judge Comerford's blue-ribbon committee was made up of forty-three lawyers and business leaders, all respected members of the community. The chairman was Mitan's lawyer—Jerold Solovy, fifty-eight, a Harvard Law School graduate and a senior partner in Jenner and Block, a prestigious law firm. The group quickly became known simply as the Solovy commission.

The Solovy commission, which had neither subpoena power nor the power to take testimony under oath, was almost guaranteed to end up talking about abstract administrative issues. It would look into the courts and recommend many things that at one time or another had probably been recommended before. Maybe the court should have fewer divisions or more, or be more computerized or less, or have more clerks or fewer.

The commission's first action, in January of 1985, was

to recommend a Circuit Court rule against *ex parte* communications. Illinois Supreme Court rules, binding on all lower courts, already forbade *ex parte* communications, and had for longer than anyone could remember. The problem was not the lack of a rule, but that the existing rule was ignored. Responding to that problem with an additional rule was like responding to judicial bribery convictions with a court rule forbidding bribes.

Next, Solovy criticized the Illinois Judicial Inquiry Board and Illinois Courts Commission for failing to take strong disciplinary action against Judge John Laurie. Although Laurie had been acquitted, undisputed evidence showed that he had engaged in serious improper conduct. The famous "We'll see" / "Sure" conversation with Hake had been unethical, whatever had actually been said. First, it was an unethical *ex parte* conversation. Second, a judge who is offered a bribe has an ethical obligation to report it. Laurie didn't.

Giving Laurie only a one-month suspension was ridiculous, as far as Solovy was concerned, and he said so publicly. "The organized bar is asleep," he said. "It doesn't care about its duty to its profession or to citizens. Our judicial system stinks."

Around the same time, Solovy was privately critical of the Attorney Registration and Disciplinary Commission. In offhand conversations with lawyers and journalists, he complained that the disciplinary commission had gone easy on ill-behaved lawyers, dragged its feet in investigations, and failed to take complaints seriously.

Members of the disciplinary commission staff reacted to Solovy's criticism at first with open resentment, and then they counterattacked.

The vehicle of the counterattack was W. Jason Mitan.

On December 31, 1986, Mitan had filed a motion with the Illinois Supreme Court requesting reinstatement to the

bar, and listing as counsel Solovy and two other lawyers—
Dan Pierce and one of Pierce's young associates, Jeffrey P.
DeJong.

After the motion was filed, DeJong went to review the
disciplinary commission's files on Mitan. The files contained allegations that Mitan had continued to practice
law after his disbarment. After being told what was in the
files, Mitan realized he had no realistic chance of reinstatement and directed his lawyers to withdraw the reinstatement motion.

That was all the disciplinary commission needed. It filed
a petition with the Illinois Supreme Court charging that
the reinstatement motion had been "manifestly fraudulent
and frivolous" and that the lawyers who filed the motion
had failed to adequately investigate Mitan's behavior after
his disbarment. The petition asked the court to impose
monetary sanctions against Solovy and the others.

Solovy exploded. "It was a totally unprofessional sand-
bag," he said. "The message they sent to the public and
the bar is, 'Don't criticize us or we'll come after you.' What
type of chilling effect does that have on the average person?"

It was ironic, to say the least, that Solovy, the outspoken
critic of the bar's failure to cleanse itself, should be involved in an effort to arm a man like Mitan with a law
license. Nonetheless, the whole flap showed the difficulty
of reforming the Cook County court system. The agency
responsible for punishing the dozens of attorneys who were
shown by the Greylord investigation to be shifty and
unethical, if not outright felons, was more concerned with
punishing its critic. Other targets of disciplinary action
were at least accorded confidentiality until their review
was over. But not Solovy.

As for the Solovy commission itself, its recommendations, as predicted, were mostly unstartling.

Its most dramatic accomplishment was to get the presiding judge of the domestic relations division, Richard H. Jorzak, replaced. Jorzak, who had been responsible for the assignments of sensitive cases to Allen Rosin, was reassigned to personal-injury cases after the Solovy commission released a report saying, in part: "There is a general perception that many lawyers are able, one way or another, to get their cases assigned to certain judges, that certain judges show favoritism to certain lawyers, that case assignments are not made on a random basis, and that cases are not always decided on their merits."

The Solovy commission recommended that the financial disclosure requirements for judges be expanded; it recommended a bill that would allow prosecutors to demand jury trials for some serious crimes; it recommended that more court sessions be held in the afternoons in the First Municipal District. Those recommendations were all followed.

The commission recommended—once again—that the political selection of judges be replaced with a merit system, but the Illinois General Assembly kept that idea on indefinite hold. Commission recommendations for adding judges, physical facilities, and support personnel were taken under advisement by the appropriate bodies.

The commission said nothing directly critical of the man who established it, Chief Judge Comerford. It did not question why for so many years he had not only been oblivious to suspected thievery, but had also promoted some of the most notorious judges, enhancing their opportunities for corruption—putting Olson in narcotics court, Holzer in chancery, Rosin in divorce.

There was a conspicuous absence of any recommendation concerning the method of selecting the chief judge—probably the first thing that needed to be changed in a serious effort to get at the roots of corruption. As long as the chief judge was elected by the full judges, he would be accountable to them, his subordinates—a situation that made it virtually impossible for him to deal with the entrenched patterns and practices that led to Greylord.

In November 1987, the full judges of the Circuit Court overwhelmingly reelected Comerford to another three-year term as chief judge.

In the spring of 1985, Anton R. Valukas succeeded Dan Webb as U.S. attorney for the Northern District of Illinois. William Kunkle, the first assistant state's attorney of Cook County and one of the insiders of the Greylord investigation, had lobbied for the job. In the end it went to Valukas, then forty-one, because of his old-boy ties to the office. Valukas, a partner in Jenner and Block, Tom Sullivan's firm, had been an assistant U.S. attorney under Jim Thompson and was a close friend of Webb's.

Valukas, whose round face, small mustache, and rimless glasses made him look disconcertingly like Heinrich Himmler, vowed to continue the Greylord probe, the third in the line of U.S. attorneys to do so.

And the indictments did, indeed, continue. By the summer of 1988, by the government's count, eighty-seven judges, lawyers, and court personnel had been charged with crimes in the investigation, which was then almost a decade old. Included in the indictments were seventeen sitting or former judges. Twelve of the judges had been convicted, one had been acquitted, and four remained to be tried. All of the judges awaiting trial were involved in traffic or branch court kickback schemes.

The government totals did not include Frank Salerno, the judge who gave a hot mink to his sixteen-year-old girlfriend—but not because he escaped prosecution. Although Salerno was one of the targets of Greylord, having been implicated in bribe taking in both traffic court and at the branch court at Belmont and Western, he was indicted in a different investigation, this one code-named Operation Phocus.

Phocus focused on Salerno's tenure in license court, where violations of municipal licensing laws were prosecuted. His bagman, Victor Albanese, was one of the main witnesses in Phocus, in which Salerno and thirty-one others, mostly city inspectors, were accused of taking bribes. Salerno pleaded guilty in June of 1987 and was sentenced to nine years in prison.

Valukas's office was under a deadline crunch of sorts. The statute of limitations for Greylord-related crimes, like extortion and bribery, was five years. Since the investigation became public knowledge in August 1983—when the first television and newspaper stories appeared—it was assumed most indictable activity around the traffic and branch court had ceased. Therefore, August 1988 was the outside limit for indictments involving events that occurred before Greylord became public knowledge.

Valukas, however, had broadened the investigation into other divisions—including divorce court, where the government was looking into more recent conduct involving Allen Rosin, Wayne Olson, and John Reynolds. Also, some crimes, such as tax offenses, had longer statutes of limitation.

In announcing additional branch court indictments in March of 1988, Valukas said Greylord was "far from over." But it was nevertheless thought that those indictments, which included Judge John J. McDonnell, were the last for the colorful gang that had once starred in traffic court.

Valukas announced his indictments from the same room in the Dirksen Building where Webb had announced his. The place had been increasingly gussied up for the cameras through the years. Now it had a backdrop of colorful departmental seals—FBI, Treasury, and so forth.

Standing there, Valukas looked quite nice himself. He had shaved off his mustache and replaced his rimless spectacles with tortoise shell ones, and he no longer looked like someone who might call out the Gestapo.

"There is nothing more insidious than judicial corruption," he said.

One by one, the convicted judges lost their appeals and went off to prison. Murphy faced ten years, Dollars Devine fifteen, LeFevour twelve, Olson twelve, Holzer eighteen, Reynolds ten, Sodini eight, McCollom eleven.

Michael McNulty, a onetime traffic court judge who resigned from the bench after his indictment, took a voluntary disbarment, and publicly repented, received a three-year term. James L. Oakey, Jr., a former associate judge who was convicted of paying bribes as a lawyer but not of anything he had done as a judge, received eighteen months. Oakey had been removed from the bench by the Illinois Courts Commission a decade earlier for secretly running a business on the side.

Oakey had originally been convicted on several counts of mail fraud, but that conviction had been thrown out, and he had been retried for not filing personal income tax returns for two years. Oakey was bitter and defiant at his sentencing.

"I refused to become a government witness, and that is why I am before this court," said Oakey, a white-haired man of more than three hundred pounds who had been a brilliant public defender before becoming a judge. "I could never become a government witness and I don't respect anyone who does. I'm the son of a tough South Side Irish cop. I never squealed or ratted on my fellow man."

Cooperation was what the government was after, no doubt about it. Tremendous pressure was put on the convicted judges to become government witnesses.

The government wanted Dick LeFevour to cooperate against Reynolds in the hope that Reynolds would be the key to divorce court the way Jimmy LeFevour had been to traffic court. Dick LeFevour was reluctant. He was placed in solitary confinement and shuffled back and forth between the federal penal farm at Oxford, Wisconsin, and the Metropolitan Correctional Center in Chicago, near the U.S. attorney's office.

This shuffling is known as "diesel therapy." Uncooperative prisoners are placed on a prison bus, in manacles and leg irons, ostensibly to be taken to some other facility for some administrative reason. In reality they are taken nowhere. They are driven about, sometimes for several days at a time, in chains, out of touch with their families and lawyers, for no purpose other than to make their lives uncomfortable.

Robert L. Tucker, a lawyer serving a sentence at Oxford for a fraud conviction unrelated to Greylord, recalled seeing John Devine subjected to diesel therapy in early 1987 while dying of cancer.

"I saw this person struggle off of the bus, bent over, obviously swollen in the midsection from something other than calories, hardly able to put one foot in front of the other," said Tucker, who worked in the prison bakery.

"Later I saw him come in for one of the meals, and I saw him try to hold onto one of the railings in order to steady himself and get through the line. I could see that he was jaundiced. He took his tray and ambled over to a table where he was later joined by Dick LeFevour. It bothered me that a man obviously that ill had simply been sent into the population, apparently to behave like everybody else, when it was clear that he needed attention—indeed, daily assistance.

"So I talked to Dick LeFevour and asked what in the world Devine was doing here. LeFevour told me that Devine had been a victim of diesel therapy and had just come out of a hole somewhere.

"Well, in the next several days I saw him continue to deteriorate so rapidly that I later offered Dick LeFevour to have him come into the dining room and sit down. I said I would personally see that his tray was prepared and brought over to him. We were just sitting there watching a man die. I told LeFevour that somebody needed to petition the court to have him brought before Judge Getzendanner just to see if she would recognize the man she sentenced some months ago. I thought she wouldn't. Devine was just that bad off."

A short time later, Devine was transferred to the federal prison at Springfield, Missouri, where he lapsed into a coma and died on April 2, 1987, without ever receiving treatment for his cancer.

Dick LeFevour finally agreed to cooperate, which caused Reynolds to plead guilty and accept a ten-year sentence for bribes he took at Belmont and Western.

The government's next step was to try to flip Reynolds and crack divorce court. When Reynolds refused to cooperate, he was reindicted—this time for perjury. The indictment said he lied when he claimed under oath before a federal grand jury that he did not know about corruption in traffic court. Rather than cooperate, Reynolds pleaded guilty to the second indictment.

He clung to the only dignity he had left—not to be a government informer. The price was another two years tacked onto his sentence.

A recurrent theme emerged in Greylord: An exceptional number of those involved in the corruption were heavy, if not uncontrollable, drinkers.

The list of problem drinkers started with Harold Conn, the traffic court clerk who went on trial first in Greylord, and ran through McDonnell, one of the last indicted.

John J. Jiganti, president of the Chicago Bar Association, commented on the drinking of Greylord judges in the September 1987 issue of the *Chicago Bar Record*, the association's publication: "Substance abuse does not necessarily equate to corruption, but it invariably leads to poor performance, and it unequivocally leads to an appearance of impropriety. The public record, however, does not reflect any attempt by the bench or bar to assist the afflicted judges. An examination of our failure to adequately respond to this professional and human dilemma may tell us a great deal about the origins of Greylord."

On June 24, 1987, the United States Supreme Court held in a Kentucky case known as *U.S.* v. *McNally* that the mail fraud statute did not apply to intangible rights—such as the right of citizens to the honest services of their public officials. In other words, the mail fraud theory worked out by Matt Lydon in 1970 had been wrong. The mail fraud statute could only be used to prosecute crimes in which the victims were deprived of real property, said the Supreme Court.

The *McNally* ruling affected several Greylord convictions, most notably that of Judge Holzer, who had been found guilty of twenty-three counts of mail fraud, three of extortion, and one of racketeering.

In an effort to salvage the Holzer mail fraud counts in view of *McNally*, prosecutors argued that the state of Illinois had an equitable right to the bribe money Holzer received. There was, said the government, a constructive trust obligating Holzer to turn the money over to the state; by failing to do so, he had deprived the state of its tangible right to the money. The U.S. Court of Appeals for the Seventh Circuit couldn't buy that. It vacated the mail fraud counts.

253

Holzer's lawyers, Ed Foote and Duane M. Kelley, contended that the government's evidence so overlapped the three types of counts that the entire conviction had to be overturned. The Seventh Circuit disagreed. It let the extortion and racketeering counts stand, keeping Holzer behind bars, although his sentence was reduced by Judge Marshall from eighteen years to thirteen years.

As it turned out, the *McNally* decision kept only one Greylord defendant out of jail—John J. Ward. Four others—Harlan Becker, Bob Daniels, Harry Jaffe, and James Oakey—got mail fraud counts dismissed or set aside, but racketeering, extortion, or tax charges stuck.

Only two defendants had been convicted solely of mail fraud—attorneys Jay I. Messinger and Ward. Messinger, who had been sentenced to two years in 1986 on a lone mail fraud count, was already out on parole before the *McNally* decision was handed down. Ward, who had received a sentence of a year and a day shortly before *McNally*, was the only Greylord defendant who actually escaped jail because of the decision.

Terry Hake was mentioned as a possible Republican candidate for either Cook County state's attorney or clerk of the Circuit Court in 1988, but he decided to stay out of politics. Republican chances were not good anyway.

After his cover as a Greylord mole was blown in 1984, Hake had become a full-fledged FBI agent. The work was boring, and there was resentment in the office about the way he was able to enter the agency, circumventing normal channels.

In February of 1988, Hake quit the FBI and took a job as "inspector general" of the Regional Transit Authority, the body that oversees public transportation in the Chicago metropolitan area. It was headed by Samuel K. Skinner, a former U.S. attorney whose image suffered periodic damage when scandals erupted in the agency.

Hake's job change prompted Tom Sullivan, Dan Webb, and Anton Valukas to write a letter to the *Chicago Tribune*.

"The word 'hero' is derived from the Greek 'heros,' meaning 'embodiment or composite of ideals'—one who sacrifices personal needs for those of the community. In our opinion, and in the opinion of those who worked with Terry in the FBI, the United States attorney's office, and the state's attorney's office, he is a hero in the classic sense of that word. He has sacrificed for the common good."

That was one view. Another was presented in the graffiti on the men's room walls at traffic court.

"Stool Pigeon Hall of Fame," said a graffito over the urinals.

"Hake was here and he had a wire," said one near a toilet-paper dispenser.

After Greylord became public knowledge, Brocton Lockwood was never again assigned to Chicago as a fill-in judge. He had ended up testifying in only one trial, that of traffic court bagman Ira Blackwood. Even though Blackwood was convicted, the case was made less on the undercover work Lockwood did than on payments David Ries claimed he had made to Blackwood over a seventeen-month period.

Lockwood sat during the Blackwood trial and listened to a defense lawyer call him a "hillbilly" for believing Blackwood's boasts about fixing cases: "This country boy from down South was hearing just what he wanted to hear. But no one with a semblance of intelligence would have believed it."

The months of wearing a microphone in his boot and reading Ludlum and Follett novels had not amounted to much in the end.

Lockwood went back to the quiet of Marion, Illinois. In April 1984, he resigned his associate judgeship and returned to private practice. He devoted his spare time to writing a personal memoir, to be published by a university press.

He had been disillusioned by the corruption he had seen in Chicago and felt more disillusioned because there was little prospect of change.

"Chicago has a one-party, totalitarian system that operates for the benefit of the government and not for the people," Lockwood said. "Lawyers compromise so that nobody's a clear winner, nobody's a clear loser, and everybody stays a little happy."

Everybody but Brocton Lockwood.

If he had it to do over again, he said, he probably would not become a mole.

Dan Webb returned to private practice in 1985, joining Winston and Strawn, a firm known for political influence. The firm's chairman, Thomas A. Reynolds, Jr., was a close friend of Jim Thompson. When Thompson left the U.S. attorney's office, he practiced briefly at Winston and Strawn before running for governor. The firm also had Democratic connections. Walter Mondale was a partner for several years after Jimmy Carter lost the White House.

Webb was frequently mentioned as a possible Republican candidate for one office or another, but there was nothing appealing for him in the 1988 elections.

He became a fervent campaigner for merit selection of judges.

"There is no question in my mind that you can make all the changes you want in the brick and mortar of the system, but it's the people you appoint to the bench who choose to become corrupt," said Webb.

"There is only one way to prevent that from happening in the future, and that is to try to find a better way to select the men and women who serve as judges."

Webb said that after he successfully prosecuted corrupt policemen in the early 1970s, when he was a Thompson assistant, he had boasted to the press that the case would have a far-reaching impact in preventing future police corruption.

No longer was he so naive.

His expectation for Greylord was not high. He said he originally thought it would be responsible for only one substantial reform—merit selection.

By 1988, he sounded bitter; the General Assembly had failed him.

"In terms of convictions, Greylord is the most successful undercover operation in the history of undercover operations," he said. "But in terms of institutional impact, Greylord has been a miserable failure."

As the Greylord cases were still winding their way through the courts, the government launched three more stings in Chicago.

Several city inspectors were nailed in Operation Phocus along with Judge Salerno. The FBI opened a gambling and prostitution parlor in the suburbs of Chicago in Operation Safebet. Operation Incubator, the biggest of the post-Greylord stings, snared several allies of the late Mayor Harold Washington.

Incubator starred Michael Raymond, alias Michael Burnett, who came to Chicago as a representative of Systematic Recovery Service, a New York–based company that was trying to get a contract from the city to collect overdue parking tickets. Raymond was authorized by Bernard Sandow, president of the New York company, to bribe whomever it took to get the contract. Raymond was doing similar bidding on behalf of Sandow with New York City officials.

Raymond carried on the high standards of perfidy established by the Greylord cast. He was a swindler, con

257

man, burglar, robber, home invader, murder suspect, and, generally, one of the great recidivists of our time. The Justice Department took to him immediately. U.S. attorneys in both Chicago and New York put him to work as a mole.

Raymond was established in a plush Chicago lakefront apartment, outfitted with hidden taping equipment. He began passing out money to anyone he could get to take it. Aldermen and other Washington administration insiders began a parade to the apartment.

Several officials were indicted. The evidence against them included tapes that, like many of the tapes in Greylord, were poor in clarity. Much, in fact, was indecipherable. Again, the government thoughtfully provided transcripts of the tapes, transcripts that contained the government's version of what was said. As in Judge Laurie's case, there were disputes over what one could hear and what the government said one was hearing.

The pattern was reminiscent of the scene from *Guys and Dolls*, in which Nathan Detroit, proprietor of the oldest floating crap game in New York, is forced into a game with a gun-toting torpedo called Big Jule—using Big Jule's dice.

"But these—these dice ain't got no spots on 'em," says Detroit. "They're blank."

"I had the spots taken off for luck," answers Big Jule. "But I remember where the spots formerly were."

Big Jule won. In Operation Incubator, the government also won, using its indecipherable tapes. The juries apparently chose to believe that the government remembered where the spots were.

Aldermen and city inspectors went to jail, while admitted criminals went free for cooperating with the government. Anton Valukas was happy to have Michael Raymond on his side. Raymond's criminal escapades did tend to be somewhat embarrassing, but that was the price of justice.

APPENDIX 1

OPERATION GREYLORD—CONVICTED JUDGES AS OF JUNE 1, 1988

Defendant	Position	Conviction	Sentence
John J. Devine	Associate Judge	Convicted Oct. 8, 1984, on one racketeering/conspiracy count, 25 extortion counts, and 21 mail fraud counts.	15 years prison
Reginald J. Holzer	Circuit Judge	Convicted Feb. 18, 1986, on one racketeering/bribery count, three extortion counts, and 23 mail fraud counts. Racketeering/bribery and mail fraud convictions reversed by the Seventh Circuit Court of Appeals on Feb. 19, 1988.	Resentenced to 13 years prison
Richard F. LeFevour	Presiding Judge, First Municipal District	Convicted July 13, 1985, on one racketeering/bribery count, 53 mail fraud counts, and five tax counts.*	12 years prison

Source: Special Commission on the Administration of Justice in Cook County.
*"Tax counts," unless otherwise indicated, refer to the felony charge of filing false income tax statements.

Appendix 1

Defendant	Position	Conviction	Sentence
John H. McCollom	Circuit Judge	Pleaded guilty May 1, 1987, to eight racketeering/conspiracy counts and two tax counts.	11 years prison, 5 years probation
Michael E. McNulty	Former Associate Judge	Pleaded guilty Dec. 16, 1987, to three tax counts.	3 years prison, $15,000 fine, 3 years probation, 600 hours community service
Wayne W. Olson	Circuit Judge	Pleaded guilty July 18, 1985, to one racketeering/bribery count, one extortion count, and one mail fraud count.	12 years prison, $35,000 fine, 5 years probation
John F. Reynolds	Circuit Judge	Convicted May 7, 1986, on one racketeering/bribery count, one racketeering/conspiracy count, six extortion counts, 25 mail fraud counts, and three tax counts. Pleaded guilty April 8, 1988, to two perjury counts.	10 years in prison, $33,000 fine (Sentencing pending)
Roger E. Seaman	Former Associate Judge	Pleaded guilty Dec. 16, 1987, to two mail fraud counts and one tax count.	(Sentencing pending)

260

Defendant	Position	Conviction	Sentence
Raymond C. Sodini	Circuit Judge	Pleaded guilty Jan. 20, 1987, to one racketeering/ conspiracy count and one tax count.	8 years prison, 5 years probation, 750 hours community service

APPENDIX 2

OPERATION GREYLORD—CONVICTED ATTORNEYS AS OF JUNE 1, 1988

Defendant	Position	Conviction	Sentence
Hugo Arquillo	Attorney	Pleaded guilty Dec. 16, 1987, to two tax counts.	2 months work release, $1,300 fine, 3 years probation, 200 hours community service
Lee Barnett	Attorney	Pleaded guilty Jan. 15, 1987, to one racketeering/conspiracy count and one mail fraud count.	6 months prison, 2 years probation
Lebert D. Bastianoni	Attorney	Pleaded guilty July 6, 1987, to two tax counts.	30 days work release, $5,000 fine, 4 years probation, 500 hours community service, ordered to pay back taxes and penalties
Harlan Becker	Attorney	Convicted Feb. 17, 1987, on two tax counts. Pleaded guilty Nov. 6, 1987, to one racketeering/conspiracy count and one racketeering/bribery count.	6 years prison, $60,000 fine, 5 years probation, ordered to pay $63,000 in back taxes and penalties
Jerry B. Berliant	Attorney	Pleaded guilty April 15, 1985, to three tax counts.	20 weekends in jail, 3 years probation

Source: Special Commission on the Administration of Justice in Cook County.

Defendant	Position	Conviction	Sentence
Neal Birnbaum	Attorney	Pleaded guilty Oct. 14, 1987, to one racketeering/ conspiracy count, one racketeering/bribery count, and one mail fraud count.	(Sentencing pending)
Dale Boton	Attorney	Pleaded guilty Mar. 23, 1988, to four misdemeanor tax counts for failure to file income tax returns.	(Sentencing pending)
Howard M. Brandstein	Attorney	Pleaded guilty Sept. 19, 1986, to one racketeering/conspiracy count and one tax count.	1 year and one day prison, $56,000 forfeiture, 5 years probation, 200 hours community service
Houston Burnside	Attorney	Pleaded guilty June 5, 1985, to three tax counts.	30 weekends in prison, $3,000 fine, 3 years probation
Bruce L. Campbell, Jr.	Attorney	Pleaded guilty Feb. 4, 1987, to one racketeering/ bribery count and one tax count.	1 year prison, 6 months of which is work release; 5 years probation
James I. Canoff	Ass't. Corporation Counsel	Pleaded guilty April 17, 1984, to one racketeering/ bribery count, 18 mail fraud counts, and one obstruction of justice count.	6 months work release, 300 hours community service, $5,000 restitution to the City of Chicago

Defendant	Position	Conviction	Sentence
James J. Costello	Attorney	Pleaded guilty July 18, 1985, to one racketeering/bribery count and one mail fraud count.	8 years prison, $100 fine, 5 years probation
Robert Daniels	Attorney	Convicted Feb. 17, 1987, on two tax counts. Pending trial on one racketeering/bribery count and one racketeering/conspiracy count.	6 years prison
Vincent E. Davino	Attorney	Pleaded guilty Jan. 16, 1987, to one racketeering/conspiracy count and one mail fraud count.	4 years prison, 5 years probation, 500 hours community service
Thomas M. Del Beccaro	Attorney	Pleaded guilty April 11, 1986, to two mail fraud counts.	90 days in prison, later revoked; $1,000 fine; 5 years probation
Thurman Gardner	Attorney	Pleaded guilty April 1, 1985, to four tax counts.	6 months prison, 3 years probation, 750 hours community service
Richard H. Goldstein	Attorney	Pleaded guilty Feb. 4, 1987, to one racketeering/conspiracy count and one tax count.	1 year prison, 6 months of which is work release; 5 years probation; 400 hours community service

Defendant	Position	Conviction	Sentence
Alphonse C. Gonzales	Attorney	Pleaded guilty June 25, 1986, to two tax counts and on July 8, 1986, to one extortion count.	3 years prison, later reduced to 1 year; $2,000 fine; 5 years probation
William H. Kampenga	Attorney	Pleaded guilty Mar. 23, 1988, to two tax counts.	(Sentencing pending)
Melvin Kanter	Attorney	Pleaded guilty Dec. 17, 1986, to one racketeering/ bribery count.	90 days work release, $25,000 fine, 5 years probation, 400 hours community service
Edward Kaplan	Attorney	Pleaded guilty Jan. 28, 1985, to three tax counts.	2 years prison, 5 years probation
Paul G. Kulerski	Attorney	Pleaded guilty March 18, 1985, to two tax counts.	3 months prison, 5 years probation, 400 hours community service
Bernard N. Mann	Attorney	Pleaded guilty Feb. 25, 1987, to one racketeering/ bribery count and one tax count.	6 months prison, $25,000 fine, 5 years probation, 400 hours community service
Joseph E. McDermott	Attorney	Pleaded guilty Dec. 10, 1986, to one racketeering/ bribery count and one tax count.	1 year and one day prison, $30,000 fine, 5 years probation

Appendix 2

Defendant	Position	Conviction	Sentence
Ralph E. Meczyk	Attorney	Pleaded guilty July 6, 1987, to two tax counts.	30 days work release, $5,000 fine, 4 years probation, 500 hours community service, ordered to pay back taxes and penalties
Jay I. Messinger	Attorney	Convicted May 8, 1986, on one mail fraud count.	2 years prison, $1,000 fine
James E. Noland	Attorney	Pleaded guilty March 27, 1987, to one racketeering/bribery count and one tax count.	15 months prison, $15,000 fine, 5 years probation, 400 hours community service
Edward E. Nydam	Attorney	Pleaded guilty April 29, 1985, to two tax counts and on Feb. 25, 1986, to one mail fraud count.	6 months prison, 5 years probation (on tax counts only)
James L. Oakey	Attorney, Former Associate Judge	Convicted May 15, 1987, on two tax counts. Pending trial on one racketeering/bribery count and one racketeering/conspiracy count.	18 months prison, $5,000 fine, 5 years probation, ordered to pay back taxes and penalties

Defendant	Position	Conviction	Sentence
William F. Reilly	Attorney	Pleaded guilty March 27, 1987, to one racketeering/bribery count and one tax count.	14 months prison, $5,000 fine, 5 years probation, 400 hours community service
Mark Rosenbloom	Attorney	Pleaded guilty March 11, 1988, to two tax counts.	2 years probation, 300 hours community service
Bruce Roth	Attorney	Convicted Aug. 24, 1987, on two extortion counts, one racketeering/bribery count, and one racketeering/conspiracy count.	10 years prison, 5 years probation
Martin Schachter	Attorney	Pleaded guilty July 5, 1984, to one mail fraud count.	4 years probation
R. Frederic Solomon	Attorney	Pleaded guilty April 8, 1986, to four tax counts.	2½ years prison, 5 years probation
Dean S. Wolfson	Attorney	Pleaded guilty Jan. 25, 1985, to one racketeering/bribery count and three mail fraud counts.	7½ years prison, $3,000 fine, 5 years probation
Cyrus Yonan, Jr.	Attorney	Pleaded guilty May 14, 1987, to one racketeering/bribery count and two tax counts.	1 year and one day prison, $15,000 fine, 3 years probation, 400 hours community service, ordered to pay $12,300 in back taxes and penalties

Appendix 2

Defendant	Position	Conviction	Sentence
Arthur Zimmerman	Attorney	Pleaded guilty Dec. 22, 1987, to two tax counts.	3 years prison, $10,000 fine, 3 years probation, 300 hours community service

APPENDIX 3

OPERATION GREYLORD—CONVICTED COURT PERSONNEL AS OF JUNE 1, 1988

Defendant	Position	Conviction	Sentence
Gaetano Bianco	Deputy Sheriff	Pleaded guilty to one misdemeanor count for civil rights violation.	(No information available; court file sealed.)
Ira J. Blackwood	Police Officer	Convicted Aug. 10, 1984, on one racketeering/ bribery count and ten extortion counts.	7 years prison, $20,000 fine, 5 years probation
Harold J. Conn	Deputy Clerk	Convicted March 15, 1984, on one racketeering/ bribery count and nine extortion counts.	6 years prison, $2,000 fine, 5 years probation
James F. Hegarty	Police Officer	Pleaded guilty Feb. 28, 1986, to one tax count.	3 years probation, 300 hours community service
Leopoldo Hernandez	Deputy Sheriff	Pleaded guilty July 31, 1985, to one extortion count.	6 months work release, 5 years probation, 500 hours community service
Paul B. Hutson	Deputy Sheriff	Pleaded guilty Feb. 25, 1986, to one misdemeanor tax count for failure to file income tax returns.	60 days work release, 5 years probation

Source: Special Commission on the Administration of Justice in Cook County.

Appendix 3

Defendant	Position	Conviction	Sentence
Alan Kaye	Deputy Sheriff	Convicted March 1, 1985, on official misconduct, theft, bribery, and intimidation counts (in state court).	5 years (state prison)
Jerome R. Kohn	Deputy Sheriff	Pleaded guilty Jan. 26, 1987, to one racketeering/ conspiracy count and one tax count.	18 months prison, $10,000 fine, 5 years probation
Nick La Palombella	Deputy Clerk	Pleaded guilty Feb. 25, 1986, to one tax count.	60 days work release, 5 years probation
James R. LeFevour	Police Officer	Pleaded guilty Dec. 4, 1984, to three tax counts.	30 months prison
Arthur W. McCauslin	Police Officer	Pleaded guilty Dec. 4, 1984, to two tax counts.	18 months prison
Lawrence E. McLain	Police Officer	Pleaded guilty Dec. 4, 1984, to two tax counts.	15 months prison
Frank L. Mirabella	Deputy Sheriff	Pleaded guilty Sept. 19, 1986, to two racketeering/bribery counts and one tax count.	7 months prison, $15,000 fine, 5 years probation, 300 hours community service
Steve Ruben	Deputy Sheriff	Pleaded guilty Feb. 25, 1986, to one tax count.	(Sentencing pending)

Defendant	Position	Conviction	Sentence
Patrick J. Ryan	Deputy Sheriff	Pleaded guilty Feb. 25, 1986, to one racketeering/ bribery count and one tax count.	60 days work release, 5 years probation
James V. Trunzo	Police Officer	Pleaded guilty Sept. 5, 1984, to two tax counts.	1 year prison, $10,000 fine, 3 years probation
Joseph Trunzo	Police Officer	Pleaded guilty Sept. 5, 1984, to two tax counts.	1 year prison, $10,000 fine, 3 years probation
Ernest Worsek	Receiver	Pleaded guilty Oct. 22, 1985, to one mail fraud count and one misdemeanor tax count for failure to file income tax returns.	6 months prison
Nick Yokas	Deputy Sheriff	Pleaded guilty Feb. 25, 1986, to one tax count.	60 days work release, 5 years probation